101 Great Hikes
of the
San Francisco Bay Area

101 Great Hikes of the San Francisco Bay Area
First edition

Printing History
1st Edition March 2000

5 4 3

Some photos are used by permission and are
the property of the original copyright owners.

All photographs by Ann Marie Brown,
except p. 319 by Bill Rhoades.

Front cover photo: © Robin Mitchell

Editors: Bill Lechat, Sam Moran
Cartography: Ann Pettit

ISBN: 1-57354-068-4
ISSN: 1078-8921

Published by
Avalon Travel Publishing
5855 Beaudry Street
Emeryville, CA 94608 USA

Printed in the United States of America by Malloy Lithographing, Inc.

Please send all comments, corrections,
additions, amendments, and critiques to:

101 Great Hikes of the San Francisco Bay Area
Foghorn Outdoors
5855 Beaudry Street
Emeryville, CA 94608 USA
e-mail: info@travelmatters.com
www.foghorn.com

Distributed in the United States and Canada by Publishers Group West

FOGHORN ✖ OUTDOORS

101 Great Hikes
of the
San Francisco Bay Area

Ann Marie Brown

INTRODUCTION

I'm a nature lover, a wildlife watcher, a committed hiker, and a card-carrying member of the Sierra Club. I run my life's appointment calendar by the timing of the wildflower bloom, the flow of waterfalls, and the show of autumn colors. I spend my work days and play days doing basically the same thing—exploring the natural world.

This being the case, it may seem odd that I choose to live in a large urban area with six million neighbors. But my home—the San Francisco Bay Area—is the most wild metropolitan area in the United States. Although grizzly bears no longer roam the Bay Area as they did 150 years ago, coyotes still gallop across the grasslands, herds of tule elk wander the coastal hills, and mountain lions and bobcats stalk their prey. Elephant seals still breed on the Bay Area's beaches, river otters ply the waterways, wild pigs root for acorns, and golden eagles and peregrine falcons soar overhead.

In the course of hiking the 101 trails in this book, I saw all of these creatures and more.

If you hike much in the Bay Area, you will be awed by the beauty and grace of centuries-old virgin redwoods. You'll wonder at the sight of rare and precious wildflowers, some of which grow here and nowhere else in the world. Your ears will be filled with the sound of crashing surf against miles of jagged coastal bluffs. You'll gaze at waterfalls coursing down basalt cliffs, pouring over sandstone precipices, and even dashing to the sea. You'll stand on summits and look down thousands of feet to the valleys below. In autumn, you'll watch black oaks and big leaf maples turn bright gold, and in winter, you'll see a dusting of snow fall on the Bay Area's high peaks and ridges.

Quite possibly, you'll wind up spending some of the best days of your life on Bay Area trails. I know I have.

Speaking of hiking, take a look out the window. Chances are good that it's a nice day for a walk. See you out there—

Ann Marie Brown

HOW TO USE THIS BOOK

This book is organized geographically, with each hike numbered from 1 to 101. Use the map on page 6 to locate where in the San Francisco Bay Area you want to hike. Then find the trails' stories by using the table of contents, the index, or just by thumbing through the book. (The trails are arranged in numerical order.)

Or you can simply turn to the chapter covering the Bay Area region where you'd like to hike and read the stories in that chapter.

Each trail has one or a series of graphic icons listed with it, which give you a snapshot of the trail's features. They are:

 The trail visits a beach.

 The trail climbs to a high overlook offering wide views.

 The trail leads through a unique or special forest.

 The trail travels to a waterfall.

 The trail offers an opportunity for wildlife watching.

 The trail features wildflower displays in spring.

 Leashed dogs are permitted on the trail.

Each trail is rated for round-trip mileage, time required for hiking, and total elevation change over the entire round-trip trail. The following difficulty designations have been assigned: easy, moderate, or strenuous. An **easy** trail is less than five miles long and has less than a 750-foot elevation change. A **moderate** trail is between five and eight miles long and has between 750 and 1,500 feet of elevation change. A **strenuous** trail is more than eight miles long and has an elevation change of more than 1,500 feet.

To qualify for the book, each trail had to be one of the Bay Area's greatest. The trails are further ranked with a rating of two, three, or four stars for overall quality and scenic beauty.

★ ★ ★ ★   one of the Bay Area's top 25 trails
★ ★ ★   worth driving out of your way
★ ★   a great hike for people living nearby

101 GREAT HIKES of the SAN FRANCISCO BAY AREA

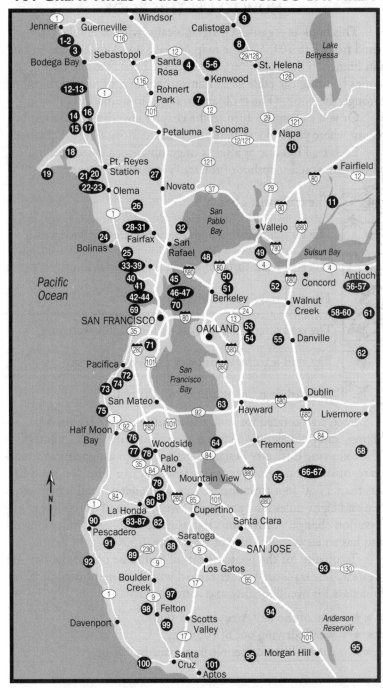

CONTENTS

• Napa & Sonoma •

• Marin •

• Marin, cont. •

• East Bay, cont. •

• Peninsula & South Bay •

• Peninsula & South Bay, cont. •

Napa
& Sonoma

1. POMO CANYON TRAIL
Sonoma Coast State Beach

DISTANCE: 5.8 miles round-trip; 3 hours   **LEVEL:** Moderate

ELEVATION CHANGE: 1,000 feet   **RATING:** ★ ★ ★

DIRECTIONS: From Highway 1 in Bodega Bay, drive north for seven miles to the Shell Beach parking lot on the west side of the road. Park in the lot, then walk across Highway 1 to access the trail on its east side.

If the wind is howling on the Sonoma Coast or the fog has smothered the beaches in a cool, white-gray blanket, you don't have to pack up your car and head inland. A first-rate hiking trip is possible on the Pomo Canyon Trail from Shell Beach, where wind and fog can't ruin the trip.

Pomo Canyon Trail heads northeast from the coast, meanders over coastal grasslands covered with spring wildflowers, then visits a beautiful grove of second-growth redwoods in a wind-protected canyon. Although the trail offers great views of the ocean and the Russian River when the weather is clear, it also provides a destination that doesn't require sunshine to be good. In fact, a hike to Pomo Canyon's redwood groves in dense fog or light rain may be the most romantic walk you've ever taken.

Wildflower lovers take note: the coastal hills and grasslands along Pomo Canyon Trail are well known for erupting in blooms in April, May, and June. During the peak bloom time, more than 100 different species may be flowering at one time. Although the grasslands don't exhibit vast, showy carpets of individual species, the great diversity of species draws flower worshippers every year.

Start your trip at the Shell Beach parking lot north of Bodega Bay. You'll have to cross Highway 1 to access the Pomo Canyon trailhead; do so with care. The trail begins as an old paved road that has eroded into part gravel, part pavement, and part grasses. It makes easy walking as you head uphill away from the coast. Although the noise of the highway stays with you for the first half mile, it will soon disappear. Unfortunately, with it goes the expansive ocean views. Turn around occasionally to gaze at the wide blue Pacific while you can.

At a junction at 0.7 miles, where the path reaches a grassy plateau punctuated by a few large rock formations, bear right, then bear left shortly afterward. You'll leave the worn pavement behind and follow grassy double-track. Soon this narrows to single-track. Bright blue and pale white Douglas iris dot the grasslands in early spring; blue gentian and tarweed follows later in summer.

The path rolls along the ridge top, heading generally downhill toward Willow Creek's canyon. As you go farther north, you'll gain fine views of the Russian River's graceful curves and Goat Rock Beach beyond. Watch for a short spur trail on the left that leads to a grassy knoll. There you gain a more open view of the 110-mile-long river at its junction with the sea.

Hike past dense blackberry vines and coastal chaparral that is sometimes taller than you are. The trail crosses several seeps and springs that provide year-round water for lichen-covered Douglas firs and Monterey pines.

Reach the first redwood grove at 1.6 miles. It's a bit of a shock: the redwood trees' bark is not the usual reddish-brown color. Their trunks are completed covered with a gray-green lichen, making the trees appear ghostlike. This is a mysterious forest indeed. You might expect a leprechaun to pop out at any moment.

Pomo Canyon Trail wanders along the edge of the grove, then opens out to more grasslands with wide views of the deep green Willow Creek drainage and Russian River canyon. In another half

View of Russian River from Pomo Canyon Trail

mile, you're back in the redwoods and you begin a steep descent to the trail's end. The narrow second- and third-growth trees create a lovely ambience and a soft carpet of needles under your feet. Ferns of many varieties line the woodland floor.

The path ends anticlimactically at Pomo Campground, a walk-in or environmental camp. Less than two dozen sites are scattered among the trees; campers must walk in a few hundred feet from the parking lot. If the campground is empty, you might choose a picnic table for a rest stop. Otherwise, just turn around and head back over the ridge. The beauty of this trail is worth seeing all over again.

Trip notes: There is no fee. Dogs and bikes are not allowed. A trail map is available for $1 at park headquarters at Salmon Creek or at the kiosk at Wright's Beach. For more information, contact Sonoma Coast State Beach, Bodega Bay, CA 94923; (707) 875-3483 or (707) 865-2391. Website: www.mcn.org/1/rrparks

2. KORTUM TRAIL
Sonoma Coast State Beach

DISTANCE: 4.6 or 7.6 miles round-trip; 2-4 hours   **LEVEL:** Easy

ELEVATION CHANGE: 500 feet   **RATING:** ★ ★ ★

DIRECTIONS: From Highway 1 in Bodega Bay, drive north for seven miles to the Shell Beach parking lot on the west side of the road. The trail begins on the northwest side of the parking lot (another section of the trail begins on the southwest side).

Sonoma Coast State Beach encompasses 13 miles of coastline stretching from Bodega Bay to the Russian River. Located north of Marin County's coastline and west of the Sonoma County towns of Petaluma and Santa Rosa, the Sonoma Coast is on the road to few other places. And that's exactly what makes it appealing.

The best way to get to know this beautiful stretch of coast is to take a walk on the Kortum Trail, which skirts grassland bluffs from Blind Beach to Wright's Beach over a distance of 3.8 miles one-way. By starting in the middle of the trail at Shell Beach, you can choose to hike out and back along the entire trail or follow only the most scenic, northern portion for a 4.6-mile round-trip.

The path is named for environmentalist and veterinarian Bill Kortum, who worked as a volunteer for 30 years to protect this stretch of coast. Numerous issues threatened the area, including the building of a nuclear power plant at Bodega Bay and the closure of public access to the coast at Sea Ranch. Thanks to the efforts of Kortum and others like him, thousands of acres of Sonoma coastline have remained unspoiled and open for enjoyment.

Heading north from the Shell Beach parking lot, immediately you'll notice two parallel trails: the wider, more obvious path is routed slightly inland and runs a straighter course, and a narrower use trail meanders along the jagged edge of the bluffs. Take your pick; the paths eventually converge.

Kortum Trail leads across classic California coastal bluff terrain, with open grasslands intersected by brushy drainages and ravines. Views of offshore outcrops and spring wildflowers will wow you as you walk. Douglas iris, lupine, and Indian paintbrush gild the grasslands. To the south you can see Bodega Head and the northern tip of Point Reyes on clear days. To the west, the shimmering Pacific extends as far as your gaze can follow.

A highlight of the trip is the massive rock outcrop rising from the grasslands at 1.3 miles, which invites a climb to its summit. Coastal views are superb from the top of the lichen-covered and fern-dotted rock formation, which was once undersea. Beyond it, Kortum Trail leads away from the ocean and ascends a coastal hill (take the short spur to its summit for more views), then drops back down the other side. Views of the wave-pounded tunnel at Arched

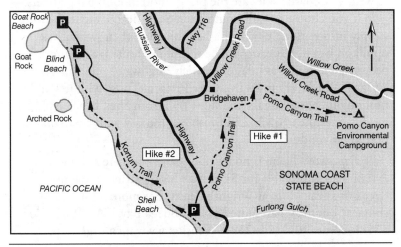

Sonoma Coast view from a rock outcrop on Kortum Trail

Rock are excellent. The path ends about 100 feet from Blind Beach's parking lot; you can take a short trail from the lot down to the beach. From there, it's a half-mile stroll north to Goat Rock Beach. (Goat Rock is a massive offshore outcrop that is connected to the mainland by a paved road, now closed to cars.)

Birdwatchers will want to bring their binoculars for this hike. Numerous raptors hunt in the grasslands. Watch for harriers, red-shouldered hawks, black-shouldered kites, and even great-horned owls. Don't be surprised if you see a human bird soar overhead as well. The coastal skies are the playground of local hang gliders.

If you choose to walk south from Shell Beach, the trail drops steeply into Furlong Gulch at a half mile out, then switchbacks uphill on wooden stairsteps. The rest of the route is a bit more pedestrian as it curves inland, parallels Highway 1, and travels to Wright's Beach, 1.5 miles from Shell Beach. Those with less ambition might choose to take the short trail from Shell Beach parking lot down to Shell Beach, and finish out the day with a nap on the brayed tan sands.

Trip notes: There is no fee. Dogs and bikes are not allowed. A trail map is available for $1 at park headquarters at Salmon Creek or at the kiosk at Wright's Beach. For more information, contact Sonoma Coast State Beach, Bodega Bay, CA 94923; (707) 875-3483 or (707) 865-2391. Website: www.mcn.org/1/rrparks

3. BODEGA HEAD TRAIL
Sonoma Coast State Beach

DISTANCE: 2.0 miles round-trip; 1 hour   **LEVEL:** Easy

ELEVATION CHANGE: 400 feet   **RATING:** ★ ★ ★

DIRECTIONS: From Highway 1 in Bodega Bay, turn west on East Shore Road. (The turnoff is signed for Bodega Head.) Drive a half mile, then turn right on West Shore Road. Drive 3.5 miles to Bodega Head; take the right fork in the road and head to the west parking lot.

Say "Bodega Bay" and most people's thoughts turn to Alfred Hitchcock movies. And birds. Better they should think of hiking instead, and wildflowers, whale watching, and coastal vistas.

Bodega Head is the tip of the curving peninsula of land that juts out from the coast west of Santa Rosa and Sebastopol. Bodega Head extends toward the ocean, then curves back around toward the land like the fingers of a hand turning inward. From a high point on Bodega Head you can wave to the wide open Pacific, the sheltered harbor at Bodega Bay, the northern tip of Point Reyes, and the rolling hills and farms of western Sonoma. On a clear day, there's nothing quite like it.

The clear day is the tricky part. Bodega Bay is almost as famous for fog as it is for the Hitchcock thriller *The Birds*. When it isn't foggy in Bodega Bay, it's usually windy. But there's a way to beat the system: Plan your trip for autumn or winter, and try to arrive in the morning, not the afternoon. This gives you the best chance at a sunny, windless hike.

Start your trip at Bodega Head's west parking lot (bear right at the fork on the drive in). The view from the parking lot is mesmerizing enough. The sea crashes against dark sandy beaches and rugged bluffs and outcrops. Tenacious sea palms grip the offshore rocks, holding on for dear life with each passing breaker. As soon as the wave dissipates, the plants spring back to an upright position, as if made of rubber.

Take the trail on the north side of the parking lot signed as "Bodega Head Trail." It climbs uphill on grassy bluffs to the highest point on Bodega Head, where a 360-degree view is yours for the

---

taking. A left fork at the start of the trail leads a short distance to the bluffs' eroded edges. This colorful miniature badlands area looks like something straight out of Death Valley.

Follow the main path uphill to a signed junction. Take the left fork for Horseshoe Cove Overlook; the right fork continues to Salmon Creek Beach and Bodega Dunes Campground. The overlook trail deadends at a high, rock-covered point, where you can look down at rightfully named Horseshoe Cove and the University of California Marine Laboratory alongside it. To the east, you can see the town of Bodega Bay and the RVs lined up along Doran Park on the sand spit that protects Bodega Harbor. It's fascinating to watch the fishing boats leave Bodega Bay, cruise through the harbor, squeeze through the narrow channel between Doran Park and Bodega Head, then motor out to freedom in Bodega Bay.

When you've soaked in the view, retrace your steps to the parking lot, then take the unsigned trail that begins to the left of the rest rooms. This footpath circles around the "enclosed hand" shape that is Bodega Head. It climbs initially to a memorial site for Bodega Bay's commercial fishermen, then hugs the edge of the bluffs as it

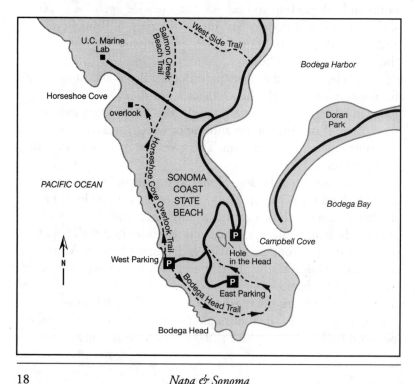

Horseshoe Cove Overlook on Bodega Head

curves around the south of the Head. On windy days, some hikers find refuge in a grouping of cypress trees.

At the southern tip of the head, you see what looks like an island rising from the sea. It's Tomales Point, the northern tip of the Point Reyes peninsula. Geographically speaking, Point Reyes is directly south of Bodega Head. The two peninsulas are separated by only five miles of sea, although Point Reyes' peninsula is immense in comparison to tiny Bodega Head. (On the clearest days, tiny Bird Rock island is also visible, just off the coast of Tomales Point.) If you've ever visited the tule elk preserve at the northern tip of Point Reyes or hiked the Tomales Point Trail, you were standing just opposite here, looking back at Bodega Head. (See the Tomales Point story on pages 44 to 46).

Where the trail turns away from the sea, make a choice: You can continue in a looping circle past the east parking lot and back to your car, or you can simply turn around and retrace your steps. The latter option is the most scenic. You'll get to see Bodega Head's crashing surf, offshore outcrops, and secluded coves all over again.

Trip notes: There is no fee. Dogs and bikes are not allowed. A trail map is available for $1 at park headquarters at Salmon Creek or at the kiosk at Wright's Beach. For more information, contact Sonoma Coast State Beach, Bodega Bay, CA 94923; (707) 875-3483 or (707) 865-2391. Website: www.mcn.org/1/rrparks

4. LAKE ILSANJO LOOP
Annadel State Park

DISTANCE: 5.3 miles round-trip; 3 hours   **LEVEL:** Easy

ELEVATION CHANGE: 500 feet   **RATING:** ★ ★ ★

DIRECTIONS: From U.S. 101 in Santa Rosa, take the Fairgrounds/Highway 12 exit. Highway 12 becomes Farmers Lane as it heads through downtown Santa Rosa. Turn right on Montgomery Drive and follow it for 2.7 miles (veering to the right), then turn right on Channel Drive. Follow Channel Drive into the park, stop and pay the fee at the self-registration station, then drive to the end of the road and park in the lot (it's a total of 2.2 miles on Channel Drive).

Annadel State Park is a horsey kind of place. When you count the horse trailers in the parking lot, the hoofprints all over the place, and the horse "evidence" along the trail, you might think more horses visit here than people.

Then again, Annadel is also a mountain biker's kind of place. Most of the trails at Annadel are open to bikes (not just the usual wide fire roads). The bikers and equestrians share the trails with great equanimity, and trail conflicts are rare to nonexistent.

Considering all this, it's surprising that Annadel is also a hiker's kind of place, but it is. Annadel's 5,000 acres are filled with woodlands, meadows, creeks, wildflowers, and even a 26-acre lake, all of which are worth seeing on foot. One of the park's paths, called Steve's S Trail, is designated for hikers only. Combine it with a few of the park's fine multi-use trails and you have a great loop trip in the park.

The trip starts at the trailhead at the end of Channel Drive. On one trip, we arrived there and heard a loud ruckus. Two dozen male turkeys, separated into two groups, were having it out over a flock of hens alongside the parking lot. It was like *West Side Story* with feathers.

Take the hikers-only trail from the far side of the parking lot or the wide fire road from its center; both meet up in a few hundred feet. At that junction, head uphill on narrow Steve's S Trail, leaving the road for the cyclists and horses. The trail makes a good climb over a mile with just enough of a pitch to get your heart rate up.

It weaves through a dense and shady Douglas fir forest, with a few redwoods and bay laurels for variety. The woodland floor is completely lined with sword ferns. In early spring, look for rare redwood orchids among them.

After gaining a ridge, Steve's S Trail meets up with Louis Trail heading left. Stay right and travel south into an open meadow lined with bright yellow mule's ears in the spring and early summer. Around the meadow's edges you'll find a variety of oaks—canyon, blue, and valley. Continue on Lower Steve's S for six-tenths of a mile to the northern edge of Lake Ilsanjo. You'll head back into the forest again, but this time it's a mixed oak and madrone woodland. (The black oaks turn bright colors in the fall.) Enjoy lovely views of a wide, spreading meadow to your right.

Go left to circle the lake clockwise. You'll gain the best views of blue water, tules, and paddling water birds as you walk across Lake Ilsanjo's earthen dam. The natural-looking reservoir is a lovely contrast to the manzanita and chaparral surrounding it. If you're wondering about the origin of the lake's name, "Ilsanjo" is a combination of Ilsa and Joe, the names of the land's former owners.

Although you may not have had much company on your hike, expect lots of people at the lake. Its tule-lined shores are popular with bikers, hikers, picnickers, swimmers, and anglers. More than a few visitors make this a combination hiking/fishing trip, stalking

Lake Ilsanjo, Annadel State Park

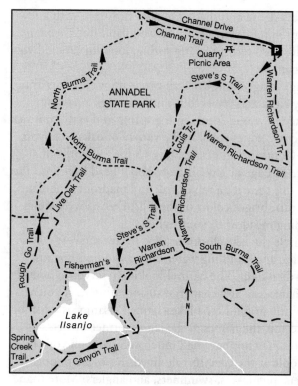

Ilsanjo's shoreline to cast for good-sized largemouth bass and plentiful bluegill.

At the far side of the dam, you'll wind up on wide Rough Go Trail. Follow it around the west side of the lake, then bear left on North Burma Trail. The latter heads north to Channel Trail, which runs parallel to the road you drove in on. Follow level Channel Trail three-quarters of a mile back to the parking lot and your car.

With all the possible trails at 5,000-acre Annadel State Park, a park map is essential. Buy one at the self-registration area where you pay your day-use fee. If you want to add on a few more miles to this hike, an option is to take single-track Spring Creek Trail from the west end of Lake Ilsanjo's dam. The trail follows Spring Creek for 1.3 miles to Canyon Trail, then connects to Rough Go Trail and eventually rejoins the loop described above. This option will add just under three miles to your loop.

Trip notes: A $2 day-use fee is charged per vehicle. Pay the fee at the self-registration station on Channel Drive, a half mile before the trailhead parking area. Dogs are not allowed. Bikes are allowed on all trails except Steve's S. Park maps are available for 75 cents at the self-registration station. For more information, contact Annadel State Park, 6201 Channel Drive, Santa Rosa, CA 95409; (707) 539-3911 or (707) 938-1519.

5. BALD MOUNTAIN LOOP
Sugarloaf Ridge State Park

DISTANCE: 7.0 miles round-trip; 4 hours   **LEVEL:** Moderate

ELEVATION CHANGE: 1,500 feet   **RATING:** ★ ★ ★ ★

DIRECTIONS: From U.S. 101 in Santa Rosa, take the Fairgrounds/Highway 12 exit. Highway 12 becomes Farmers Lane as it heads through downtown Santa Rosa. Continue on Highway 12 for 11 miles to Adobe Canyon Road and turn left. (Or, from Highway 12 in Sonoma, drive 11 miles north to Adobe Canyon Road, then turn right.) Drive 3.5 miles to the park entrance kiosk. Park in the lot about 100 yards past the kiosk, on the left. Take the trail signed as "Lower Bald Mountain Trail."

While the grassy summit of Bald Mountain at 2,729 feet is the crowning glory of this loop trip in Sugarloaf Ridge State Park, each leg of the route has its own gifts to offer. Take the most direct path to the summit, then loop back downhill on a series of trails that provide a roundabout tour of the park's varied and lovely terrain.

On the saddle below Bald Mountain

Start your trip on Lower Bald Mountain Trail from the parking lot just past the entrance kiosk. At its start, the well-graded path climbs a grassy slope. Deer frequently graze in the open meadow, which is covered with wildflowers in the spring, especially Douglas iris, California poppies, brodiaea, and blue-eyed grass.

Tunneling through a hardwood forest, the

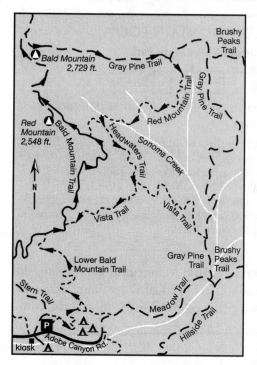

path meets up with Bald Mountain Trail, a paved service road leading to the summit. The paved road makes less pleasant hiking, but it ascends quickly through slopes covered with ceanothus, manzanita, chamise, and toyon. The blooming, scented chaparral will take your attention away from the asphalt.

At 2.3 miles, reach the pavement's end at a saddle and trail junction. The left fork leads to microwave-covered Red Mountain at 2,548 feet. You'll go right for Bald Mountain, now following a dirt fire road. The final half mile to the summit ascends grassy slopes with occasional outcrops of green serpentine. The dirt road curves around the north side of the mountain to junction with Gray Pine Trail. Take the short spur on the right to reach the 2,729 foot summit. It's bald indeed; not a single tree obstructs the sweeping panoramic view.

Two signs at the top identify all the neighboring landmarks, including Mount St. Helena, Mount Diablo, Bodega Bay, Mount Wittenberg in Point Reyes, Snow Mountain, Mount Tamalpais, the Golden Gate Bridge towers, Angel Island, and the Bay Bridge. Most impressive is the glimpse of the Sierra Nevada, 130 miles away. A posted quote from author Robert Louis Stevenson sums it up: "There are days in a life when thus to climb out of the lowlands seems like scaling heaven."

From the summit, take wide Gray Pine Trail east, descending along a ridge. In three quarters of a mile, turn right on single-track Red Mountain Trail. The trail dips and climbs through chaparral for nearly a mile. Watch for the left turnoff for Headwaters Trail; take it and enjoy a lovely downhill stretch along the headwaters of Sonoma Creek. In a half mile, bear right on Vista Trail. The path skirts lovely meadows with fine views of the Sonoma Creek canyon and Sugarloaf Ridge, then ends at paved Bald Mountain Trail. Follow the pavement downhill for only a quarter mile to the left turnoff for Lower Bald Mountain Trail, the single-track path you started on. The final mile is an easy descent back to your car.

Trip notes: A $5 day-use fee is charged per vehicle. Dogs are not allowed. Bikes are allowed only on fire roads. A trail map is available at the entrance kiosk for $1. For more information, contact Sugarloaf Ridge State Park, 2605 Adobe Canyon Road, Kenwood, CA 95452-9004; (707) 833-5712 or (707) 938-1519.

6. GOODSPEED TRAIL to GUNSIGHT ROCK
Sugarloaf Ridge State Park & Hood Mountain Regional Park

DISTANCE: 7.0 miles round-trip; 4 hours   **LEVEL:** Strenuous

ELEVATION CHANGE: 1,900 feet   **RATING:** ★ ★ ★ ★

DIRECTIONS: From U.S. 101 in Santa Rosa, take the Fairgrounds/Highway 12 exit. Highway 12 becomes Farmers Lane as it heads through downtown Santa Rosa. Continue on Highway 12 for 11 miles to Adobe Canyon Road and turn left. (Or, from Highway 12 in Sonoma, drive 11 miles north to Adobe Canyon Road, then turn right.) Drive 2.2 miles to the small parking area on the left at a bridge over Sonoma Creek (it's 1.3 miles before the entrance kiosk for Sugarloaf Ridge State Park).

Mount Hood is a 2,730-foot peak in Sonoma County, located just outside the border of Sugarloaf Ridge State Park. Despite its respectable size, Mount Hood has one problem—its summit view is a big disappointment. Manzanita and pine trees cover its wide, rounded top, and you just can't see a darn thing from up there.

Fortunately, Mount Hood has Gunsight Rock located a quarter mile and three hundred feet below its summit. From lofty Gunsight Rock, you can see just about everything in Sonoma County, plus the big mountains of Napa and Marin. Not only that, but Gunsight Rock's bouldery outcrop is perched so dramatically on the slope of Mount Hood that its steep dropoff makes the wide view even more impressive.

A bonus is that getting to Gunsight Rock is just as good as being there. The Goodspeed Trail, which accesses it, is a study in diversity. Redwoods, laurels, manzanitas, oaks, grasslands, wildflowers, serpentine, wildlife, and vistas—you get a little bit of everything on the seven-mile round-trip to Gunsight Rock. Pick a clear, cool day, preferably in spring when the wildflowers are blooming, and don't miss this trip.

Goodspeed Trail's trailhead and first two miles are located in Sugarloaf Ridge State Park. The trail's final mile and a half are located in Hood Mountain Regional Park. From the trailhead at the bridge on Adobe Canyon Road, you enter a shady redwood forest and take a mellow stroll through the big trees. Two footbridges carry you across Sonoma Creek and Bear Creek. The first quarter-mile of redwood forest is so lovely that you may be tempted not to go farther. But press on and you quickly leave the shade of the stream canyon and head into drier, rockier terrain. The trail begins its moderate but steady ascent, heading out into the sunlight. Blue and white Douglas iris line the path in April.

At nearly one mile out, you'll cross a dirt road, then pick up the single-track trail on the far side. The trail drops down to a stream crossing that is dry in summer but a wide flow in winter and spring. Huge and pretty boulders line the stream. This, too, seems like a fine destination by itself.

Valley view from Gunsight Rock on Hood Mountain

Napa & Sonoma

The trail climbs out of the canyon, then continues through an alternating progression of sunshine and shade, grasslands and forest. The exposed slopes of Mount Hood are dotted with serpentine and wildflowers, including red paintbrush, California poppies, brodiaea, blue-eyed grass, and red thistles. The forested slopes include a mix of bay laurel, oaks, manzanita, and pines, plus flowers such as hound's tongue and shooting stars.

The trail gets progressively steeper as you go. Two conical-shaped summits come into view at two miles. One is very green and grassy, the other is covered with chaparral and woodland, but neither of these is Mount Hood. (They're lesser summits at 2,350 feet.) Goodspeed Trail climbs along the southwest shoulder of the grassy summit, then makes a series of short, steep switchbacks to rise over it. Look for plentiful poppies and lupine in the grasslands in springtime.

You're given a brief rest at a small saddle, then—surprise—the trail drops back down on the northeast side of the forested summit, then climbs again. Fortunately, this final ascent is shaded. At last you come out to a broader saddle between the two small summits and Mount Hood. Shortly thereafter is the left turnoff for Gunsight Rock. Turn left and walk a few hundred yards to your destination.

A cluster of boulders with a wide notch in the middle, suitably named Gunsight Rock offers sweeping views to the south, west, and north. Mount St. Helena in Napa and Mount Tamalpais in Marin are easy landmarks. The whole of Sonoma Valley can be seen in one glance. The city of Santa Rosa lies to the west.

The dropoffs are extreme from this rocky promontory, so use caution. Find a flat boulder and sit down to admire the view.

If you choose to hike the final quarter mile to the summit of Mount Hood, just follow the trail uphill. Its grade steepens and you enter a dry, brittle forest of manzanita and knobcone pines. The summit consists of a wide dirt clearing, possibly a turnaround for fire engines, encircled by tall shrubs and chaparral. A visit here will probably inspire you to head back down to Gunsight Rock.

Trip notes: A $5 day-use fee is charged per vehicle. Dogs and bikes are not allowed. A trail map is available at the entrance kiosk for $1. For more information, contact Sugarloaf Ridge State Park, 2605 Adobe Canyon Road, Kenwood, CA 95452-9004; (707) 833-5712 or (707) 938-1519.

7. LAKE & FALLEN BRIDGE LOOP
Jack London State Historic Park

DISTANCE: 4.2 or 6.6 miles round-trip; 2-4 hours   **LEVEL:** Moderate

ELEVATION CHANGE: 600 feet or 1,600 feet   **RATING:** ★ ★ ★

DIRECTIONS: From Sonoma on Highway 12, drive north for 4.5 miles to Madrone Road and turn left. At the end of Madrone Road, turn right on Arnold Drive and follow it for three miles into Glen Ellen, then turn left on London Ranch Road. Follow London Ranch Road for one mile to the park entrance kiosk. Park in the day-use area on the right (not in the visitor center lot on the left). The trail leads from the parking area.

Jack London wanted beauty, and so he "bought beauty, and was content with beauty for awhile." That's how he described his ranch and the surrounding hills, which are now part of Jack London State Historic Park. London's vision of beauty is the basis for this hike from the ranch's vineyards. An easy four-mile loop leads through a pretty woodland to a small lake and high vistas. If you're feeling ambitious, a more strenuous trail travels 6.6 miles round-trip to the summit of 2,463-foot Sonoma Mountain.

London, the most popular and highest paid fiction writer of the early 1900s, wanted to build his home in Glen Ellen to escape city life. After two years of construction, his ranch dream house mysteriously caught fire and burned to the ground just days before he and his wife were to move in. London continued to live on the ranch in a small wood-frame house until his death in 1916. Be sure to begin or end your trip with a visit to the Jack London Museum at the visitor center, which has interesting exhibits and photographs from the author's life.

Take the paved trail from the parking lot to the picnic area, then pick up the dirt fire road signed as Lake Trail. Follow it to the right past the barns and winery buildings. Turn right at the sign for "Pig Palace," London's extravagant pig pen. Check out this elaborate stone structure, then return to the main path. Skirting around carefully tended vineyards, the road forks at a gate; hikers should take the right turnoff on single-track Lake Trail. You'll climb for a half mile through mixed hardwoods and Douglas firs to the lake's edge. (Several paths junction with Lake Trail; all lead to the lake.)

London's prized lake is more of a pond nowadays. With sediment continually encroaching, it has shrunk to half its original size. A redwood log cabin that was used as a bathhouse still stands. The Londons swam, fished, and entertained guests at the lake.

Beyond the lake, you get to the park's "real" hiking. From the ranch road on the southeast edge of the lake, take single-track Quarry Trail east. A quarter-mile of walking leads you to a bench and a lovely vista point that overlooks the Valley of the Moon and green ridges behind it. Enjoy this spot, then continue on Quarry Trail, turn left and loop back on Vineyard Trail and Vineyard Road.

Back near the lake again, follow the wide ranch road uphill through a few switchbacks. (The road is now called "Mountain Trail.") At a large clearing and second vista point, you gain another fine view of Sonoma Valley. This is also the intersection with Fallen Bridge Trail, where you'll make a 1.3-mile loop. Take the left fork first, crunching through the leaves lining the path. The route tunnels through madrones and oaks, then meets up with Asbury Creek and parallels it. Bear right to loop back on Upper Fallen Bridge Trail, now climbing steeply through the redwood-lined creek canyon. At a junction with Mountain Trail, turn right and follow the dirt road back to the clearing, then continue downhill through the switchbacks to the lake.

Those who seek a more strenuous trip can continue uphill on wide Mountain Trail for 2.5 miles to the summit of

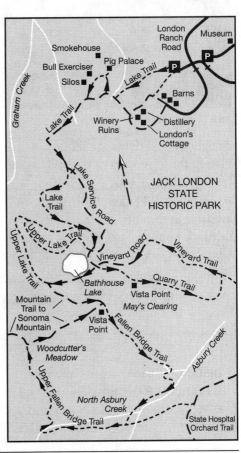

Sonoma Mountain. The path climbs moderately but steadily through a mix of forests and meadows. A popular rest stop is 1.4 miles from the top amid the redwoods at Deer Camp. Sonoma Mountain's actual summit lies just outside the park boundary on private property and is lined with barbed wire, but a short right spur leads to a panoramic overlook on an eastern ridge 100 feet below the top. Excellent views are provided of Mount St. Helena, San Pablo Bay, and Mount Tamalpais. (Note that heading straight up and down the mountain makes a 6.6-mile round-trip. Hiking the lower part of the trail as described adds 1.8 miles.)

Jack London's lake

Trip notes: A $6 day-use fee is charged per vehicle. Dogs are not allowed. Bikes are allowed only on fire roads. A park map is available at the entrance kiosk for $1. For more information, contact Jack London State Historic Park, 2400 London Ranch Road, Glen Ellen, CA 95442; (707) 938-5216 or (707) 938-1519.

8. RITCHEY CANYON & COYOTE PEAK
Bothe-Napa Valley State Park

DISTANCE: 5.0 miles round-trip; 3 hours   **LEVEL:** Moderate

ELEVATION CHANGE: 900 feet   **RATING:** ★ ★ ★

DIRECTIONS: From Highway 29/128 in St. Helena, drive north on Highway 29/128 for five miles to the entrance to Bothe-Napa Valley State Park on the left side of the highway. (It's 3.5 miles south of Calistoga.) Turn left and drive a quarter mile to the entrance kiosk, then continue past the visitor center to the horse trailer parking lot on the right. The trail begins on the right side of the horse trailer parking lot.

Even the most devoted and enthusiastic Napa Valley wine-tasters eventually tire of their task. If it's a hot summer day, perhaps they start daydreaming of a shady redwood forest where they could walk for a while or sit by a stream. Such a daydream might seem preposterous. Where in the midst of the sun-baked vineyards could a redwood tree possibly grow?

At Bothe-Napa Valley State Park, that's where. Ritchey Canyon and Redwood trails take you through a lovely stand of them, one of the most eastern groves of coastal redwoods in California. Paired with a visit to the summit of Coyote Peak, this loop trip will leave you even more intoxicated with Napa Valley's wine country.

Joining the redwoods are plenty of Douglas firs, buckeyes, and bigleaf maples, plus ferns galore. Look carefully among the branches of the trees: five different kinds of woodpeckers dwell within the park's borders. We spotted the largest of these, the pileated woodpecker, on a tree right by the picnic area. He was working his way up and down a big Douglas fir like a telephone lineman on triple overtime.

Start your hike by heading up Ritchey Canyon Trail from the horse trailer parking lot. (You can also start by the small bridge near the visitor center, or access the trail from the park campground.) The first half mile is somewhat noisy due to the proximity of the highway and campground, but soon you leave those distractions behind. Ferns, wild grape, and blackberry bushes line the path. Second-growth redwoods are mixed in with Douglas firs. Black oaks and big-leaf maples form a canopy over the trail and Ritchey Creek, which runs dependably year-round. (The oaks and maples wear bright yellow coats in autumn.) Keep the creek on your right;

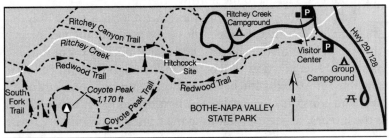

Coyote Peak view

the trail narrows and junctions with Redwood Trail, which you follow. Ritchey Canyon Trail crosses to the north side of the stream.

Three-quarters of a mile from the start, reach a junction with Coyote Peak Trail and bear left. The trail begins a fair climb but remains pleasantly shaded most of the way. Halfway up the trail you leave the conifers and enter drier slopes and a bay and live oak forest. Slowly the oaks give way to low-growing chaparral and some interesting rock formations. Wide views open up on your right of conifer-covered Ritchey Canyon below.

Near the top you reach a junction; the right fork will be your return. Bear left and make a short but steep climb to a knoll just below Coyote Peak's summit. You're rewarded with a pastoral view of the vineyards and valley far below. This is your best view of the day. The summit is a short distance farther, but its vista is mostly obstructed by trees. Peering through the branches, you can make out Mount St. Helena to the northwest.

Return to the junction with the western leg of Coyote Peak Trail and follow it steeply down the opposite side of the mountain. You'll soon leave toyon, chamise, and ceanothus in favor of shady redwoods. At a junction with South Fork Trail, turn right. Follow a concrete apron across Ritchey Creek, then turn right on Redwood Trail and cross the creek again. The next half mile on Redwood Trail is the loveliest of the trip, featuring the densest redwoods and ferns.

If Ritchey Creek isn't running too wide, you can cross it at an obvious (but unbridged) spur, then follow Ritchey Canyon Trail for part of your return. On the opposite bank of Ritchey Creek, Ritchey Canyon Trail passes the old Hitchcock home site, where Lillie Hitchcock Coit and her parents lived in the 1870s. Lillie Coit is probably best known for lending her name and money to Coit Tower on Telegraph Hill in San Francisco, but she also threw some grand parties for the San Francisco elite here at her country estate.

Spring is the best season to hike at Bothe-Napa, preferably in April or May when the buckeyes are in fragrant bloom and the creek is running strong. Wildflowers, including solomon's seal and redwood orchids, bloom in the cool shade. Park volunteers manage a small native plant garden near the visitor center for those who want to brush up on plant identification before or after the trip.

Trip notes: A $5 day-use fee is charged per vehicle. Dogs and bikes are not allowed. Trail maps are available at the entrance kiosk or visitor center for $1. For more information, contact Bothe-Napa Valley State Park, 3801 St. Helena Highway North, Calistoga, CA 94515; (707) 942-4575. Website: www.napanet.net/~bothe

9. MOUNT ST. HELENA
Robert Louis Stevenson State Park

DISTANCE: 10.0 miles round-trip; 6 hours   **LEVEL:** Strenuous
ELEVATION CHANGE: 2,100 feet   **RATING:** ★ ★ ★
DIRECTIONS: From Highway 29/128 in Calistoga, turn north on Highway 29 and drive eight miles (through the town of Calistoga) to the signed trailhead. Park in the pullouts on either side of the road. The trail begins on the left side of the road.

Normally a trail that is eighty percent fire road would not interest me in the slightest. But the spectacular view from the top of Mount St. Helena makes the climb on its wide, exposed road completely worthwhile. And unlike other Bay Area peaks bearing world-class vistas like Mount Diablo and Mount Tamalpais, Mount St. Helena has no automobile access to its summit. Its view must be earned with some effort.

For the best possible trip, pick a cool, clear day in late autumn, winter, or spring—forget the hot days of summer. Then pack along the finest picnic lunch you can imagine, drive to the trailhead, and start climbing.

At its start, the trail is called the Stevenson Memorial Trail, named for author Robert Louis Stevenson. He and his wife honeymooned at an abandoned mine site along this trail in the summer of 1880. The first mile consists of well graded single-track through a densely wooded canyon. Except for some road noise from the highway below, this stretch is a delightful stroll past giant madrones, bay laurels, Douglas firs, and black oaks. The switchbacks are plentiful, making the ascent a breeze. Enjoy the good trail and the shade, because both will come to an end in short order.

One mile up the trail is a stone monument marking the spot where the Stevensons honeymooned. It's carved with a Stevenson quote, but the words have been worn illegible. Lacking the finances for a fancier vacation, the Stevensons camped here for a month in an old cabin, using hay for bedding. While they honeymooned, Stevenson took extensive notes on both the mountain landscape and the couple's camping experience. These scribblings became the basis for his book *The Silverado Squatters*. Mount St. Helena later became the model for Spyglass Hill in Stevenson's *Treasure Island*.

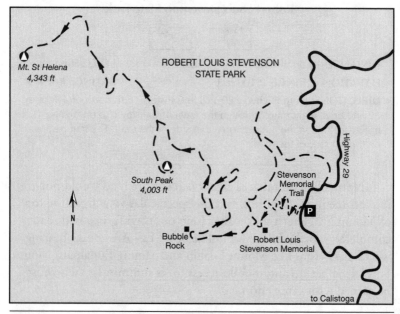

Say farewell to the shade and single-track. Shortly beyond the Stevenson monument the trail joins Mount St. Helena Fire Road. Turn left on the dirt road (this is one of only two junctions on the entire route). Take a look around and notice the terrain change. You're in big knobcone pines and manzanita now, combined with some serious sunshine and views of the Napa Valley.

Keep climbing. At a major switchback at 1.6 miles, you reach Bubble Rock, where rock climbers strut their stuff. The grade is surprisingly moderate, and the remaining miles to the summit go by quickly (provided you aren't hiking on a hot day). You don't have to wait until you reach the summit to be rewarded; you gain fine vistas of Napa Valley, the Vaca Mountains, Lake Berryessa, and the volcanic rock of the Palisades at several points along the road.

The trail's second major trail junction shows up at 3.1 miles, along the ridgeline of Mount St. Helena. The road to the left leads to South Peak, a lesser summit at 4,003 feet. Continue straight for the mountain's higher summit, but not without first oohing and aahing over the vista from this saddle. This is your most expansive view so far.

Save your film, because now it's less than two miles to Mount St. Helena's summit at 4,343 feet. When you reach the top, pay no attention to the buildings and microwave equipment. Instead stroll around and take in the amazing 360-degree scenery. There's Lake Berryessa and the Sierra Nevada to the east. To the southeast lies Mount Diablo, 60 miles away. Most impressive of all—and this is the part that gives the whole trip an A-plus grade—is the clear-day view of Mount Shasta to the north, nearly 200 miles distant. Often Mount Lassen is visible as well, with 7,056-foot Snow Mountain in the northern foreground. Pull out a map of Northern California, a pair of binoculars, and your picnic lunch.

You may notice some odd-shaped rocks under your feet on the northwest side of the wide summit. If you've ever visited Devils Postpile National Monument in the Eastern Sierra, you'll recognize them—they're the five-sided tops of lava columns. Although Mount St. Helena is com-posed of volcanic rock, it's not a volcano. It's part of a large ancient lava flow.

One more tip on climbing Mount St. Helena: Every winter, usually during the coldest days in December or January, the peak receives a thorough dusting of snow. If you can keep your eye on the

Volcanic rock on Mount St. Helena's summit

Napa & Sonoma

winter weather and take off on a moment's notice, you could have the exhilarating experience of climbing mighty Mount St. Helena in the snow.

Trip notes: There is no fee. Dogs are not allowed. Bikes are allowed only on fire roads. For more information, contact Robert Louis Stevenson State Park c/o Bothe-Napa Valley State Park, 3801 St. Helena Highway North, Calistoga, CA 94515; (707) 942-4575 or (707) 938-1519. Website: www.napanet.net/~bothe

10. SUGARLOAF MOUNTAIN LOOP
Skyline Wilderness Park

DISTANCE: 7.4 miles round-trip; 4 hours   **LEVEL:** Moderate

ELEVATION CHANGE: 1,500 feet   **RATING:** ★ ★ ★

DIRECTIONS: From Highway 29 in Napa, turn east on Imola Avenue. Follow Imola Avenue four miles to its end at Fourth Avenue. Turn right into the park entrance.

Napa Valley hikers speak of Skyline Wilderness Park in hushed tones. Several Napa friends told me repeatedly that Skyline Park had the best hiking in the region. So imagine my surprise when I drove up and discovered that the trailhead for this "wilderness park" is located in an RV camp packed with trailers, lawn chairs, and plastic flowers and flamingos.

So it is, and there's no way to reach the park's fine trails except to walk by the RVs, past the park's social hall and picnic areas, and through an eighth-mile corridor of chain-link fencing. (The latter passes by neighboring state hospital property.) Finally, after about 10 minutes of this strange meandering, you leave it all behind and enter the quiet, steep-walled canyon of Marie Creek.

Trail choices are plentiful. The park isn't large, so by connecting a series of paths you can see a good portion of it. This 7.4-mile loop tours both high walls of Marie Creek canyon, visits the summit of Sugarloaf Mountain, then finishes out alongside pretty Marie Creek.

After passing through the maze of well marked paths to reach the actual trailhead, make your first trail choice based on the day's weather. If visibility is good, take Skyline Trail for the first leg of

Descending Sugarloaf Mountain's grassy slopes

the loop. Skyline Trail, a part of the Bay Area Ridge Trail and open to horses and bikes as well as hikers, climbs to the top of the park's southwest ridge and follows it for four miles. The trail offers good views of Napa Valley and San Pablo Bay.

If it's cloudy, take Buckeye Trail for the loop's first leg. Buckeye Trail is narrow single-track and open to hikers only. It climbs half-way up the southwest canyon wall, then contours along this steep slope for its entire three-mile distance. The path wanders through a series of oak and buckeye groves, grasslands, and fern-covered rock walls. Buckeye Trail is drop-dead gorgeous after a period of rain, when all the tiny ferns come to life.

Buckeye Trail and Skyline Trail meet up just before Lake Marie, a long, narrow reservoir on Marie Creek. The lake is popular with bass fishermen, most of whom access it by hiking on wide, level Lake Marie Road. If you wish, you can take the spur trail from Skyline Trail down to the lake's edge. Then follow Skyline Trail as it curves around the lake and crosses Marie Creek. You'll hike a pleasant stretch along the stream, then turn left on Rim Rock Trail. Prepare for a healthy climb up Sugarloaf Mountain.

Rim Rock Trail traverses open, grassy slopes—an ideal setting for spring wildflowers. Lichen-covered outcrops of volcanic rock are scattered among the grasses. The trail makes a steep climb through oaks and manzanitas to the mountain's summit. Be sure to turn around as you ascend to check out the gorgeous views of Marie canyon below you. As you gain elevation, Mount Diablo peeks out above the hills to the south.

Sugarloaf Mountain has two peaks—the west peak at 1,630 feet, which you're climbing, and the east peak at 1,686 feet, which is covered with microwave towers. Your summit is broad and dotted with coast live oaks, so you have to wander around a bit to get the best views. (Head downhill to the west to reach an open clearing.) While the peak's perspective on the Napa Valley, Napa River, and the northern tip of San Pablo Bay is interesting, the long-distance vista south is the real draw. You can clearly make out the looming outline of Mount Tamalpais in Marin County, as well as the towers of the Golden Gate Bridge and the San Francisco skyline. Nowhere is it more obvious that Mount Tamalpais is a ridge, not a single peak, than from this angle. Looking west and northwest, you can see Mount Veeder and Mount St. Helena.

Continue hiking on Rim Rock Trail, now descending the west side of Sugarloaf Mountain. The trail makes a steep drop through several switchbacks to the canyon bottom. Remarkably tall manzanita bushes border the trail. Cross Marie Creek on a footbridge, then continue straight to junction with Lake Marie Road. A right turn will lead you through a final level mile back to the edge of the RV park and eventually to your car.

Sprawling live oaks on Sugarloaf Mountain

Trip notes: A $4 day-use fee is charged per vehicle. Dogs are not allowed. Bikes are allowed only on fire roads. A free park map is available at the entrance kiosk. For more information, contact Skyline Wilderness Park, 2201 Imola Avenue, Napa, CA 94510; (707) 252-0481.

11. MARSH & SOUTH PASTURE LOOP
Rush Ranch, Solano County Open Space

DISTANCE: 4.6 miles round-trip; 2 hours   **LEVEL:** Easy
ELEVATION CHANGE: Negligible   **RATING:** ★ ★ ★
DIRECTIONS: From Interstate 80 near Fairfield, take Highway 12 east. Drive four miles on Highway 12 to Grizzly Island Road. Turn right and drive 2.2 miles to the sign for Rush Ranch on the right. Turn right and drive to the parking area.

It takes more than an hour's drive from the Golden Gate to reach the northeast edge of immense San Francisco Bay. Although it bears a different name here, the final stretch of bay water before it disperses into the narrow waterways of the delta lies some 40 miles distant from the Golden Gate.

The place is called Suisun Marsh, and it's an important and distinct component of the San Francisco Bay ecosystem. Unlike in most of the East Bay and South Bay, where diking and filling have destroyed the bay's natural wetland edges, the North Bay's Suisun Marsh remains relatively untouched. Such tidal wetland areas have become so rare that Suisun is considered to be the largest contiguous estuarine marsh in the United States.

Although much of Suisun Marsh is run by the California Department of Fish and Game as a wildlife management area, one section of it is operated by a Solano County foundation specifically as a nature preserve. That's Rush Ranch, a former sheep and cattle ranch that is now a 2,000-acre open space area, including more than 1,000 acres of wetlands. At least 12 rare or endangered species can be found at Rush Ranch, including the salt marsh harvest mouse, the Suisun shrew, the Suisun Marsh song sparrow, the black rail, and the clapper rail. Many rare marsh plants may also be seen.

Suisun Slough at Rush Ranch

Rush Ranch offers educational programs and has three trails open to hikers. Visiting the ranch feels like a trip to the country—the weathered, picturesque ranch buildings look much as they did when the Rush family lived here in the early 20th century. Despite the proximity of bustling Fairfield and Suisun City, the ranch land feels remote and peaceful. Its acreage on Suisun Marsh is mostly flat as a pancake, punctuated by the rounded Potrero Hills and bordered by two distant mountains—Mount Diablo to the south at 3,849 feet and Mount Vaca to the north at 2,819 feet.

Bring your binoculars along for this walk—wildlife sightings are nearly guaranteed. More than 230 species of birds reside in or pass through this marsh. By combining two trails that begin at the ranch buildings, you can make a figure-eight loop of 4.6 miles. Start your trip by picking up interpretive brochures at the visitor center, then set out from the back of it on Marsh Trail. The path leads around a managed freshwater marsh and along Suisun Slough, an unaltered salt marsh. Be sure to climb to the top of the small hill near interpretive post #3. You'll get up high enough to gain some perspective on this wide, flat, marshy plain and its waterways. Small boats cruise up the slough occasionally; the Department of Fish and Game allows hunting and fishing on its piece of the marsh.

Much of this walk follows levees just a few feet from the water's edge. Although tall cattails and blackberry vines block views along some of the trail, they soon give way. Keep your eyes on the waterways; it's not uncommon to see a river otter swim by in either the freshwater on your right or the saltwater on your left.

Amid all this nature, one man-made surprise may confront you. Every now and then a huge, gray military plane from nearby Travis Air Force Base will cruise overhead slowly and almost silently. These planes' very slow maneuvering makes them capable of taking off and landing on short runways.

Marsh Trail's final stretch crosses the grasslands to return by the barn and parking area. Head to your right to set out on the second half of the figure-eight on South Pasture Trail. (The trail begins near the water tower and windmill on the south side of the ranch.)

South Pasture Trail circles a restored seasonal pond and offers more views of Suisun Marsh. Birdwatching is excellent. Red-tailed hawks are commonly seen flying over the grasslands and tidal marsh, searching for prey. Other common raptors are northern harriers, osprey, barn owls, American kestrels, and golden eagles. Butterfly watching is also good, especially when the wildflowers bloom in spring.

Trip notes: There is no fee. Dogs and bikes are not allowed. Free trail maps and brochures are available at the visitor center. For more information, contact Rush Ranch, P.O. Box 115, Fairfield, CA 94533; (707) 432-0150.

Marin

12. TOMALES POINT TRAIL
Point Reyes National Seashore

DISTANCE: 9.4 miles round-trip; 5 hours   **LEVEL:** Moderate

ELEVATION CHANGE: 900 feet   **RATING:** ★ ★ ★ ★

DIRECTIONS: From San Francisco, cross the Golden Gate Bridge and drive north on U.S. 101 for 7.5 miles. Take the Sir Francis Drake Boulevard exit west toward San Anselmo, and drive 20 miles to the town of Olema. At Olema, turn right (north) on Highway 1 for about 150 yards, then turn left on Bear Valley Road. Drive 2.2 miles on Bear Valley Road until it joins with Sir Francis Drake Highway. Bear left on Sir Francis Drake and drive 5.6 miles, then take the right fork onto Pierce Point Road. Drive nine miles to the Pierce Point Ranch parking area.

If seeing wildlife is one of the reasons you enjoy hiking, the Tomales Point Trail is sure to satisfy. You'll have a good chance at spotting big, furry animals before you even get out of your car (and not just the usual Point Reyes bovines).

The wildlife is abundant because Tomales Point Trail is located in Point Reyes National Seashore's tule elk preserve. Before 1860, thousands of native tule elk roamed Tomales Point, but in the late nineteenth century the animals were hunted out of existence. The preserve is the park service's attempt to re-establish the elk in their native habitat. Their efforts have been successful; today the herd is numbered at 200 and going strong.

Seeing the magnificent tule elk is almost a given. Frequently they're hanging out in large numbers near the trailhead parking lot, and often you spot them as you drive in on Pierce Point Road. Once you're out on the trail, you'll probably see more elk as well as other wildlife. If you hike early in the morning, before many other people have traipsed down the trail, check the dirt path for footprints. I've seen mountain lion tracks as well as more common raccoon and elk prints. While hiking, I've encountered large jackrabbits, various harmless snakes, big fuzzy caterpillars, and a variety of birds. Once I had to make a wide circle off the path to avoid a big skunk who was walking down the trail ahead of me. He was just moseying along, indifferent to my presence.

It's 4.7 miles to the trail's end at the tip of Tomales Point, but you don't have to walk that far to have a great trip. Only a mile or two of hiking will provide you with splendid coastal and Tomales Bay views, plus a probable wildlife encounter. Set your own trail distance and turn around when you please. Just make sure you pick a clear day for this trip; although you may still see tule elk in the fog, you'll miss out on the trail's world-class views. And be sure to carry a few extra layers. If the weather is clear, it's almost guaranteed to be windy.

The Tomales Point Trail begins at Pierce Point Ranch, one of the oldest dairies in Point Reyes. The ranch manufactured milk and butter for San Francisco dinner tables in the 1850s. Begin hiking around the western perimeter of the ranch, or take a few minutes to inspect its buildings. Interpretive signs describe the history of the ranch and its dairy business. The trail curves uphill around the ranch, then heads northwest along the blufftops toward Tomales Point, the northernmost tip of Point Reyes. Wildflowers bloom profusely in the spring, particularly poppies, gold fields, tidy tips, and bush lupine.

The trail is wide, smooth, and easy to hike from beginning to end. At a half mile out, you reach the first short climb, in which you gain about 100 feet. Turn around and look behind you as you ascend—you've got the ocean on one side and Tomales Bay on the other. Views are spectacular on clear days. Look for forested Hog Island in Tomales Bay, a popular pull-up spot for kayakers.

Tule elk at Tomales Point

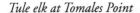

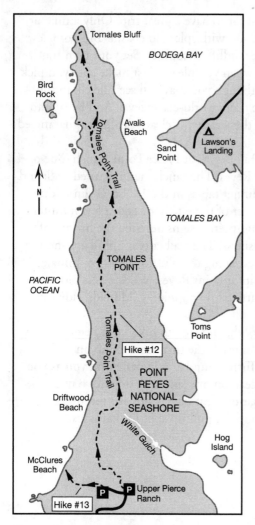

At 1.8 miles, the path starts to descend, offering a good view of Bird Rock out at sea and the town and campground at Lawson's Landing across Tomales Bay. At 2.5 miles, the trail reaches its highest point. Views of Bodega Bay and the Sonoma Coast to the north are excellent. Many hikers make this high knoll their turnaround point for a five-mile round-trip. If you continue, you'll descend to the site of an outpost of Pierce Point Ranch, then pass by windswept Bird Rock, usually covered with pelicans and cormorants.

In the final three-quarters of a mile past Bird Rock, the trail becomes a bit sketchy. Yellow bush lupine carpets the sandy soil in April and May. Amid a series of low dunes, the trail peters out, then vanishes. But the route is obvious; just keep hiking until the land runs out. When it does, you are rewarded with breathtaking views of Bodega Head and Tomales Bay. Look closely and you can make out little tiny boats leaving the harbor at Bodega Bay.

Trip notes: There is no fee. Dogs and bikes are not allowed. A free park map is available at the Bear Valley Visitor Center on Bear Valley Road. For more information, contact Point Reyes National Seashore, Point Reyes, CA 94956; (415) 663-1092.

13. McCLURES BEACH
Point Reyes National Seashore

DISTANCE: 1.0 mile round-trip; 1 hour   **LEVEL:** Easy

ELEVATION CHANGE: 250 feet   **RATING:** ★ ★ ★

DIRECTIONS: Follow the directions on page 44 to the town of Olema in western Marin County. At Olema, turn right (north) on Highway 1 for about 150 yards, then turn left on Bear Valley Road. Drive 2.2 miles on Bear Valley Road until it joins with Sir Francis Drake Highway. Bear left on Sir Francis Drake and drive 5.6 miles, then take the right fork onto Pierce Point Road. Drive 8.9 miles to the left turnoff for McClures Beach, just before you reach Pierce Point Ranch. Turn left and park in the lot.

Most people don't make the long drive out to the northern tip of Point Reyes just to hike to McClures Beach. The majority of visitors show up because they've come to visit the Pierce Point Ranch or hike the Tomales Point Trail (see the previous story). But McClures Beach is worth a trip all by itself, especially during periods of low tides when its most precious secrets are revealed. In addition, because of its remote location and relatively small size, McClures Beach often provides a chance for solitude along its rocky stretch of sand.

The trail from the parking lot leads steeply downhill to the beach in a half-mile. This same stretch will get you huffing and puffing on the way back up, but it's short enough so that anybody can handle it. Starting out as loose sand, the path gets firmer as it winds its way downhill. Buckwheat, ice plant, and morning-glories border the path. You'll walk parallel to the eroding streambed of a steep ravine, which can roar with water during winter storms but is usually just a trickle in summer. Near the end of the trail, on the left, is a fascinating stretch of sculpted sandstone and mudstone. The granite on the right side of the path is much harder and more resistant to erosion.

McClures' rocky beach is a prime area for tidepools, especially if you are fortunate enough to show up during a minus tide. The south end of the beach has the best tidepool areas. During regular low tides, a narrow passageway on the southern end of McClures Beach is revealed. By walking through the rock-lined gap, you'll

Narrow passageway at McClures Beach

gain access to another sandy beach, which is connected to McClures by a narrow peninsula of rock extending from the coastal bluffs.

A small metal sign warns of the dangers of climbing on this rocky extension of the land, but with careful footing you can easily ascend it and find yourself 100 feet above the crashing waves. From this perspective, you can look back and see both McClures Beach and its neighboring beach simultaneously. Tunnels and blowholes in the rock allow the sea to rush in, depositing continually refreshed pools of salt water in the rock's deep hollows. The pools are lined with bright green sea anemones.

Even at high tide, when sand and water have closed off the passageway and covered many of McClures' tidepools, you'll find shards of abalone shells, mussels, and assorted body parts of crabs as you walk along the sand. You don't have to walk far to see all there is to see—McClures Beach is only about three-quarters of a mile long, and bounded by granite cliffs.

Swimming is definitely not recommended, although some hardy surfers attempt to claim the winter waves here. McClures Beach is considered to be one of the most dangerous beaches in Point Reyes because of its rocky shores and crashing breakers.

Trip notes: There is no fee. Dogs and bikes are not allowed. A free park map is available at the Bear Valley Visitor Center on Bear Valley Road. For more information, contact Point Reyes National Seashore, Point Reyes, CA 94956; (415) 663-1092.

14. KEHOE BEACH
Point Reyes National Seashore

DISTANCE: 1.0 to 3.0 miles round-trip; 1-2 hours   **LEVEL:** Easy

ELEVATION CHANGE: Negligible   **RATING:** ★ ★ ★

DIRECTIONS: Follow the directions on page 44 to the town of Olema in western Marin County. At Olema, turn right (north) on Highway 1 for about 150 yards, then turn left on Bear Valley Road. Drive 2.2 miles on Bear Valley Road until it joins with Sir Francis Drake Highway. Bear left on Sir Francis Drake and drive 5.6 miles, then take the right fork onto Pierce Point Road. Drive 5.5 miles to the Kehoe Beach Trailhead on your left. Park along either side of the road in the pullouts.

At most beaches in California, you just drive up, park your car in the paved parking lot, walk a few feet, and plop down in the sand. Kehoe Beach beats that by a mile. Exactly a mile, in fact, because that's how far it is to hike there round-trip. The distance is just long enough for a pleasant, level walk, and it can be combined with another mile or so of sauntering along Kehoe's wide strip of sandy beach.

The trail proves that the journey can be as good as the destination. The fun starts right where you park your car. In late summer you'll find a huge patch of blackberries across the road from the trailhead. If you're wearing long sleeves and long pants, you can pick enough berries to sustain you as you hike.

The trail is gravel, almost completely level, and wide enough for holding hands with your hiking partner. The path runs alongside Kehoe Marsh, a freshwater marsh that provides habitat for birds and birdwatchers. Songbirds are nearly as abundant as the non-native iceplant that weaves thick cushions of matted foliage alongside the trail. Grasses and vines grow in profusion, encouraged by the proximity of the marshy creek and its underground spring. As you near the ocean, the marsh land transforms to sandy dunes, where you may see big jackrabbits hopping among the grasses.

Before you sprint down to Kehoe's brayed tan sands, take the spur trail that cuts off to the right and up the bluffs above the beach. In springtime, the bluffs are painted bright blue and gold with prolific lupine and poppies. It's a glorious sight to behold.

Grass-covered dunes at Kehoe Beach

Once you've admired the flowers, head to the beach to hike farther or have a picnic lunch. You'll return on the same trail.

Dogs are allowed on leash at Kehoe Beach. This is a great bonus for dog-lovers and their canine companions because there are few places in all of Point Reyes where dogs are permitted. Keep your canine friend leashed, though. The strict leash rules protect harbor seals that occasionally haul out on Kehoe Beach. Take care not to disturb them—they nurse pups on land from late March through June, and they need to rest for an average of seven hours per day.

Trip notes: There is no fee. Leashed dogs are allowed. Bikes are not allowed. A free park map is available at the Bear Valley Visitor Center on Bear Valley Road. For more information, contact Point Reyes National Seashore, Point Reyes, CA 94956; (415) 663-1092.

15. ABBOTTS LAGOON
Point Reyes National Seashore

DISTANCE: 2.4 to 6.0 miles round-trip; 1-3 hours   **LEVEL:** Easy

ELEVATION CHANGE: Negligible   **RATING:** ★ ★ ★

DIRECTIONS: Follow the directions on page 44 to the town of Olema in western Marin County. At Olema, turn right (north) on Highway 1 for about 150 yards, then turn left on Bear Valley Road. Drive 2.2 miles on Bear Valley Road until it joins with Sir Francis Drake Highway. Bear left on Sir Francis Drake and drive 5.6 miles, then take the right fork onto Pierce Point Road. Drive 3.3 miles on Pierce Point Road to the Abbotts Lagoon Trailhead on the left side of the road.

If the wind is howling and you've been blown off the path on other Point Reyes trails, drive over to Abbotts Lagoon for a trip through a sheltered watery paradise. The trail itself isn't long, but it leads to Point Reyes Beach where you can hike along the sand for miles. The result is a spectacular two-part trip: first, an easy 1.2-mile stroll through protected lagoons teeming with bird life; second, a windswept walk to the north or south along wide open coastline.

Abbotts Lagoon is huge—more than 200 acres—and joined by a spillway to two freshwater ponds. The lagoon is only rarely influenced by tides, during the few times a year when harsh winter storms break through its low sand bar and open it to the ocean. Soon thereafter sand will accumulate and seal off the lagoon, but these brief openings result in water that is continually brackish—a mix of saltwater and freshwater—and a haven for many species of birds, mammals, and plants.

The trail is equally loved by beach lovers and birdwatchers. The latter are thrilled by the amount and diversity of bird habitat in a relatively small area; the former enjoy the level trail and easy access to Point Reyes Beach, also known as Ten-Mile Beach or the Great Beach. If you're a birding novice and want to give the sport a try, look for these easy-to-spot species: western grebes (large, gray and white diving birds with a long, swanlike neck and yellow bill); pie-billed grebes (similar to western grebes but with a short, rounded bill and no white patch); coots (dark grey or black hen-like birds that skitter across the water when they fly, dragging their feet); and caspian terns (like seagulls but more angular and elegant, with large red bills). The autumn migration season is the best time to bird-watch, although birds are present at the lagoon year-round.

The first half-mile of trail is level and hard-packed for wheel-chair use, and the rest of the route is wide, level, and sandy. The scenery is pretty from the start, leading through coastal scrub and open grasslands that are gilded with wildflowers in the spring. A bucolic-looking white farmhouse, perched on a distant hillside, keeps watch over the scene.

At one mile out, shortly before you cross a small footbridge that separates the two parts of the lagoon, you'll notice a spur trail that leads up the hillside to the left. Take this spur and climb up to the top of the bluff. High on this grassy knoll is the best spot to gain perspective on the immense size of Abbotts Lagoon and its distinctive two-part shape. It's also an excellent spot to birdwatch, picnic, or just admire the beauty of the place. Beyond the lagoon, you'll see bright white ocean waves crashing on the sandy beach.

If you want to hike along Point Reyes Beach, walk back downhill to the footbridge and pick up the spur trail that leads west from the lagoon to the ocean, only a quarter mile away. Or you can just walk across the dunes, but watch your step around the many fragile dune plants. Look for yellow bush lupines, beach strawberry, morning glories, and yellow sand verbena.

Beach explorers should carry an extra layer of clothing—the coast is much windier than the protected lagoon. Head north or south and walk as long and far as you please. You may see harbor seals and sea lions; they often haul out on the sand.

Wildflower season from March through May brings spectacular shows of poppies and lupine along the Abbotts Lagoon Trail. Also look for cobweb thistle, a native thistle that is brilliant red, and prolific Douglas irises. But perhaps the best time to visit Abbotts Lagoon is on a crystal-clear day in late fall or winter, when the fog

A bird's-eye view of Abbotts Lagoon

has vanished and the rich, primary colors of water, sky, and grasslands are thoroughly saturated.

Trip notes: There is no fee. Dogs are not allowed. Bikes are
allowed. A free park map is available at the Bear Valley Visitor
Center on Bear Valley Road. For more information, contact Point
Reyes National Seashore, Point Reyes, CA 94956; (415) 663-1092.

16. MARSHALL BEACH
Point Reyes National Seashore

DISTANCE: 2.4 miles round-trip; 1.5 hours   **LEVEL:** Easy

ELEVATION CHANGE: 300 feet   **RATING:** ★ ★ ★

DIRECTIONS: Follow the directions on page 44 to the town of Olema in
western Marin County. At Olema, turn right (north) on Highway 1 for
about 150 yards, then turn left on Bear Valley Road. Drive 2.2 miles on
Bear Valley Road until it joins with Sir Francis Drake Highway. Bear left on
Sir Francis Drake and drive 5.6 miles, then take the right fork onto Pierce
Point Road. In 1.2 miles you'll see the entrance road for Tomales Bay State
Park. Drive just past it to Duck Cove/Marshall Beach Road; turn right and
drive 2.6 miles. The road turns to gravel and dirt; stay to the left where it
forks. Park in the gravel parking area, taking care not to block any of the
dirt roads that connect here.

The Marshall Beach Trail is one of the best kept secrets in
Point Reyes. Few visitors know about Marshall Beach because the
trailhead is situated on a dirt road to nowhere, at the northeastern
tip of the Point Reyes peninsula. While thousands of visitors pour
into neighboring Tomales Bay State Park for its protected bay
waters and stunning white beaches, few realize that right next door
is Marshall Beach, with all the same advantages but none of the
crowds and no entrance fee.

On your first trip to the Marshall Beach trailhead you may
question if you're going the right way. The road leads through cow
country with no beach in sight. The paved road turns to dirt and
you keep driving along grassy coastal bluffs until you reach a non-
descript trailhead sign. Then you start hiking through cow pastures.
Be sure to keep a vigilant lookout for meadow muffins—the stuff
can stay on your boot soles for days.

Hiking down to Marshall Beach

Why do we have cow pastures in a national park? Because ranching is considered to be part of the "cultural history" of Point Reyes. Cattle and dairy ranches have operated in the area since the 1850s. The 1962 law that authorized Point Reyes National Seashore made allowances so that the original ranch owners could continue operating within the park's boundaries. Currently, there are seven viable dairies in the park, milking about 3,200 cows and producing over five million gallons of milk each year. Just wave and smile at Bessie as you walk to the beach.

The hike to Marshall Beach is a simple out-and-back, with no trail junctions. Just amble down the wide ranch road, which curves around the hillside and descends to the water's edge. You'll find no shade along the route, except at the edge of Marshall Beach's cove where windswept cypress trees stand guard. Thick lichen hangs from their branches.

Marshall Beach is a nearly perfect beach, with coarse white sand and azure blue Tomales Bay water. It's a small slice of paradise overlooking the hamlet of Marshall on the far side of the bay. You can swim in the calm bay waters, which are protected from the wind by Inverness Ridge. The most common visitors to the beach are kayakers who paddle over from Marshall, Inverness, or Tomales Bay State Park to the south. Other hikers are few.

Essentials for this trip include a picnic, a bathing suit, a good book, and some binoculars for birdwatching. Settle in for a perfect afternoon, then drag yourself away—and back up the hill—when it's time to leave.

Trip notes: There is no fee. Dogs are not allowed. Bikes are allowed. A free park map is available at the Bear Valley Visitor Center on Bear Valley Road. For more information, contact Point Reyes National Seashore, Point Reyes, CA 94956; (415) 663-1092.

---

17. JEPSON, JOHNSTONE, & BEACHES LOOP
Tomales Bay State Park

DISTANCE: 4.6 miles round-trip; 2.5 hours   **LEVEL:** Easy

ELEVATION CHANGE: 500 feet   **RATING:** ★ ★ ★

DIRECTIONS: Follow the directions on page 44 to the town of Olema in western Marin County. At Olema, turn right (north) on Highway 1 for about 150 yards, then turn left on Bear Valley Road. Drive 2.2 miles on Bear Valley Road until it joins with Sir Francis Drake Highway. Bear left on Sir Francis Drake and drive 5.6 miles, then take the right fork onto Pierce Point Road. Drive 1.2 miles to the access road for Tomales Bay State Park. Turn right and drive one mile down the park road. Turn left and park at the Heart's Desire Beach parking lot. Johnstone Trail begins at the south end of the beach.

Tomales Bay State Park is 1,000 acres of white sandy beaches, sparkling bay waters, and dense forests filled with botanical marvels. Most visitors come to the park for its easy access to Tomales Bay, a large, sheltered cove that is blessed with good weather. Protected by Inverness Ridge, Tomales Bay is often sunny and warm even when the nearby ocean coastline is fogged in or windy. The bay is surf-free for swimming—an activity that is nearly impossible at the turbulent beaches of neighboring Point Reyes. The water of Tomales Bay is a lovely light blue, making the white sand beaches look like a tropical paradise.

Hikers will find still more treasures at Tomales Bay State Park. A loop route starting from Heart's Desire Beach follows Johnstone Trail to secluded Pebble Beach, then gently climbs to a junction with Jepson Trail and drops back down through a unique forest of

Bishop pines. Both legs of the loop are set in a forest so tangled with curving tree branches, huckleberry vines, wax myrtle, toyon, and ferns that you can often see only a few feet ahead of you. When the loop returns to Heart's Desire Beach, you can add on a short out-and-back walk to Indian Beach.

Start your trip at the south side of Heart's Desire Beach at the trail sign for Johnstone Trail. Leave the beach crowds behind as you travel through a forest of oaks, bay, and madrone, gaining frequent views of Tomales Bay through the trees. Pass through Vista Point Group Picnic Area, which offers a stunning view of Heart's Desire Beach and Tomales Bay. At a half mile out, watch for a sign point-

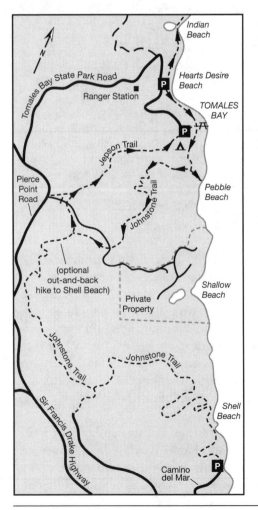

ing left to "rest rooms" where the Johnstone Trail turns right. The "rest rooms" spur trail descends to Pebble Beach, a gorgeous and secluded little beach composed of tiny—guess what?—pebbles. Because you have to walk to it, Pebble Beach always has fewer visitors than Heart's Desire. Narrow and only about 100 yards long, the scenic beach is backed by a small marsh. Views to the east are lovely; the predominant land form across the bay and to the south is Black Mountain at 1,280 feet.

After your beach visit, return to the main trail and hike gently uphill on Johnstone Trail. Note the pink lichen growing on the bark of broad oak trees

Jepson Trail, Tomales Bay State Park

near Pebble Beach. Johnstone Trail winds gradually upward, passing through several wet, marshy areas on small wooden bridges. After crossing a paved, private road, it meets up with Jepson Trail. Hikers who wish to make a long day of it can turn left to stay on Johnstone Trail and make a two-mile trip to Shell Beach. The route is an out-and-back, so you'll have to return to this junction eventually, adding four miles to your day. The suggested loop turns right on Jepson Trail and crosses the private road again near Pierce Point Road. (A small parking area is located here for hikers who don't want to drive in to the park. You could start your trip from Pierce Point Road and avoid paying the entrance fee.)

Jepson Trail makes a more direct descent to Tomales Bay. The trail passes through the park's virgin grove of Bishop pines, which bear gracefully sculpted limbs and weather-worn trunks. The trees are cousins of the Monterey pine; they're in the family of pines that requires the extreme heat of fire to break open their cones and disperse their seeds. As such, these pines do not reproduce often. Bishop pines are relatively uncommon along the California coast, but Tomales Bay and Point Reyes have healthy stands of them.

Jepson Trail deposits you at the parking lot for Vista Point Group Picnic Area. Cross it, enter the picnic area, and turn left on Johnstone Trail to head back to Heart's Desire Beach. Then cross to the north side of Heart's Desire and pick up the Indian Nature Trail to Indian Beach. The path is a half-mile interpretive trail with signs explaining the park's various plants and their uses by the coastal Miwok Indians. Stay to the right at the fork; you'll climb gently then descend to Indian Beach, a lovely strip of sand that separates an inland marsh from Tomales Bay. Three tall, bark-covered teepees stand guard at the beach; these are replicas of coastal Miwok Indian dwellings.

Birds and wildlife are plentiful both in the marsh and along the shoreline. On one trip, we stood on the footbridge over the marsh and watched a group of bat rays feeding in the oceanbound stream. The rays hovered in the water, moving their fins just enough to hold steady their position in the current while they fed on tiny organisms in the creek.

You can take the bridge at the north end of the beach to loop back to Heart's Desire Beach on a dirt service road, but that route isn't the most scenic. You're better off retracing your steps on the Indian Nature Trail.

Trip notes: A $5 day-use fee is charged per vehicle. Dogs and bikes are not allowed. A park map is available at the entrance kiosk for $1. For more information, contact Tomales Bay State Park, Star Route, Inverness, CA 94937; (415) 669-1140 or (415) 893-1580.

18. ESTERO TRAIL to SUNSET BEACH
Point Reyes National Seashore

DISTANCE: 7.8 miles round-trip; 4 hours   **LEVEL:** Moderate
ELEVATION CHANGE: 720 feet   **RATING:** ★ ★ ★ ★
DIRECTIONS: Follow the directions on page 44 to the town of Olema in western Marin County. At Olema, turn right (north) on Highway 1 for about 150 yards, then turn left on Bear Valley Road. Drive 2.2 miles on Bear Valley Road until it joins with Sir Francis Drake Highway. Bear left on Sir Francis Drake and drive 7.6 miles to the left turnoff for the Estero Trailhead. Turn left and drive one mile to the trailhead parking area.

The Estero Trail to Sunset Beach is quintessential Point Reyes. It's full of good surprises, including an exemplary display of Douglas iris in spring, a thick forest of Monterey pines, nearly non-stop views of estuary, bay, and ocean, and access to pristine Sunset Beach.

Plus, the 7.8-mile round-trip mileage is the perfect length for a day hike in Point Reyes.

The trail leads from the left side of the Estero parking lot and laterals across a grassy hillside, with little or no indication of what lies ahead. As you hike, look over your left shoulder to observe the regenerating hillsides of Inverness Ridge. After the Point Reyes wildfire of 1995, the ravaged slopes quickly turned from black to green again.

Round a corner and descend into a dense stand of Monterey pines, the remainders of an old Christmas tree farm. In another few minutes of walking through the trees, the trail opens out to blue, serene Home Bay, exactly one mile from the trailhead.

Walk across the footbridge on the edge of the bay. You'll be surrounded by bay water, or mud flats if the tide is out. On the bridge's far side, the trail rises above Home Bay and crests its first hill. At its high point you'll see where Home Bay opens up to Drakes Estero. The next stretch of trail had to be rebuilt in 1999 after several stormy winters caused a large landslide. Water views are lovely as you descend the hill's far side. Shortly you'll cross another levee in another protected cove.

Sunset Beach

Continue hiking up and down the undulating trail, paralleling the edge of calm Drakes Estero and enjoying nonstop water views and nonstop Douglas irises in spring. Their lavish, sky-blue blooms decorate the hillsides in April and May. If the tide is out when you hike, Drakes Estero's mud flats and the oyster

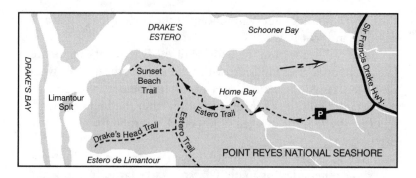

beds of nearby Johnson's Oyster Farm will be revealed. If the tide is in, you'll see miles of azure blue water. You'll climb and descend a total of three hills on this trail; the third one has a lone eucalyptus tree growing on its summit.

Your chance of seeing wildlife along the route is excellent. Waterfowl and shorebirds can be seen close-up every time the trail dips down to one of Home Bay's many coves. On one trip, I spotted an immense great blue heron, slowly beating his wings and taking off from the ground like a huge, mythical creature. Deer also frequent this section of the park, including a herd of white fallow deer that were imported by a rancher a generation ago. (Before I knew that exotic white deer roamed in Point Reyes, I was astonished to see a pure white buck on the hillside above the Estero Trail early one morning. I was sure that the fog was playing tricks on my eyes.) Many more common black-tail deer are also present.

At 2.4 miles out, you'll reach a trail sign for Drakes Head to the left and Sunset Beach straight ahead. Continuing straight on Sunset Beach Trail, the route levels out. At 1.5 miles from the junction, you'll be within view of Sunset Beach. A large, quiet pond separates it from you. You can hear the ocean waves ahead even though the water in the foreground is completely calm and still.

Hike around the left side of the pond. The trail becomes narrow and muddy, but just keep going. (Don't be tempted to head inland into the coastal scrub to bypass the mud. The brushy areas are lined with poison oak.) In a quarter mile you reach the place where Drakes Estero empties into the sea. Beautiful Sunset Beach, littered with rounded boulders and sculpted sandstone, is hikeable to your left. On many days, you'll hear the barking of sea lions who have hauled out on Limantour Spit, just across from you.

Trip notes: There is no fee. Dogs are not allowed. Bikes are allowed. A free park map is available at the Bear Valley Visitor Center on Bear Valley Road. For more information, contact Point Reyes National Seashore, Point Reyes, CA 94956; (415) 663-1092.

---

19. CHIMNEY ROCK
Point Reyes National Seashore

DISTANCE: 1.4 miles round-trip; 1 hour   **LEVEL:** Easy

ELEVATION CHANGE: Negligible   **RATING:** ★ ★ ★ ★

DIRECTIONS: Follow the directions on page 44 to the town of Olema in western Marin County. At Olema, turn right (north) on Highway 1 for about 150 yards, then turn left on Bear Valley Road. Drive 2.2 miles on Bear Valley Road until it joins with Sir Francis Drake Highway. Bear left on Sir Francis Drake and drive 17.6 miles to the left turnoff for Chimney Rock. Turn left and drive nine-tenths of a mile to the trailhead and parking area.

SPECIAL NOTE: During peak weekends, the park service may require visitors to ride a shuttle bus from Drakes Beach to the Chimney Rock Trailhead. Phone the Bear Valley Visitor Center at (415) 663-1092 for updated information.

If you like wildflowers and ocean views, there may be no better springtime hike in Point Reyes than the Chimney Rock Trail. Each year from March to May colorful wildflowers carpet the rugged coastal bluffs that lead to an overlook of Chimney Rock, an offshore sea stack. This is one of the best flower displays in all of Point Reyes. If you hike the trail earlier in the season—December to February— you're likely to see elephant seals on the beaches below Chimney Rock and the spouts of gray whales out at sea. Adding to the trail's attractions, a tidepool area is found at a rocky beach near the trail-head, offering hikers a chance to inspect the contents of the sea during low tides.

The best trip on the Chimney Rock Trail is achieved with some planning. First, know that the wind can blow fiercely at Chimney Rock. Although the first half of the trail is on the sheltered side of the headland that faces Drakes Bay, the second half extends onto the thin peninsula of land that separates Drakes Bay from the Pacific Ocean. At the point where the bay and ocean meet, you'll find

Chimney Rock—and frequently, a howling wind. Make sure you dress for it. On the up side, this trail is usually not as windy as nearby Point Reyes Lighthouse, if that's any consolation.

From the trailhead parking lot, you can head straight for the Chimney Rock Trail or you can take a couple of short, worthwhile detours. The latter requires a brief descent on the paved road that continues beyond the parking lot. In a few hundred feet you'll see a dirt trail on the left signed for Elephant Seal Overlook. Take it, go through a cattle gate, walk about a quarter-mile, then come out to a fenced overlook with a view of the southern tip of Drakes Beach. This is where elephant seals haul out in the winter months, creating a tremendous cacophony of barking and snorting. Although you are a few hundred feet above the seals, you can clearly see them brawling with each other and watch their strange, jerking movements as they go from sand to sea and back.

Elephant seals started to colonize the beaches in Point Reyes in 1981 and the annual seal population has expanded to more than 1,000 individuals. (Elephant seals were nearly extinct from hunting by the year 1900; their comeback in the last century has been quite remarkable.) The huge male elephant seals arrive in late November to claim the best spots on the beaches; the pregnant females come to shore two to three weeks later to give birth and breed. In a few months the seals disappear back into the ocean and are usually not seen again until the following winter.

After you've watched the seals' antics, continue down the paved road to see the Point Reyes Lifesaving Station, which was built in 1889 and operated until 1968. Despite the proximity of the Point Reyes Lighthouse, many shipwrecks occurred along the Point Reyes peninsula and the crews at the lifeboat station had the daring job of

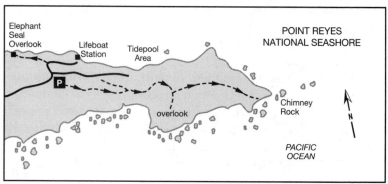

Blufftop views from Chimney Rock Trail

rescuing survivors. Just beyond the lifeboat station is a rocky beach that offers good tidepooling at low tides. (You can find out the daily status of the tides at the Bear Valley, Lighthouse, or Drakes Beach visitor centers or just by checking a local newspaper.)

With these detours completed, you're ready for the main event—the Chimney Rock Trail. The path is a narrow, dirt trail leading from the rest rooms at the trailhead parking lot. The route crosses grassy headlands, first along sheltered Drakes Bay where you can see the tall white cliffs that mark Drakes Beach. Then the trail climbs slightly to the top of the narrow bluffs that divide Drakes Bay from the sea. If it's a windy day, you'll feel it here.

At four-tenths of a mile, you'll see a faint trail leading off to the right; this path travels one-tenth of a mile to an overlook of the Point Reyes Headlands Reserve and the Farallon Islands, 20 miles away. The main trail continues another three-tenths of a mile to a fenced overlook of multiple sea stacks, the largest of which is Chimney Rock. It's impossible to see the rock's "chimney" from here, although you can see it from the south end of Drakes Beach.

On a clear day this is an excellent spot to look for passing gray whales. Even if you don't see any, you're still rewarded with stellar ocean views. A small beach just to the left of the trail's end is the temporary winter home of a group of elephant seals. You'll hear them barking and making a ruckus. Do not attempt to descend to any of the beaches near Chimney Rock; the cliffs are steep, rugged, and unstable.

Wildflower lovers, take note. In addition to the more common flowers such as poppies, owl's clover, lupine, checkerbloom, Douglas iris, and footsteps-of-spring that you'll find along the trail in spring, look for the more rare pussy's ears near the end of the Chimney Rock Trail. They're light purple or white and somewhat furry, as you might expect.

Trip notes: There is no fee. Dogs are not allowed. Bikes are allowed. A free park map is available at the Bear Valley Visitor Center on Bear Valley Road. For more information, contact Point Reyes National Seashore, Point Reyes, CA 94956; (415) 663-1092.

20. SKY TRAIL to MOUNT WITTENBERG
Point Reyes National Seashore

DISTANCE: 4.5 or 8.4 miles round-trip; 2-4 hours   **LEVEL:** Moderate
ELEVATION CHANGE: 750 feet or 1,300 feet   **RATING:** ★ ★ ★
DIRECTIONS: Follow the directions on page 44 to the town of Olema in western Marin County. At Olema, turn right (north) on Highway 1 for about 150 yards, then turn left on Bear Valley Road. Drive 1.7 miles on Bear Valley Road, then turn left on Limantour Road. Drive 3.4 miles on Limantour Road to the Sky Trailhead on the left. Turn left and park in the lot. Begin hiking on the gated dirt road.

There's an easy way and a hard way to hike to Mount Wittenberg, the tallest summit in Point Reyes National Seashore. The route from Sky Trailhead is the easy way, a 4.5-mile semi-loop with a 750-foot elevation gain. The route from Bear Valley Trailhead is the hard way, a 4.6-mile loop or out-and-back with a 1,300-foot elevation gain. Both trails are excellent and they can easily be combined for an 8.4-mile round-trip. Either way your reward is the summit of Mount Wittenberg at 1,407 feet, where on a clear day you'll have panoramic views of the coast and Olema Valley.

Notice I said on a *clear* day. I've been on Mount Wittenberg's summit nearly a dozen times, and only twice have I seen much in the way of a view. For the best experience, you need to hike to

Mount Wittenberg on one of Point Reyes' rare cloudless, fogless days. These occur most often in fall, although you might get lucky in winter or spring, especially immediately following a rainstorm.

For the Sky Trail route to the summit, begin hiking from the Sky Trailhead on Limantour Road. The path is a wide dirt fire road with a steady, moderate grade through a dense forest of Douglas firs. Only once do the trees open up sufficiently to provide a clear view to the west of Limantour Beach and Drakes Bay. This occurs at an obvious curve in the road, where a wooden railing lines the right side. Consider it a preview of coming attractions.

Keep climbing steadily for seven-tenths of a mile, where you'll crest a ridge and reach a junction of trails. Bear left on the narrow Horse Trail, which climbs through dense fir trees for a half mile to a junction with Z Ranch Trail. Turn right on Z Ranch Trail and follow its level path seven-tenths of a mile, past woods and meadows, to a grassy saddle below Mount Wittenberg's summit. Views of Drakes Bay are fine from here, but they are even better from the top. At a junction of trails, the Wittenberg Summit Trail turns sharply left and heads up the mountain. Go for it—it's less than a quarter-mile to the top.

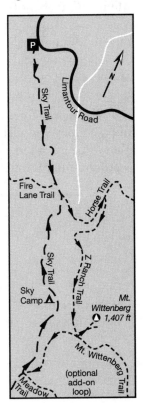

In contrast to the route you've been traveling, the summit of Wittenberg is mostly bald and grassy, with only a few trees. This turns out to be a good arrangement, because after a five-minute ascent to the top you have a 360-degree view of the entire Point Reyes peninsula. You can see Olema Valley and Bolinas Ridge to the east, sparkling Drakes Bay and the ocean to the west and south, and Tomales Bay to the north. Looking beyond the peninsula, you can make out Mount Tamalpais in Marin County, Mount St. Helena in Napa County, and Mount Diablo in the East Bay, 50 miles away. In spring, Wittenberg's exposed, grassy slopes are gilded with tidy tips, lupine, and California poppies.

When you've seen enough, backtrack down the summit trail to the saddle and turn right on Z Ranch Trail (don't go back the way you came). In four-tenths of a mile, you'll connect with Sky Trail's wide road, where you turn right and enjoy an easy jaunt to Sky Camp. Throughout this mostly level stretch you'll enjoy more views of the coast through the trees. Once you reach the camp, you can find an unoccupied campsite and relax for a while. The best sites are at the camp's far reaches near site number 10, where views extend over the fire-scarred forest to the ocean beyond. The 1995 Point Reyes fire severely burned the forests between Sky Trail and the coast but stopped right at the edge of Sky Trail and Sky Camp.

From Sky Camp, you have a mostly downhill stroll on Sky Trail back to the trailhead and your car. If you desire, you can nearly double the length of this trip by adding on a loop from Mount Wittenberg down to Bear Valley and back. After visiting the summit and returning to the junction of trails at the saddle, bear left on the Mount Wittenberg Trail and follow it downhill for 1.8 miles to Bear Valley Trail. Turn right on Bear Valley Trail and hike six-tenths of a mile to Meadow Trail, then turn right on Meadow Trail and hike 1.5 miles back uphill to a junction with Sky Trail. Turn right on Sky Trail to finish out the loop via Sky Camp as described above. This makes an excellent 8.4-mile loop.

Trip notes: There is no fee. Dogs and bikes are not allowed. A free park map is available at the Bear Valley Visitor Center on Bear Valley Road. For more information, contact Point Reyes National Seashore, Point Reyes, CA 94956; (415) 663-1092.

---

21. COAST, FIRE LANE, & LAGUNA LOOP
Point Reyes National Seashore

DISTANCE: 5.0 miles round-trip; 2.5 hours   **LEVEL:** Easy
ELEVATION CHANGE: 450 feet   **RATING:** ★ ★ ★
DIRECTIONS: Follow the directions on page 44 to the town of Olema in western Marin County. At Olema, turn right (north) on Highway 1 for about 150 yards, then turn left on Bear Valley Road. Drive 1.7 miles on Bear Valley Road, then turn left on Limantour Road. Drive 5.9 miles on Limantour Road to the left turnoff for the Point Reyes Youth Hostel. Turn left, drive a half mile (past the youth hostel) and park in the lot on the

right. Then walk back up the road for three tenths of a mile, passing the hostel again. Begin hiking on the dirt road just west of (and across the road from) the youth hostel. The road is signed as Coast Trail to Coast Camp.

If you've ever wanted to take an easy hike to a windswept beach, then find a private spot to sit on the sand and look out to sea for an hour or so, the Coast Trail provides the chance.

The Coast Trail is an L-shaped wide road that begins at the Point Reyes Youth Hostel and makes a beeline for the coast. It then turns left (south) and runs parallel to the beach for another mile to Coast Camp and beyond. An excellent loop trip is made possible by following Coast Trail to Coast Camp (2.8 miles), exploring the nearby beach, then returning to the trailhead on Fire Lane and Laguna trails (1.8 miles).

The region surrounding Coast Trail was badly burned in the Point Reyes fire of 1995, but it recovered quickly. Six months after the fire, the trail's surrounding grasslands and hillsides were green with new life as a multitude of ferns, berry bushes, and vines poked up from the ground and grasses blanketed the blackened earth. In only a few years, the coastal scrub regained its rightful place. Today, it's difficult to find any burn evidence along the trail.

Wide Coast Trail is sunny and exposed most of the way, except for a brief section near a stream where it enters a thicket of alders.

Coast Trail

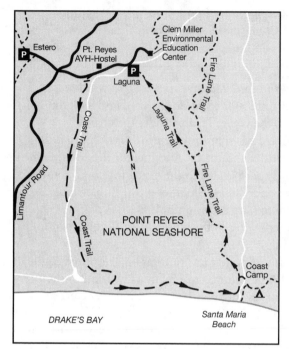

In winter, the stream creates a marsh area that is thickly lined with cattails. Hiking is easy on the wide, dirt road, taking a slight downhill grade to the coast. When you reach the shoreline, you can head straight for the sand and continue walking there, but it's easier to keep hiking on Coast Trail for another 1.1 miles to Coast Camp. (The camp makes an excellent easy backpacking destination. To reserve a spot at the 14-site campground, you must obtain a free permit from Point Reyes headquarters. Reservations are necessary on summer weekends.)

From Coast Camp, take the narrow foot trail by the rest rooms to Santa Maria Beach. From there, you can walk as far as you like in either direction—right toward Limantour Beach or left toward Sculptured Beach—with miles of uninterrupted shoreline between them. Or, if you're tired of walking, just flop down in the sand.

For your return trip, take Fire Lane Trail north from Coast Camp for one mile to a junction with Laguna Trail. You'll have a noticeable climb; keep turning around to check out the ocean views as you gain elevation. At the junction, bear left on Laguna Trail and hike a final eight-tenths of a mile back to your parked car.

Trip notes: There is no fee. Dogs are not allowed. Bikes are allowed only on Coast Trail. A free park map is available at the Bear Valley Visitor Center on Bear Valley Road. For more information, contact Point Reyes National Seashore, Point Reyes, CA 94956; (415) 663-1092. Website: www.nps.gov/pore

22. BEAR VALLEY TRAIL to ARCH ROCK
Point Reyes National Seashore

DISTANCE: 8.2 miles round-trip; 4 hours   **LEVEL:** Moderate

ELEVATION CHANGE: 400 feet   **RATING:** ★ ★ ★

DIRECTIONS: Follow the directions on page 44 to the town of Olema in western Marin County. At Olema, turn right (north) on Highway 1 for about 150 yards, then turn left on Bear Valley Road. Drive a half mile, then turn left at the sign for Seashore Headquarters Information. Drive a quarter mile and park in the large lot on the left, past the visitor center. Start hiking along the park road, heading for the signed Bear Valley Trail.

The Bear Valley Trail is hands-down the most famous trail in Point Reyes, and for that reason alone I avoided it for years. I feared the crowds at the trailhead, the noise of other chattering trail users, and the probable lack of peace in a place as sacred as Point Reyes.

But when I finally hiked it, I realized that bypassing the Bear Valley Trail had been a big mistake. The trail is incredibly beautiful and easy enough for a family hiking trip. Best of all, arriving at the trailhead before 9 A.M. assures you of some solitude along the route, even on weekends. Winter is the best season for less crowds, and the trail is prettiest then anyway, when the streams are running full and the ferns are in full leafy display.

The trail is simple to follow. It begins as a wide dirt road just beyond the Bear Valley Visitor Center and Morgan Horse Ranch. Several trails junction with Bear Valley Trail, but just stay on the wide, main road and meander your way through the mixed bay and Douglas fir forest, following the path of Bear Valley Creek. Ferns of many kinds adorn the creek's banks, including delicate five-finger ferns. You'll notice a slight uphill grade in the first mile, but the entire route never gains or loses more than 200 feet in elevation.

At 1.5 miles from the trailhead, you reach the edge of large Divide Meadow, a lovely spot for a rest or a picnic on your return trip. Deer are often sighted here. Divide Meadow marks the divide in this valley: Bear Valley Creek, which flows north, is left behind, but soon the trail parallels Coast Creek, which flows south all the way to the sea. More forest, ferns, and lush streamside foliage keep you company as you walk. In spring, the buckeye trees along this

Bear Valley Trail's Divide Meadow

stretch bloom with perfumy white flower clusters. Also in spring, the trail is bordered by a profusion of blue forget-me-nots and tasty miner's lettuce.

At 3.2 miles you reach a junction of trails. Glen Trail leads to the left and Baldy Trail leads to the right, but you simply continue straight on Bear Valley Trail to Arch Rock. Although at present you are deep in the forest, surrounded by alders, bay laurel, and Douglas fir, you will soon leave the shade. A half mile farther the trail opens out to coastal marshlands and chaparral, and soon you spot the ocean straight ahead.

Near the sea the Bear Valley Trail splits off, meeting up with Coast Trail. You can take either path to Arch Rock—continue straight ahead, or go right and then jog left 100 yards farther. The junction is not well-signed, so keep in mind that you want to end up at the bluffs' edge overlooking the ocean. (If you keep heading to the right on Coast Trail, you'll miss Arch Rock altogether and wind up at Kelham Beach in eight-tenths of a mile.)

The final steps of the hike are dramatic and memorable as you traverse the top of Arch Rock's precipitous, jade-green bluff jutting out into the sea. Coast Creek, the previously gentle stream you were following, now cuts a deep and eroded gorge on its way to the ocean. After hiking in the peaceful, sheltered forest, the frequent raging wind on top of Arch Rock can be a shock to your system.

A spur trail leads down the cliffs by Coast Creek to the beach. Some hikers plan their trip so they can descend to the beach, then crawl through Arch Rock's tunnel at the mouth of Coast Creek during very low tides. Most hikers are content to stay on top of Arch Rock and enjoy the view, which includes numerous rock outcrops, the shoreline below, and the perpetually rolling surf.

I have a long-standing ritual I perform on Arch Rock. I sit on the jagged bluff edge and wait until a sea lion swims by in the surf below. Then I follow its bobbing and rolling progress through the kelp beds and surging waters as far as my eyes will allow. When the sea lion disappears from sight, I wait for another, and then another. It's remarkable how quickly and pleasantly an afternoon can pass this way.

Trip notes: There is no fee. Dogs are not allowed. Bikes are allowed on the first 3.2 miles of Bear Valley Trail. A free park map is available at the Bear Valley Visitor Center on Bear Valley Road. For more information, contact Point Reyes National Seashore, Point Reyes, CA 94956; (415) 663-1092. Website: www.nps.gov/pore

23. BEAR VALLEY, OLD PINE, WOODWARD VALLEY, & COAST LOOP
Point Reyes National Seashore

DISTANCE: 12.0 miles round-trip; 7 hours   **LEVEL:** Strenuous

ELEVATION CHANGE: 1,700 feet   **RATING:** ★ ★ ★ ★

DIRECTIONS: Follow the directions on page 44 to the town of Olema in western Marin County. At Olema, turn right (north) on Highway 1 for about 150 yards, then turn left on Bear Valley Road. Drive a half mile, then turn left at the sign for Seashore Headquarters Information. Drive a quarter mile and park in the large lot on the left, past the visitor center. Start hiking along the park road, heading for the signed Bear Valley Trail.

You say you're looking for an epic day hike in Point Reyes National Seashore? Well here it is. If you like variety, this loop trail provides it. You'll hike past forest, meadows, and ocean over the course of 12 miles. Pack along a good lunch and make a day of it.

The loop begins just past the Bear Valley Visitor Center. Follow Bear Valley Trail for 1.5 miles to Divide Meadow (see the previous story for details on this stretch). Leave the crowds behind at the scenic meadow and turn right on Old Pine Trail, which begins next to the rest rooms. In contrast to the wide Bear Valley Trail, Old Pine

Trail is a narrow footpath closely bordered by dense Douglas firs and an undergrowth of elderberries and huckleberries. Because it's much less traveled than other nearby trails, you may even have this peaceful forest all to yourself. You'll climb steadily for 1.5 miles through the trees, then descend for just under a half-mile. Here, at a trail junction, turn right on Sky Trail. In three-tenths of a mile, you'll meet up with Woodward Valley Trail, where you turn left.

Woodward Valley Trail has long been considered the most lush, greenery-filled trail in Point Reyes, a park not lacking in trails of this sort. When the Point Reyes fire raged in 1995, Woodward Valley Trail was largely spared, although parts of it bordered the major burn area. You'll notice only a minimum of fire evidence along the trail.

Follow Woodward Valley Trail for almost two lovely miles to the coast, passing through an assortment of shady conifer forests, open hillsides, and grassy meadows. In spring, the meadow areas are verdant green and buzzing with life; they are ringed by Douglas firs. The path is downhill all the way except for occasional short rises. In the last half mile, you'll switchback more steeply down the open coastal hills, heading for Drakes Bay and the ocean. A level stretch followed by a brief climb brings you to a sweeping overlook point

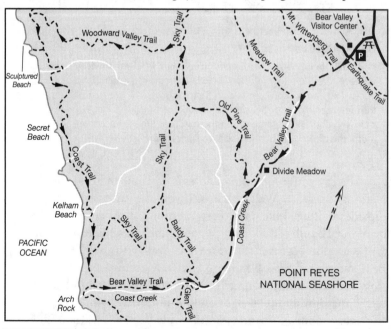

Sculptured Beach

where you can see the Farallon Islands 20 miles out to sea, Double Point and Alamere Falls to the south, Chimney Rock to the north, and a 10-mile-long arc of curving coastline in between.

At a junction with Coast Trail, turn left and parallel the bluffs along the shoreline. Spectacular ocean views are yours for the taking every step of the way. After a half-mile on Coast Trail, you'll reach the signed turnoff for Sculptured Beach. Be sure to take this short spur; Sculptured Beach features some fascinating eroded sandstone terraces and good tidepools. It's a perfect place for lunch and a rest about halfway through the loop.

Two miles farther is the turnoff for Kelham Beach. The spur trail is clearly marked by an immense eucalyptus tree. You're likely to have company at Kelham Beach; many hikers walk along the sand from Arch Rock to Kelham during low tides.

The 3.5-mile stretch on Coast Trail is followed by a left turn on Bear Valley Trail just north of Arch Rock. If you've never visited Arch Rock, take a short side trip and do so now. A quarter-mile walk on the spur trail to your right leads to a spectacular ocean overlook on a jagged, grassy bluff.

At Arch Rock, with a deep sigh, wave a sorrowful good-bye to the coast. It's time to turn inland and head home on Bear Valley Trail. A 2.4-mile walk along Coast Creek brings you back to Divide

Meadow; a final 1.5 miles along Bear Valley Creek returns you to your starting point.

If you want to add a visit to the summit of Mount Wittenberg to this loop, you can start your trip on the Mount Wittenberg Trail from Bear Valley, instead of Old Pine Trail from Divide Meadow. The Mount Wittenberg Trail climbs steeply for 1,300 feet to the tallest peak in the national seashore; take the short summit trail on the right to reach the top. (For more on Mount Wittenberg, read the story on pages 64-65.) From the base of the summit trail, follow Z Ranch Trail south to Sky Trail, then continue south on Sky Trail to pick up Woodward Valley Trail. The rest of the loop is the same as described. This loop is also 12 miles long, but it has a slightly steeper climb. On a clear day, Mount Wittenberg Trail is likely to be more crowded than Old Pine Trail, but if you've never been to the summit, you should go.

Trip notes: There is no fee. Dogs are not allowed. Bikes are allowed on the first 3.2 miles of Bear Valley Trail. A free park map is available at the Bear Valley Visitor Center on Bear Valley Road. For more information, contact Point Reyes National Seashore, Point Reyes, CA 94956; (415) 663-1092. Website: www.nps.gov/pore

24. BASS LAKE, DOUBLE POINT, & ALAMERE FALLS
Point Reyes National Seashore

DISTANCE: 8.4 miles round-trip; 4 hours   **LEVEL:** Moderate

ELEVATION CHANGE: 550 feet   **RATING:** ★ ★ ★ ★

DIRECTIONS: Follow the directions on page 44 to the town of Olema in western Marin County. At Olema, turn left (south) on Highway 1. Drive 8.9 miles on Highway 1 to Bolinas Road, which is often not signed. Turn right and drive 2.1 miles to Mesa Road. Turn right and drive 5.8 miles to the Palomarin Trailhead.

Quick—which California waterfall leaps off high coastal bluffs and cascades gracefully down to the sand and surf below? Most people think of famous McWay Falls in Big Sur, one of the most frequently visited and photographed waterfalls in the state. But don't forget the other coastal cataract that makes the same dramatic plunge from earth to sea, 150 miles up the coast in western Marin County. That's Alamere Falls in Point Reyes National Seashore.

There may be no finer way to spend a spring day than hiking to Alamere Falls and making stops along the way at Bass Lake and Double Point. If you time your trip for a clear, sunny day, when the lupine and Douglas iris are in full bloom and the waterfall is flowing with enthusiasm, this trail's scenery will knock your socks off.

Start hiking on Coast Trail from the Palomarin Trailhead in Point Reyes, the southernmost trailhead in the national seashore. Despite its off-the-beaten-track location near the town of Bolinas, the trailhead parking lot is often full of cars. The occupants of many of those cars are backpacking the 15-mile Coast Trail, a spectacular two-day trip. You'll follow a portion of that route on this hike.

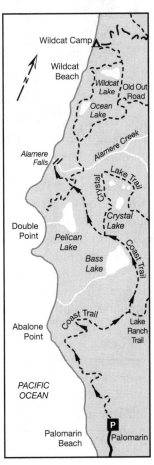

Coast Trail is a wide dirt road that begins in stands of eucalyptus. The first mile is nearly level and offers many lovely ocean views, putting you in fine spirits for the rest of the trip. Then Coast Trail turns inland, climbing slightly to a junction with Lake Ranch Trail at 2.1 miles. Stay on Coast Trail as it veers left and passes a couple of seasonal ponds, which are often covered with paddling water birds. At 2.6 miles, you'll skirt the north edge of Bass Lake. Picnicking and swimming spots are plentiful at the large blue lake; just follow the unsigned spur trail on the left amid the Douglas firs. (The spur is located about 100 yards past the point where you first glimpse the lake.)

Reach another trail junction where Crystal Lake Trail heads right to small Crystal and Mud lakes. Continue straight on Coast Trail, now heading toward the ocean. Three quarters of a mile beyond Bass Lake, prepare yourself for a stunning view of Pelican Lake, perched on a coastal bluff to your left. The Pacific Ocean forms its backdrop.

Spectacular Alamere Falls

After curving past the lake, reach an unmarked left spur trail that leads to the northern edge of Double Point. (If you take the spur, you'll come to a rocky overlook with views of the ocean and Stormy Stack, a big offshore rock outcrop. This is an excellent spot for whale watching.)

Just beyond the Double Point spur, a trail sign points straight ahead for Wildcat Camp and a second unmarked spur leads left, heading for the coastal bluffs and Alamere Falls. (Many hikers miss this turnoff. Start watching for it as soon as you pass Pelican Lake.) Follow the quarter-mile spur trail, which is quite narrow and frequently overgrown with poison oak and coastal scrub, until it meets up with Alamere Creek near the cliff edge. Although you are now practically on top of the fall, you can see little of its watery theatrics.

To see more, you must proceed with caution. Scramble downstream, then cross the creek wherever you safely can, so you wind up on the north side of Alamere Creek. At the edge of the bluffs and alongside the fall's lip you'll find a well-worn route leading down to the beach. A rope is usually tied in place to help you down the most vertical spots. Be wary of the loose sandstone and shale as you make your way down the cliffs.

Only when you touch down on the beach does the full drama of Alamere Falls unfold. Although the pristine coastline would be stunning even without the waterfall, it's made even more impressive by the sight of Alamere Creek dropping in a wide, effusive block over its cliff, then streaming across the sand and into the sea. The fall is 50 feet high, and although its width varies greatly according to how much water is flowing in the creek, it's always enchanting. Find a spot on the beach nearby to give the falls an appreciative audience.

Trip notes: There is no fee. Dogs and bikes are not allowed. A free park map is available at the Bear Valley Visitor Center on Bear Valley Road. For more information, contact Point Reyes National Seashore, Point Reyes, CA 94956; (415) 663-1092.

25. KENT, GRIFFIN, & NORTH LOOP TRAILS
Audubon Canyon Ranch/Bolinas Lagoon Preserve

DISTANCE: 3.0 miles round-trip; 1.5 hours   **LEVEL:** Easy

ELEVATION CHANGE: 800 feet   **RATING:** ★ ★ ★

DIRECTIONS: From San Francisco, cross the Golden Gate Bridge and drive north on U.S. 101 for four miles. Take the Mill Valley/Stinson Beach/Highway 1 exit and continue straight for one mile to a stoplight at Shoreline Highway (Highway 1). Turn left on Shoreline Highway and drive 12 miles to Stinson Beach, then continue north on Highway 1 for another 3.7 miles. Look for the entrance to Audubon Canyon Ranch on the right. (It's a half-mile beyond the entrance signed "Volunteer Canyon.")

SPECIAL NOTE: Check your calendar before you go. Bolinas Lagoon Preserve is open from mid-March to mid-July, on weekends and holidays only, from 10 A.M. to 4 P.M.

When I pulled into the parking lot at Audubon Canyon Ranch at Bolinas Lagoon, I thought I was in the middle of a major event. A row of cars lined the driveway, more cars kept driving in, and somebody was trying to direct all the traffic. What was it, John Muir's birthday or something?

This was no special event, just a busy day at the ranch. The Bolinas Lagoon Preserve is one of three preserves in Marin and Sonoma counties run by Audubon Canyon Ranch. The preserve's chief attraction is the Henderson Overlook, a hike-in birdwatching platform from which you can witness the miracle of great egrets and herons nesting in the tops of redwood trees.

The preserve is open only from mid-March to mid-July, on

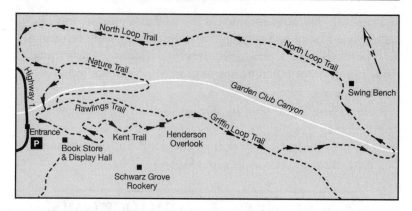

Saturdays, Sundays, and holidays, from 10 A.M. to 4 P.M. With visitation periods so limited, there's no way to avoid the crowds in the parking lot, except perhaps to show up on a rainy day. Fortunately, most of the visitors are either right by the parking lot or on their way to or from the egret overlook. If you're willing to hike a little farther, you can explore a beautiful protected wildlife preserve and find some solitude as well.

Start your trip with a visit to the Henderson Overlook. The Alice Kent Trail begins behind the preserve's buildings and it climbs moderately and pleasantly for a half mile. About halfway up you'll get your first glimpse of snow-white great egrets, nesting in their treetop colony on the neighboring hillside. At the overlook platform, you'll find a set of viewing benches, which are stacked like bleacher seats at a football game. The Audubon people have set up sighting scopes; visitors take turns looking at the birds.

What you see through the scopes depends on what month it is. By May, the egret eggs have usually hatched. Looking through the scopes you can see the baby egrets in their nests. Typically you'll see two or three per nest, all clamoring for food. If you show up in late March or April, you'll see the adult birds (both male and female) incubating the eggs. In late June or July you may see young egrets learning to fly.

In any month, the sighting scopes provide a beautiful magnified view of the adult egrets in their white feathered finery. So large that they appear almost clumsy, the adult egrets make the redwood branches sway and drop dramatically when they take off and land. The egret's delicate feathers were the reason for its near extinction. The birds were massively hunted in the early 1900s to provide plumage for ladies' hats. Efforts of the Audubon Society resulted in legislation protecting the birds from hunting.

With luck, you may also get to see a great blue heron in its nest. There are presently only nine pairs of herons in the preserve, compared to about 100 egret pairs. The herons begin nesting a month earlier than the egrets.

After you've marveled at the birds, continue beyond the overlook on Griffin Trail, which leads uphill through an oak and bay forest. The path heads straight up with no switchbacks for a half-mile. Conserve your energy by not grumbling under your breath.

When you reach the marked intersection of Griffin Trail and North Loop Trail, follow North Loop Trail downhill into a fern-filled redwood forest. Congratulate yourself on your stamina and enjoy the mostly downhill trip along Garden Club Canyon's small stream. After about 10 minutes, you'll swing away from the creek and follow the ridge on a narrow path. Climbing ever so slightly, the trail tops out at a high, open bluff. Have a seat on the strategically placed wooden swing, which is wide enough for about four people, and enjoy the fine view of Bolinas Lagoon and the ocean. Sway back and forth to your heart's content as you review the day's wonders.

Finally, follow the trail back downhill along the sloping hillside. The path curves gently all the way back to Audubon Ranch headquarters, providing sweeping coastal views all the way.

Great white egret

Trip notes: There is no fee, although donations are accepted. Dogs and bikes are not allowed. For more information, contact Audubon Canyon Ranch Headquarters, 4900 Highway 1, Stinson Beach, CA 94970; (415) 868-9244.

26. BARNABE PEAK LOOP
Samuel P. Taylor State Park

DISTANCE: 6.0 miles round-trip; 3 hours   **LEVEL:** Moderate

ELEVATION CHANGE: 1,300 feet   **RATING:** ★ ★ ★ ★

DIRECTIONS: From San Francisco, cross the Golden Gate Bridge and drive north on U.S. 101 for 7.5 miles. Take the Sir Francis Drake Boulevard exit west toward San Anselmo, then drive about 15 miles (through the towns of Ross, Fairfax, and Lagunitas) to the entrance to Samuel P. Taylor State Park. Don't turn here; continue on Sir Francis Drake for one mile beyond the main park entrance. Park in the dirt pullout across the road from Devil's Gulch Horse Camp. Walk across the road and take the paved road to the campground.

Samuel P. Taylor State Park is overshadowed by its large and famous neighbor, Point Reyes National Seashore. Even when the state park's campground is filled to the limit on summer weekends, it's rare to find many people on its hiking trails. But that's just fine with those who know and love the park; they get to enjoy a little solitude along with the scenery. Samuel P. Taylor's best hike is a loop trip to Barnabe Peak, a six-mile trek that leads through a ferny, mossy bay forest, passes by a waterfall, and then bags the summit of Barnabe Peak at 1,466 feet.

The trailhead isn't at the main Samuel P. Taylor park entrance; it's a mile west on Sir Francis Drake Boulevard at Devil's Gulch Horse Camp. Park in the dirt pullout across the road from the camp, then walk up the paved camp road for 100 yards until you spot a trail cutting off to the right along Devil's Gulch Creek, paralleling the road. Follow it and immediately you descend into a stream-fed canyon filled with Douglas firs, tanoaks, bay laurel, and about a million ferns. By April, the ground near the stream is covered with forget-me-nots, buttercups, and milkmaids.

A few minutes of upstream walking brings you to a footbridge

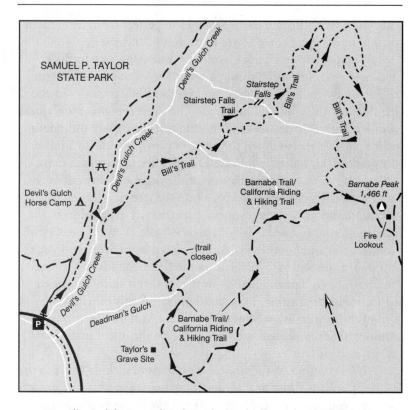

over Devil's Gulch. Just ahead is a huge, hollowed-out redwood tree. It's the only redwood around, situated among many other kinds of hardwoods. Go ahead, climb inside; everybody does it. The tree's charm is irresistible.

Turn right and cross the footbridge, then turn left on the far side of the bridge, following the sign marked "Bill's Trail to Barnabe Peak." You'll climb very gently above the creek, marveling at the walls of ferns and the long limbs of mossy oaks, and gaining 350 feet over three-quarters of a mile. Soon you gain a nice view of the bald, grassy ridge on the far side of the canyon.

After crossing a bridge over a feeder stream, look for the Stairstep Falls Trail cutting off to the left from the main trail. Bear left and in 10 minutes of walking, you'll reach the trail's end near the base of Stairstep Falls. True to its name, 40-foot-tall Stairstep Falls drops in three main cascades, with a rocky "staircase" at its base producing dozens of rivulets of water. Trail maintenance crews try to keep the area cleared of fallen trees and branches so you can stand near the base of the falls. It's a lovely spot, perfect for quiet contemplation in the good company of ferns, forest, and water.

When you've seen enough, retrace your steps back to Bill's Trail and continue uphill through dozens of switchbacks. The trail is beautifully graded—maybe even *too* beautifully graded—so you hardly even realize you're climbing. (The route is popular with local runners, especially on weekend mornings.) The patient meandering of the path slows you down so you have plenty of time to admire the graceful bay laurels, immense Douglas firs, and prolific ferns.

At 3.7 miles, you near the top of the ridge and the trail opens out to a small meadow. A dip back into the trees is followed by another meadow, and then you are permanently expelled from the shade onto the exposed ridge of Barnabe Peak. Wow! What a view! Tomales Bay and Point Reyes are spread out before you, and you're not even at the top yet. Turn left on the fire road to hike the final quarter-mile to Barnabe Peak's summit, which is easily identified by its fire lookout tower. This lookout, one of only two in Marin County (the other is on Mount Tamalpais), is fully operational. Although the tower itself is closed to the public, the view from its base is magnificent.

At the summit, your panorama expands to include views to the south of Bolinas Ridge and Mount Tamalpais. That sparkling patch of water with the large spillway is Kent Lake in the Marin Munici-

Barnabe Peak's summit vista

Marin

pal Water District. To the east, you can see Mount Diablo, and in the foreground lies the town of Lagunitas and the San Geronimo Valley. Are those little tiny boats on Tomales Bay to the west? Yes indeed. The big hill on the southeast side of Tomales Bay is Black Mountain at 1,280 feet.

The story goes that Barnabe Peak was named for explorer John Fremont's mule. After many great traveling expeditions with Fremont, Barnabe lived out his final days as the pet of the Samuel P. Taylor family.

On your return trip down the open, exposed fire road, enjoy the vistas as long as you have them. The return leg of the loop is only two miles, compared to the four miles you hiked to reach the summit, so expect a much steeper grade downhill. (Hikers with bad knees might consider walking this loop in reverse, saving the long switchbacks for the downhill stretch.) At 1.3 miles from the peak, you'll notice a small white picket fence in a clearing 100 feet off the trail. This is Samuel P. Taylor's grave site; he lived from 1827 to 1896. Taylor was famous for establishing the first paper mill on the West Coast and producing newsprint for the San Francisco dailies. He built the town of Taylorville on the site of the present-day park and opened Camp Taylor, a popular weekend recreational resort.

Trip notes: There is no fee if you park in the roadside pullout across from Devil's Gulch Horse Camp. A $5 per vehicle day-use fee is charged if you park in the main paved parking areas. Dogs are not allowed. Bikes are allowed on fire roads only. A park map is available at the ranger kiosk for 75 cents. For more information, contact Samuel P. Taylor State Park, P.O. Box 251, Lagunitas, CA 94938; (415) 488-9897 or (415) 893-1580.

27. MOUNT BURDELL
Olompali State Historic Park

DISTANCE: 5.8 miles round-trip; 3 hours   **LEVEL:** Moderate
ELEVATION CHANGE: 1,500 feet   **RATING:** ★ ★
DIRECTIONS: From San Francisco, cross the Golden Gate Bridge and drive north on U.S. 101 for 28 miles to Novato. Continue another 2.5 miles north of Novato on U.S. 101; the park entrance is on the west side of the highway. Note: the park is accessible only to southbound traffic

from U.S. 101. Driving north, you must continue to the first safe place
to make a U-turn (San Antonio Road), then go south on U.S. 101 to the
entrance.

Olompali is the state park with the funny name that thousands
of commuters drive by daily on U.S. 101. Located a few miles north
of Novato and a few miles south of Petaluma, the park's entrance is
right along the freeway corridor. You might expect this would mean
that the place is packed with visitors year-round, but in fact, the
opposite is true. Olompali is one of the least visited state parks in
the San Francisco Bay Area.

Maybe that's because nobody can pronounce its name. It's oh-
lomp-o-lee, with the accent on the second syllable.

Olompali is also a historic park with a colorful past. This land
was a major Miwok Indian trade center for hundreds of years. The
Coast Miwoks inhabited at least one site within the present-day
park from about 500 A.D. This site was probably one of the largest
Indian sites in what is now Marin County. The name Olompali
comes from the Miwok language and means something like "southern village" or "southern people."

In more recent history, the land was owned by the Burdell
family, a prominent San Francisco dentist and his wife. In the late
1800s they built a 26-room mansion with formal gardens here.
In the twentieth century, the land was rented to various tenants,
including the band The Grateful Dead in 1966. (One of their
album covers features the hills of Olompali.) In the 1970s, a series
of archeological digs in the parkland uncovered an Elizabethan
silver six-pence dated 1567, possibly related to Sir Francis Drake's
landing in Marin County.

In the last decade, park personnel have sunk some money and
effort into Olompali's trail system. Where ten years ago there were
only frustratingly steep, rutted paths, not much better than deer
trails, today there are carefully built, beautifully switchbacked trails.
The park's best offering is a gently sloped trail that climbs 1,500 feet
to the summit of Mount Burdell, a grassy, rounded peak with lovely
views of northern Marin County and southern Sonoma and Napa
counties. It's the fifth highest peak in Marin County.

One caveat: Olompali's inland hills can bake in the summer
and early fall. Even though the Mount Burdell Trail is mostly

The grassy summit of Mount Burdell is covered with poppies in spring

shaded, the hike can be quite hot and unpleasant in the summer months. The best times to visit are spring, when the wildflowers bloom, or fall, when the oaks' leaves turn gold. Clear winter days can also be lovely.

Take the trail leading uphill from the parking lot (not the path that heads toward the ranch buildings). The trail starts in the sun but soon enters the wooded eastern slopes of Mount Burdell. Oak savanna gives way to forests of bay laurels, madrones, and deciduous oaks. The only negative is the constant rumble of cars on the highway; at least you can relish the fact that you're not in one of them.

At 1.3 miles, the path reaches a junction of trails. A right turn is the completion of a short loop through the park; you'll turn left on the signed trail for Burdell Mountain Summit. (A closed trail at this junction is the old summit trail; it made a beeline straight uphill and was subject to terrible erosion in winter rains.)

As you continue the climb, you'll get peek-a-boo views of the Petaluma River to the east and its surrounding marshlands. A few more switchbacks uphill and you'll be able to see where the river empties into San Pablo Bay. Small planes take off and land at Gnoss Field airport, just across U.S. 101, and a steady parade of cars streams north and south on the freeway.

Where the switchbacks lead you into the mountain's many small canyons, all sights and sounds of civilization disappear. The quiet of the leafy woodland is punctured only by the movements of the many deer who inhabit it. (On one trip, I counted a total of 37 deer, all in separate groups of twos and threes.)

The trail switchbacks all the way up to a metal gate marking the park's boundary. Here, the parkland adjoins Burdell Mountain Open Space Preserve. Pass through the gate, then follow the trail down to the paved Burdell Mountain Ridge Fire Road. This road provides your best views to the southwest of the tree-lined streets of Novato. The shimmering blue water body is Stafford Lake. Far off to the south, you can see the tips of the tallest buildings in downtown San Francisco. If you follow the paved road all the way to the mountain's AT&T transmitter towers, you can walk around them and look to the west to Nicasio and Point Reyes. But the best view comes from following use trails to the north side of the summit ridge. At a low stone wall along the 1,500-foot ridgeline, you can look east toward the Petaluma River and San Pablo Bay and north toward Napa and Sonoma. This wall was built by Chinese laborers in the 1870s to mark the border between two large ranchos.

On your return trip, retrace your steps for 1.5 miles and then be sure to take the opposite side of the park's short loop. You'll descend through a canopy of oak and bay trees, pass a meandering creek, then reach a replica of a Miwok Village that was built by park volunteers and local Native Americans. Finally the trail curves down through the Burdell ranch buildings and finishes out back at the parking lot.

Trip notes: A $2 day-use fee is charged per vehicle. Dogs and bikes are not allowed. For a park map, send 75 cents and a self-addressed, stamped envelope to Olompali State Historic Park, P.O. Box 1016, Novato, CA 94948. For more information, contact Olompali State Historic Park at (415) 892-3383.

---

28. CASCADE CANYON
Marin County Open Space District

DISTANCE: 1.5 or 4.8 miles round-trip; 1-2 hours   **LEVEL:** Easy

ELEVATION CHANGE: 100 feet or 700 feet   **RATING:** ★ ★ ★

DIRECTIONS: From San Francisco, cross the Golden Gate Bridge and drive north on U.S. 101 for 7.5 miles. Take the Sir Francis Drake Boulevard exit west toward San Anselmo, then drive six miles to the town of Fairfax.

Turn left by the "Fairfax" sign (on unsigned Pacheco Road), then turn right immediately on Broadway. In one block, turn left on Bolinas Road. Follow Bolinas Road for three-tenths of a mile to a three-road intersection. Bear right on Cascade Drive (the middle road) and continue for 1.5 miles. The road becomes very narrow and ends at Elliott Nature Preserve. Parking is extremely limited. Park alongside the road (be careful to avoid blocking driveways and obey the "no parking" signs in the last 100 feet before the trailhead). Begin hiking at the gate.

Here's proof that the true measure of a waterfall is not how big it is or how much water flows over it, but the overall impression it creates. Little Cascade Falls in Fairfax is no Niagara, but it's perfectly situated in a rocky grotto nestled in a deep, forested canyon. It's the kind of place where once you arrive, you never want to leave.

At its start, the path through Cascade Canyon doesn't seem like it could possibly lead to a waterfall. To reach the trailhead, you follow a narrow road through a suburban neighborhood. Parking is difficult; take care to obey all signs and don't block anyone's driveway. When you start hiking, you head out on an often dry and dusty fire road. The water in San Anselmo Creek's first stretch is rarely more than a few inches deep. Things don't look promising.

But they get better. Keep San Anselmo Creek on your left as you hike, avoiding the wide fire road where possible and taking the single-track hiking paths. (The fire road is often submerged by the creek.) Cross a wooden footbridge a half-mile in and head to your right into a lovely oak and bay forest, now walking alongside Cascade Creek. The stream has many quiet pools and pretty rocky sections.

In a quarter mile, you'll round a bend and hear the sound of falling water, then get your first glimpse of the waterfall. Cascade Falls tumbles 18 feet over a rough rock face to a small pool below. The pool is surrounded by many large and small mossy rocks, perfectly placed for waterfall-watching.

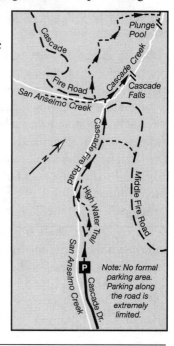

Note: No formal parking area. Parking along the road is extremely limited.

Cascade Falls

If you'd like to see more of Cascade Canyon, you could follow the informal trail up and over Cascade Falls. But the path quickly becomes rough, steep, and lined with poison oak. A better option is to backtrack a quarter-mile to the footbridge you crossed on the way in, then turn right (west) on Cascade Fire Road. In only 100 yards, you'll see a single-track trail on the right signed as "no bikes." (It's shortly beyond another single-track trail on the left). Built by devoted Fairfax nature lovers, this 1.7-mile trail was initially labeled "illegal" by local officials and was scheduled for closure in early 1996. But public support for the trail was so strong that the Open Space District eventually adopted it as one of their own.

Follow this narrow path up a wooded ridge. The climb is steady but moderate and relents at points where the trail opens out to grassy, open slopes and lovely views of the opposing ridge. Finally the trail heads downhill to rejoin Cascade Creek. Where it forks, turn right and walk about 100 feet, then cross the creek. You'll come out at the brink of a beautiful two-tiered waterfall and swimming hole called the Plunge, the Ink Well, or just plain Upper Falls.

Trip notes: There is no fee. Leashed dogs are allowed. Bikes are allowed only on fire roads. A detailed map of the area is available for a fee from Olmsted Brothers Map Company, P.O. Box 5351, Berkeley, CA 94705; (510) 658-6534. For more information, contact the Marin County Open Space District, 3501 Civic Center Drive, San Rafael, CA 94903; (415) 499-6387.

29. BON TEMPE & LAGUNITAS LAKE LOOP
Marin Municipal Water District

DISTANCE: 5.0 miles round-trip; 2.5 hours   **LEVEL:** Easy

ELEVATION CHANGE: 200 feet   **RATING:** ★ ★ ★

DIRECTIONS: From San Francisco, cross the Golden Gate Bridge and drive north on U.S. 101 for 7.5 miles. Take the Sir Francis Drake Boulevard exit west toward San Anselmo, then drive six miles to the town of Fairfax. Turn left by the "Fairfax" sign (on unsigned Pacheco Road), then turn right immediately on Broadway. In one block, turn left on Bolinas Road. Drive 1.5 miles on Bolinas Road to Sky Oaks Road, where you bear left. Drive straight for four-tenths of a mile to the ranger station and entrance kiosk, then continue for three-tenths of a mile to a fork in the road. Bear right on the gravel road. (The left fork takes you to Lake Lagunitas.) Drive four-tenths of a mile until you reach another fork, then bear left and park in the gravel parking area next to a gated fire road. Start hiking at the gate, heading uphill to Bon Tempe Dam.

When most people think of public parkland around Mount Tamalpais, they think of the towering redwoods of Muir Woods National Monument or the grasslands, forests, and stunning coastal views of Mount Tamalpais State Park. But fewer people know that five sparkling lakes are also a part of the Mount Tam landscape. Located in the Mount Tamalpais watershed on the northwest side of the mountain, the five lakes are Alpine, Bon Tempe, Phoenix, Kent, and Lagunitas. Together they provide five more reasons why the Mount Tamalpais area is so spectacular for outdoor recreation.

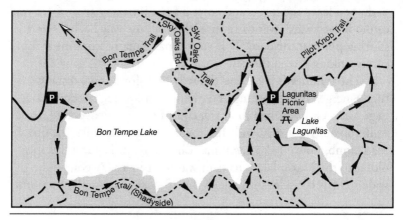

The best lakes for a hiking excursion are Bon Tempe and Lagunitas. By linking together a couple of trails, you can walk all the way around both lakes' perimeters in a couple of hours. The prime seasons are winter, spring, and early summer, when the reservoirs are filled to the brim (and sometimes overflowing down their spillways).

Start your trip by walking uphill to Bon Tempe Lake's dam. From the top, you'll gain pretty views of bright blue Bon Tempe Lake on your left and the marshes and lowlands of Alpine Lake on your right. The unmistakable profile of Mount Tamalpais looms to the southeast. The long, wide dam is an excellent spot to birdwatch. In addition to the more common cormorants, egrets, ducks, and coots, osprey are often spotted at Bon Tempe Lake. The large raptors are amazing fishermen, with razor-sharp eyes that can spot a fish in the lake from high up in the air. They plunge feet first into the water for their prey. Black-tailed deer are also commonly seen around the lake's edges.

Bon Tempe Lake is stocked with trout by the Department of Fish and Game from November to April. However, because it is a reservoir, no boating, swimming, or wading is allowed. Fishing is permitted from shoreline only. Although your dog is allowed to accompany you at the lake, he or she must be kept leashed and out of the water.

Walk across the dam, then pick up the single-track trail that leads left along the lakeshore. It climbs imperceptibly as it travels into a dense mixed forest of oaks, madrones, firs, and redwoods. This is a peaceful, shady stretch of trail, punctuated only by the sound of water lapping against the shore. About a mile down the path, you leave the forest and enter a grassy, marshy area where you can look westward over the entire lake—all the way back to your starting point at the dam. This vista is particularly stunning if the sun is sinking low in the sky.

The trail heads back into the redwoods for a short distance, then emerges at the parking and picnic area for neighboring Lake Lagunitas. Cross a small footbridge just before the pavement, then walk to your right on a wide fire road. In a quarter mile, the dirt road climbs above Lake Lagunitas' earthen dam. Lagunitas is the oldest of the Marin lakes; its dam was built in 1873. Follow the wide road as it circles the edge of the 22-acre lake. At all junctions,

Bon Tempe Lake

just take the path closest to the water. The shallower edges of the lake are crowded with reeds, tules, and cattails. Families of ducks are often seen paddling along the water surface in spring.

Pass a couple of houses along the north edge of Lake Lagunitas, then take the fire road downhill past the picnic area to the parking lot. Here you must locate the final leg of the loop along Bon Tempe Lake; head west across the parking lot to access the trail. Where the fire road splits off with a single-track trail leading left along the lake, follow the single-track. (Just ignore all trails that don't stay close to the water.) There's only one short section on Bon Tempe Lake's north side where a feeder stream and marsh force the route away from the water. You'll have to walk along the edge of paved Sky Oaks Road for 200 yards. Where you see a gravel pullout for cars on the right side of the road, look to your left to find the single-track trail again, which returns to the water's edge.

The final mile along the north shore of Bon Tempe Lake is the best stretch of the trip in springtime. The sunny, grassland slopes are covered with wildflowers, particularly patches of blue and white Douglas irises.

Trip notes: A $3 day-use fee is charge per vehicle on weekdays, $4 per vehicle on weekends from April to October, and $3 per vehicle on weekends from November to March. Leashed dogs are allowed. Bikes are allowed only on fire roads. For more information and a $2 map, contact Marin Municipal Water District at 220 Nellen Avenue, Corte Madera, CA 94925; (415) 945-1195. Or phone Sky Oaks Ranger Station at (415) 945-1181.

30. PINE MOUNTAIN & CARSON FALLS TRAILS
Marin Municipal Water District

DISTANCE: 3.0 miles round-trip; 1.5 hours   **LEVEL:** Moderate

ELEVATION CHANGE: 800 feet   **RATING:** ★ ★ ★

DIRECTIONS: From San Francisco, cross the Golden Gate Bridge and drive north on U.S. 101 for 7.5 miles. Take the Sir Francis Drake Boulevard exit west toward San Anselmo, then drive six miles to the town of Fairfax. Turn left by the "Fairfax" sign (on unsigned Pacheco Road), then turn right immediately on Broadway. In one block, turn left on Bolinas Road. Drive 3.8 miles on Bolinas Road, past the golf course, to the trailhead parking on the left side of the road. Park and walk across the road to the trailhead.

Quiz question: Name three waterfalls located on or nearby Mount Tamalpais, all within six miles of each other, that start with the letter C.

Answer: Cascade Falls in Marin County Open Space land off Bolinas-Fairfax Road (see pages 86-88), Cataract Falls near Laurel Dell, just over the border from Mount Tamalpais State Park (see pages 95-97), and Carson Falls in Marin Municipal Water District.

It's a good idea to learn them all and know which is which, because it saves a lot of confusion when you tell your co-workers about the great waterfall you saw. Carson Falls? Isn't that the one with the trail that starts at Alpine Dam and climbs the whole way? Nope, that's Cataract. Cataract Falls? Isn't that the one that falls in a long, stair-stepped plunge through a steep, rocky canyon? Nope, that's Carson. Cascade Falls? Isn't that the one that's just outside the Fairfax suburbs? Well, you got one right.

Let's set the record straight. Carson Falls is an unusual waterfall set in the middle of a dry grassland canyon in Marin Municipal Water District land, high above Alpine and Kent lakes on the north-west slope of Mount Tamalpais. It's a long chain of four pool-and-drop cataracts that pour into rock-lined pools. The trail to reach the waterfall is not well-marked so it gets less traffic than other waterfalls in Marin County. To reach Carson Falls you must hike up a ridge, then descend into a canyon, and you must have some idea where you're going because there are few signs.

Carson Falls

Carson Falls' main trailhead is located along Bolinas-Fairfax Road at 1,078 feet in elevation. From the parking area, cross Bolinas Road and pick up Pine Mountain Fire Road. Climb uphill for one mile, gaining more than 300 feet in elevation. Be sure to pause and look over your right shoulder as you climb. Check out the wide views of Mount Diablo, San Pablo Bay, Marin County, the East Bay, and even the Richmond Bridge. The ascent will get your heart pumping but the views are fine compensation for your efforts.

Keep your eyes and ears attuned for mountain bicyclists on this fire road. They sometimes come flying downhill, usually after experiencing the agony and ecstasy of climbing Pine Mountain.

After a mile of climbing, you'll reach a high point on the ridge and turn left on Oat Hill Road, also a fire road. (Before you turn, look due north for a surprising view of Mount St. Helena in Napa, 45 miles distant.) As you descend on Oat Hill Road, pay attention to the telephone lines strung up above your head. These are your indicators of where to turn to reach Carson Falls' watershed. Where the telephone lines turn right, you should, too. (The telephone pole at the turnoff is marked with a "no bikes" sign.) Leave the fire road and begin walking downhill on a steep single-track path into the

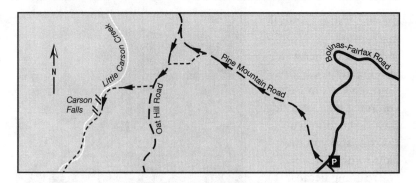

Carson Creek drainage. Watch your footing, especially if it's wet.

After descending a couple hundred feet in elevation, you'll notice a change in the landscape. Although you're still in wide open grasslands, with no hint of a waterfall nearby, you'll notice some trees growing in a little slot in the hillside—evidence of an underground spring. Get closer and you'll see they are buckeye trees, which flower exuberantly in the late spring and go dormant in the late summer. Buckeye trees are a dead giveaway that water is close at hand. Now you're in the watershed, and within moments you're right on top of the falls.

Don't expect that usual thunderous moment of wow!—a waterfall!—because Carson Falls is more subtle, more mysterious than that. This waterfall reveals its pleasures slowly, one pool at a time. To see the fall in its entirety, descend along the rough trail that parallels its cascades, dropping in elevation along with the stream. The waterfall pours in four tiers, but the lowest one is quite difficult to reach. Use extreme caution descending along the steep, rocky path. Carson Falls' green-grey rock looks like serpentine, but it's actually a type of greenstone basalt.

After your exploration, choose a rock near one of the waterfall pools, have a seat, and listen to the water music for a while. Even in summer, when Carson Falls is reduced to a mere trickle, sitting by it feels restorative, like resting in a Zen garden with the sound of the wind and the tinkling of water as your only companions.

Trip notes: There is no fee. Leashed dogs are allowed. Bikes are allowed only on fire roads. For more information and a $2 map, contact Marin Municipal Water District at 220 Nellen Avenue, Corte Madera, CA 94925; (415) 945-1195. Or phone Sky Oaks Ranger Station at (415) 945-1181.

31. CATARACT TRAIL to CATARACT FALLS
Marin Municipal Water District

DISTANCE: 3.2 or 7.5 miles round-trip; 2-4 hours   **LEVEL:** Moderate

ELEVATION CHANGE: 800 feet or 1400 feet   **RATING:** ★ ★ ★ ★

DIRECTIONS: From San Francisco, cross the Golden Gate Bridge and drive north on U.S. 101 for 7.5 miles. Take the Sir Francis Drake Boulevard exit west toward San Anselmo, then drive six miles to the town of Fairfax. Turn left by the "Fairfax" sign (on unsigned Pacheco Road), then turn right immediately on Broadway. Drive one block and turn left on Bolinas Road. Drive 7.8 miles on Bolinas Road to the dam at Alpine Lake. Cross the dam and continue one-tenth mile farther to the hairpin turn in the road. Park in the pullouts along the turn; the trailhead is on the left.

From the first rains in November until the final run-off in May or June, the multiple cascades of Cataract Falls plunge down the fern-covered hillsides of western Mount Tamalpais. Cataract Trail, which traces a path alongside Cataract Creek, provides hikers with easy access to these numerous handsome falls.

Reaching the trailhead at Alpine Lake requires a winding drive on Bolinas Road, but it's a scenic cruise in the country. You're more likely to stop for deer crossing the road than traffic. After parking at the hairpin turn near Alpine Lake's dam, begin hiking at the sign for Cataract Trail. You're treated to pretty lake views for the first quarter-mile before the trail enters a dense forest of redwoods, ferns, maples, and tanoaks. Soon the path heads steeply uphill through the woodland, at times following rock stairsteps.

You can hike as much or as little as you like, because Cataract Falls is a series of cascades spread out over 1.6 miles of Cataract Trail. As soon as the trail leaves the lake and starts to climb, you start seeing waterfalls. Half a dozen of them cascade in the first three-quarters of a mile between the lake's edge and a narrow footbridge crossing Cataract Creek. Just beyond the footbridge, you'll find a signed turnoff for Helen Markt Trail.

Most of the cascades are between 20 and 30 feet high, but their shapes and appearances are all completely different. The common element they share, besides the life-giving flow of Cataract Creek, is that each one is completely surrounded by ferns. After a good rain,

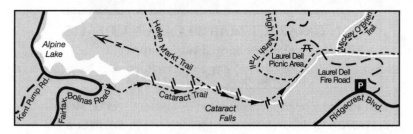

Cataract canyon is truly breathtaking, with the continual sound and sight of waterfalls providing nonstop excitement through every curve and turn of the trail. Discovering each new cascade is thrilling enough that you often forget the steepness of the climb.

The last waterfall appears just before a junction with High Marsh Trail; this is the most impressive of the group and the one most people consider to be the *true* Cataract Falls. Here, Cataract Creek makes a dramatic tumble over car-sized boulders as it rushes downhill.

From the big fall, it's less than a quarter-mile on Cataract Trail to Laurel Dell, a fine picnic area in a large, meadowy clearing. Most people are content to picnic at Laurel Dell, then turn around and hike back downhill on Cataract Trail, witnessing the waterfall show all over again. If you seek more than this 3.2-mile round-trip, you can make a 7.5-mile loop by backtracking only as far as High Marsh Trail. Follow High Marsh Trail gently uphill for 2.2 miles, gaining surprising views of San Pablo Bay. At a confusing series of trail junctions near High Marsh and Willow Meadow, turn left (north) on Kent Trail and head downhill for 1.4 miles, nearly to the edge of Alpine Lake. Turn left on Helen Markt Trail and hike two miles through the redwoods to the lower stretch of Cataract Trail. Turn right and walk a half mile back to your car. If you choose to make this loop, be sure to bring a good map with you. There are numerous junctions along the route and not all of them are signed.

Trip notes: There is no fee. Leashed dogs are allowed. Bikes are not allowed. For more information and a $2 map, contact Marin Municipal Water District, 220 Nellen, Corte Madera, CA 94925; (415) 945-1195. Or phone Sky Oaks Ranger Station at (415) 945-1181. A more detailed map of the area is available for a fee from Olmsted Brothers Map Company, P.O. Box 5351, Berkeley, CA 94705; (510) 658-6534.

32. SHORELINE TRAIL
China Camp State Park

DISTANCE: 7.0 or 11.0 miles round-trip; 3-6 hours   **LEVEL:** Moderate

ELEVATION CHANGE: 100 feet or 900 feet   **RATING:** ★ ★ ★

DIRECTIONS: From San Francisco, cross the Golden Gate Bridge and drive north on U.S. 101 for 11 miles to San Rafael. Take the North San Pedro Road exit and drive east for 3.5 miles. Turn right at the sign for Back Ranch Meadows Campground and park in the campground parking lot. Shoreline Trail is located on the bay side of the lot, signed as "no dogs."

Most people know China Camp State Park as a historic park that showcases the remains of a Chinese shrimp fishing village from the 19th century. It's the kind of place that's popular for school field trips. But don't forget about China Camp's scenic location on San Pablo Bay, which allows for blue-water vistas at every turn of the park's Shoreline Trail. With more than 1,500 shoreline acres, plus a pretty forest of oaks, bays, and madrones, the park is an island of natural beauty just outside the busy city of San Rafael.

China Camp is also a rare animal in the California State Park system. It's one of the few state parks that allows bike riders on its single-track trails. The park is rarely too crowded, and most bikers and hikers mind their manners and seem to get along fine. Just be forewarned that if you don't like sharing the trail with bikes, avoid hiking here on weekends when the park gets its heaviest use.

An out-and-back on the park's Shoreline Trail is a seven-mile round-trip that's nearly level. A more strenuous tour of the park is an 11-mile loop on Shoreline Trail, Oak Ridge Trail, and Bay View Trail. The latter hike leads you into the "backcountry" of the park, far from San Pedro Road. Whatever route you choose, begin your hike on Shoreline Trail from near Back Ranch Meadows Campground. You'll walk past a cattail-filled marsh and have immediate views of the tranquil blue waters of San Pablo Bay. The open grasslands are punctuated by a few spreading valley oaks.

In only a quarter mile, cross San Pedro Road and take Turtle Back Nature Trail (this trail is closed to bikes). When bay waters were higher, Turtle Back was an island, but now it's a shoreline hill surrounded by saltwater marsh. In late autumn, the marsh's pickle-weed turns a brilliant red color, accenting wide views of San Pablo Bay. Ancient duck blinds dot the water's edge. From Turtle Back, you can see Jake's Island to the north, another shoreline hill that was once an island. Two other such hills exist to the east—Bullet Hill and Chicken Coop Hill.

Return to the main Shoreline Trail and continue hiking east. You'll parallel North San Pedro Road until the path heads inland, then curves around to an open meadow and the park's group picnic area, Miwok Meadows. Follow its wide dirt road back toward the bay. (You end up on Miwok Fire Trail for about 100 feet.) Pick up

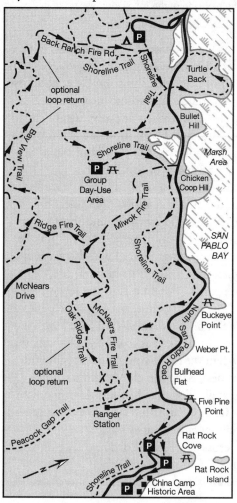

single-track Shoreline Trail again, continuing eastward. More open bay views are followed by a stint in a leafy oak and bay forest. San Pedro Road drops out of sight and sound as the trail leads through the wood-land canopy.

Three miles out, you'll switchback down-hill to China Camp State Park's ranger station, then cross the service road to pick up the trail on the opposite side. In slightly more than a half mile, you'll cross San Pedro Road to head down to China Camp Historic Area, the site of a 19th-century Chinese fishing village. China Camp was one of more than 30 such villages that sprung up on the shores of San Francisco and San Pablo bays in the 1870s.

Marsh and bay views from China Camp State Park

The Chinese villagers fished for plentiful grass shrimp in spring, summer, and fall. In winter, they mended their nets and worked on their boats. Some of the shrimp were sold at local markets, but most were exported to China. Eventually laws were passed that forbid the Chinese method of shrimp fishing with bag nets. In 1905, the export of dried shrimp was also banned, and this village along with others like it was soon abandoned.

A pier and four buildings, filled with furniture and tools from the day-to-day life of the shrimp camp, are all that remains of the village. They are fascinating to explore. A sandy beach to the west of China Camp is an excellent place for birdwatching. Great egrets and snowy egrets fish in the marsh areas and offshore of Rat Rock Island. The beach is popular with waders and swimmers in summer as the bay water is calm and relatively warm.

For your return trip, retrace your steps to the junction uphill of the ranger station. Then either bear right on Shoreline Trail for a level out-and-back, or bear left on Peacock Gap Trail to loop back on Oak Ridge and Bay View trails. If you opt for the loop, you'll climb uphill, then turn right on Oak Ridge Trail. Connect to Bay View Trail via Ridge Fire Trail. From these trails' higher elevation, bay views are far more expansive. Deciduous oaks and even some redwoods provide shade. A right turn on Back Ranch Fire Trail and a steep descent will return you to within a few yards of your car.

Trip notes: A $5 day-use fee is charged per vehicle. Dogs are not allowed. Bikes are allowed. A trail map is available at the ranger station. For more information, contact China Camp State Park, 1455A East Francisco Boulevard, San Rafael, CA 94901; (415) 456-0766 or (415) 893-1580.

33. VERNA DUNSHEE TRAIL & GARDNER LOOKOUT
Mount Tamalpais State Park

DISTANCE: 1.4 miles round-trip; 1 hour

ELEVATION CHANGE: 170 feet

LEVEL: Easy

RATING: ★ ★ ★ ★

DIRECTIONS: From San Francisco, cross the Golden Gate Bridge and drive north on U.S. 101 for four miles. Take the Mill Valley/Stinson Beach/Highway 1 exit and continue straight for one mile to a stoplight at Shoreline Highway (Highway 1). Turn left on Shoreline Highway and drive 2.5 miles, then turn right on Panoramic Highway. Drive nine-tenths of a mile until you reach an intersection where you can go left, straight, or right. Take the middle road (straight), continuing on Panoramic Highway for 4.3 more miles to Pantoll Road. Turn right on Pantoll Road and drive 1.4 miles to its intersection with Ridgecrest Boulevard. Turn right on Ridgecrest Boulevard and drive 2.9 miles to the East Peak parking area.

If it's a clear day and you're in the mood to feel on top of the world, head for the summit of Mount Tamalpais and the Verna Dunshee Trail. The trail is short, easy to walk, and features absolute top-notch views of Marin County, San Francisco, and points far beyond as it loops around the mountain's summit. To add a little challenge to the trip, you can also hike the short but steep path to the tippy-top of Mount Tamalpais' East Peak, where a closed fire lookout tower offers an all-in-one-glance panoramic view.

The drive up Mount Tamalpais is part of the adventure. From Pantoll Road upward, the coastal views are good enough that you have to remind yourself to keep your eyes on the pavement. Close attention is essential, however, because the summit road is narrow, winding, and leaves little room for error.

When at last you reach Mount Tamalpais' high ridgeline, you drive by the mountain's West Peak first. That's the one with the "huge white golf balls," or radar dishes, at 2,560 feet in elevation.

Next comes the lower Middle Peak, and finally you wind up at the road's end at the parking lot for Mount Tam's East Peak. The East Peak is the highest summit of the three at 2,571 feet. (This may not sound especially high, but when you consider that the peak is surrounded primarily by ocean, bay, and sea-level land, the 2,500-foot elevation is actually a considerable vertical rise.)

Leave your car and walk past the visitor center. If you show up on a weekend day, the center will be open and you can obtain an interpretive brochure keyed to numbers painted on the asphalt on the Verna Dunshee Trail. Locate the trail just to the right of the rest rooms; you'll walk counter-clockwise on the paved loop.

In the first few yards of trail, the manzanita grows so high and dense that the views are obscured. But not for long. Soon you emerge from the chaparral and your views extend all the way south to San Francisco and southwest to the Pacific Ocean. On the best days, the Farallon Islands are visible some 25 miles out to sea.

As you head eastward, views of southern Marin County expand to include Richardson Bay, Angel Island, and Tiburon. Before you know it you're looking at the Richmond Bridge and across it to the East Bay. Mount Diablo looms in the background. Far beyond it and rarely seen is the snowy Sierra crest.

About halfway through the loop, Temelpa Trail cuts off to the right; stay on the paved path and in a few more yards take the unsigned dirt path that leads along a northeast ridge of the summit. This puts you on a promontory directly overlooking south and east Marin County. The tall buildings of downtown San Francisco glitter in the distance like the Emerald City.

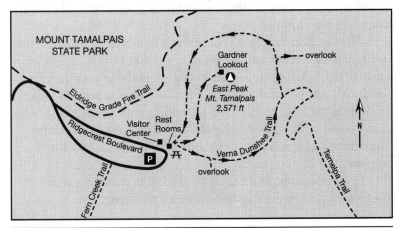

Gardner Lookout on Mount Tam's East Peak

Back on the main trail, you begin to circle around to the north, now looking toward San Rafael, Sonoma, and Napa. Yes, that's Mount St. Helena far to the northwest. The lake that glimmers in the foreground is Bon Tempe reservoir near Fairfax. Mount Tam's West Peak obscures the western view, so finish out your loop by heading south to the visitor center, then make a sharp left turn on the Gardner Lookout Trail.

The first leg of the ascending path is lined with old railroad ties. These serve as reminders of the days when "The Crookedest Railroad in the World" operated on Mount Tamalpais. In the early 1900s, no visit to San Francisco was complete without a ride on this train, which traveled up the mountain through a thrilling 281 curves. Alas, the railroad's reign ended with the advent of the automobile and the first road built to the mountain's summit.

The Gardner Lookout Trail makes a few steep switchbacks up to East Peak's summit and its closed fire lookout tower, which was built in 1937. Although you can't walk up to the tower's deck (it's lined with barbed wire), the view from its base is superb. Wander around on the East Peak's summit boulders until you find the best spot to soak in the scenery. Hopefully you brought a jacket with you; the wind often blows up here on even the balmiest days of summer.

An insider's tip: The East Peak of Mount Tamalpais is one of the finest places in the Bay Area to watch the sunset.

Trip notes: A $5 day-use fee is charged per vehicle. Dogs and bikes are not allowed. A trail map is available at the summit visitor center or Pantoll Ranger Station for $1. (The summit visitor center is open on weekends only.) For more information, contact Mount Tamalpais State Park, 801 Panoramic Highway, Mill Valley, CA 94941; (415) 388-2070 or (415) 893-1580.

34. MATT DAVIS & STEEP RAVINE LOOP
Mount Tamalpais State Park

DISTANCE: 7.0 miles round-trip; 4 hours   **LEVEL:** Moderate

ELEVATION CHANGE: 1,500 feet   **RATING:** ★ ★ ★ ★

DIRECTIONS: From San Francisco, cross the Golden Gate Bridge and drive north on U.S. 101 for four miles. Take the Mill Valley/Stinson Beach/Highway 1 exit and continue straight for one mile to a stoplight at Shoreline Highway (Highway 1). Turn left on Shoreline Highway and drive 2.5 miles, then turn right on Panoramic Highway. Drive nine-tenths of a mile until you reach an intersection where you can go left, straight, or right. Take the middle road (straight), continuing on Panoramic Highway for 4.3 more miles to the Pantoll Ranger Station and parking lot. Turn left to park in the lot, then walk across Panoramic Highway to the start of Pantoll Road. Across from the small dirt parking area, on the southwest side of Pantoll Road, is the signed trailhead for Coastal/Matt Davis Trail.

Matt Davis Trail curves a long, graceful arc from Mount Tam's Pantoll Ranger Station to the sea at Stinson Beach. Steep Ravine Trail makes a dramatic ascent alongside a boisterous stream in a steep-sided redwood canyon. Combine these two trails with a brief stretch on the Dipsea Trail and you have one of the best loop hikes in the San Francisco Bay Area.

It's a classic Mount Tamalpais day-hike, showing off the best of the state park's attributes. On weekends, the route can be quite busy, particularly the spectacular stretch of Steep Ravine Trail. (Many visitors hike this trail out-and-back, especially in the rainy season when Webb Creek is running hard.) On weekdays, you're likely to have much less company, except for a few Marin locals who walk the loop on a regular basis. Here's one of their secrets: If you start your hike around 10 A.M., you can reach the bottom of Matt Davis Trail at Stinson Beach right around noon. Don't bother pack-

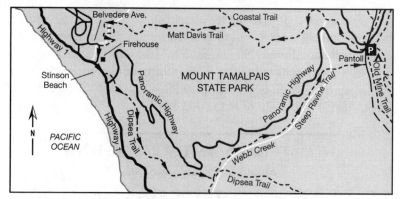

ing a picnic lunch, because you can buy a hamburger (or most anything else) at Stinson and have a leisurely lunch on the beach. After you're fueled up, you spend the afternoon hiking back uphill on Steep Ravine Trail. Now how's that for a fine day?

The loop begins near Pantoll Ranger Station on Mount Tamalpais. Exit the Pantoll parking lot, cross Panoramic Highway to the start of Pantoll Road, and pick up Matt Davis Trail on the west side of Pantoll Road across from the small dirt parking area. A bench in the first 50 feet of trail invites you to sit and enjoy a partial view of the coast. This is the last open viewing spot you'll have for a while; the trail quickly leads into the forest.

Matt Davis Trail laterals along the slope of Mount Tamalpais some 1,500 feet above the ocean, maintaining an even, easy grade. After a long stretch in a mossy oak and laurel woodland, the trail breaks out into grasslands, offering fine views of San Francisco to the south and Point Reyes to the north. In some areas it's hard to move on; you'll want to stay and relish the vistas. At 1.6 miles, you reach a trail split: Coastal Trail to the right and Matt Davis Trail to the left. Head left and begin your descent to Stinson Beach.

Hike downhill for seven-tenths of a mile through a lovely forest of Douglas firs, oaks, and the graceful branches of bay laurel. Look for tall stalks of colorful red and yellow columbine along this shaded stretch in spring. At a signed turnoff for Table Rock, follow a spur trail a few feet to a large, flat boulder with a fine overlook of the town of Stinson Beach and its long strip of sand and surf. Listen to the sound of the waves and enjoy a snack or stretching break before the final mile downhill to Stinson.

Back on the main trail, begin a series of short switchbacks, lined with wooden stairsteps to soften the steep drop. Redwood railings edge the trail. Hike down Bischof's Steps just below Table Rock (named for the trail builder who carefully constructed this stretch) and pass a lovely small cataract along Table Rock Creek. The cascading stream serenades you as you descend; you'll cross it repeatedly on wooden footbridges. Its noise competes with the roar of nearby ocean breakers.

A sign states "Caution: Rattlesnake Area" just before the trail reaches the park boundary. Turn left at the signed boundary and junction, cross a footbridge, and reach an unsigned fork in 100 yards. Turn right and walk down to Belvedere Avenue in Stinson Beach, now 3.3 miles from your start at Pantoll. Next comes a series of left turns to join the return leg of the loop. Turn left on Belvedere, walk 100 yards past the community center and firehouse, then turn left on Highway 1 (Shoreline Highway). Walk 200 yards along the road, turn left on Panoramic Highway, then walk 100 feet to join the Dipsea Trail on the right. (Or, if you wish to visit the beach at Stinson, go only to Panoramic Highway and turn right at the sign for the beach.)

Steep Ravine's lush canyon

In contrast to Matt Davis Trail's steep forested canyon, Dipsea Trail traverses sunny, exposed slopes. It provides nonstop views of the coast as it makes a gradual climb through coastal scrub and grasslands. In 1.3 miles, Dipsea Trail junctions with Steep Ravine Trail. Turn left on Steep Ravine and begin a more serious climb along Webb Creek, rising 1,000 feet in two miles. Redwoods and Douglas firs tower over the cascading stream. Chinese houses, calypso orchids, and trillium bloom in the shady understory in spring. Wooden footbridges cross the creek a half-dozen times. You'll need to duck and scramble under fallen redwood trunks, then climb a 10-foot ladder over a tricky trail stretch where Webb Creek is constricted by large boulders. All the while, you'll pause repeatedly to admire the myriad crystal pools and waterfalls on Webb Creek and the multitude of ferns that grow alongside it. Look for sword ferns, huge woodwardia ferns, and delicate five-finger ferns.

Too soon, the trail ends at the parking lot at Pantoll Ranger Station. But the entire loop is so good, you may be tempted to turn around and hike it all over again.

Trip notes: A $5 day-use fee is charged per vehicle if you park at the paved parking lot at Pantoll Ranger Station. If you park legally in any pullout along the road, there is no fee. Dogs and bikes are not allowed. A trail map is available at Pantoll Ranger Station for $1. For more information, contact Mount Tamalpais State Park, 801 Panoramic Highway, Mill Valley, CA 94941; (415) 388-2070 or (415) 893-1580.

35. MOUNTAIN THEATER & WEST POINT INN LOOP
Mount Tamalpais State Park & Marin Municipal Water District

DISTANCE: 5.0 miles round-trip; 2.5 hours   **LEVEL:** Easy
          or 8.5 miles round-trip; 4.5 hours   or Moderate
ELEVATION CHANGE: 500 feet or 1,300 feet   **RATING:** ★ ★ ★

DIRECTIONS: From San Francisco, cross the Golden Gate Bridge and drive north on U.S. 101 for four miles. Take the Mill Valley/Stinson Beach/Highway 1 exit and continue straight for one mile to a stoplight at Shoreline Highway (Highway 1). Turn left on Shoreline Highway and drive 2.5 miles, then turn right on Panoramic Highway. Drive nine-tenths of a mile until you reach an intersection where you can go left, straight, or right. Take the middle road (straight), continuing on Panoramic Highway for 4.3 more miles to the Pantoll Ranger Station and parking lot. Turn left to park in the lot, then walk across Panoramic Highway to the start of Pantoll Road. Take the paved road on the right signed "Authorized Vehicles Only"; this is the start of Old Stage Road.

Here's a trail for Mount Tamalpais history lovers. Most Bay Area residents know that Mount Tamalpais was the home of "The Crookedest Railroad in the World," which weaved its way from Mill Valley to the mountain summit through eight miles and 281 curves. The gravity car railroad, a popular tourist attraction, made Mount Tamalpais famous at the turn of the century. This five-mile loop hike visits historic mountain sites and offers first-rate views and lovely scenery along the way. If you seek a more strenuous hike, you can add on a trek along the old railroad grade to the summit of Mount Tamalpais for an 8.5-mile semi-loop trip.

Start your trip at Pantoll Ranger Station. Cross Panoramic Highway and pick up paved Old Stage Road to the right of Pantoll Road. A quarter mile of walking brings you to a series of junctions; take the path signed as "Easy Grade Trail to Mountain Theater." You'll climb steadily for eight-tenths of a mile, soon losing the noise of the nearby road as you head deeper into oak woodland. A surprise awaits when you come out of the trees and on to the stage of Mountain Theater. You'll find yourself staring up at rows and rows of stone bench seats in a forest-lined amphitheater.

Formally named the Sidney Cushing Memorial Theater after the builder of the Mount Tamalpais Scenic Railway, "Mountain Theater" is an open air, natural stone amphitheater that seats up to 3,500 people. Reconstructed in the 1930s by the Civilian Conserva-

West Point Inn

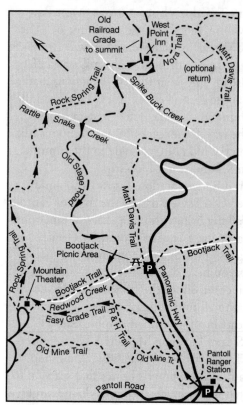

tion Corps, the theater has hosted the annual Mountain Play every summer since 1913. A Marin County tradition, the Mountain Play brings playgoers up the slopes of Mount Tam carrying blankets and picnic baskets for an afternoon of theater.

Walk to the far side of the stage, then up along the right (east) side of the rock bench seats. Near the top of the theater, on your right, is Rock Spring Trail. Follow it and enjoy a level stroll with fine lookouts toward the coast and San Francisco. In a mile and a half, the trail makes an easy descent to West Point Inn. The inn was built by the railroad in 1914 as a restaurant and stopover for passengers who were getting off the train and picking up the stagecoach to ride down to Stinson Beach or Bolinas. After the rail days ended, the building came under the jurisdiction of the Marin Water District. It is now leased and operated by a nonprofit group. You can purchase drinks and snacks at West Point Inn, which is open all day on weekends and afternoons only on weekdays (closed on Mondays). Restrooms and picnic areas are available all the time. The inn also has four cabins and seven rooms for rent. Although there is no electricity, propane is used for light, heat, and refrigeration.

A small sign on West Point Inn's front door conveys its simple philosophy: "You may use the parlor if you keep it tidy." The inn's real draw is not the parlor but the view from its deck, which takes in a wide expanse of San Francisco Bay, the Bay Bridge and Richmond

Bridge, Larkspur Landing, and San Francisco. On a clear day, the view is hard to forget.

Now it's decision time. For a five-mile round-trip, you'll want to loop back from here. Or you can continue uphill on Old Railroad Grade to Mount Tamalpais' summit, adding on an 800-foot climb and 3.5 miles of additional hiking. For the shorter loop, you have two options: You can follow Nora Trail from the front of the inn steeply downhill for a half mile to Matt Davis Trail. Turn right on Matt Davis and hike back to the base of Old Stage Road near Pantoll Ranger Station. While this is a scenic trail with coastal views and a nice stand of redwoods, it suffers from too much road noise from Panoramic Highway, especially on weekend afternoons. A quieter option that offers equal views is to follow Old Stage Road downhill from the Inn for two miles back to Pantoll. This trail is not for hikers only, however; you'll share it with mountain bikers.

Those with excess energy will want to continue uphill from West Point Inn to Mount Tamalpais' summit. Take Old Railroad Grade from the back side of the inn uphill for 1.5 steep, rocky miles to the East Peak parking lot. The wide trail is exposed and brushy, with occasional Douglas firs and Bishop pines mixed in with the chaparral. Views of the summit above and the bay below are continual inspiration.

Note that Old Railroad Grade is very popular with mountain bikers, so use care to stay out of their way. The trail is wide enough for all users, but it's difficult for bikers to control their speed on the steep descent.

Once at the 2,571-foot summit, you can hike the short, view-filled Verna Dunshee Trail or walk up to the closed Gardner Fire Lookout (see the story on pages 100-102). Both paths will reward you with some of the Bay Area's finest views.

Trip notes: A $5 day-use fee is charged per vehicle if you park at the paved parking lot at Pantoll Ranger Station. If you park legally in any pullout along the road, there is no fee. Leashed dogs are allowed on parts of the loop that are located in Marin Water District Lands, but not in Mount Tamalpais State Park. Bikes are allowed only on Old Stage Road and Old Railroad Grade. A trail map is available at Pantoll Ranger Station for $1. For more information, contact Mount Tamalpais State Park, 801 Panoramic Highway, Mill Valley, CA 94941; (415) 388-2070 or (415) 893-1580.

36. COASTAL, CATARACT, & OLD MINE LOOP
Mount Tamalpais State Park

DISTANCE: 6.4 miles round-trip; 3 hours   **LEVEL:** Moderate

ELEVATION CHANGE: 700 feet   **RATING:** ★ ★ ★

DIRECTIONS: From San Francisco, cross the Golden Gate Bridge and drive north on U.S. 101 for four miles. Take the Mill Valley/Stinson Beach/Highway 1 exit and continue straight for one mile to a stoplight at Shoreline Highway (Highway 1). Turn left on Shoreline Highway and drive 2.5 miles, then turn right on Panoramic Highway. Drive nine-tenths of a mile until you reach an intersection where you can go left, straight, or right. Take the middle road (straight), continuing on Panoramic Highway for 4.3 more miles to the Pantoll Ranger Station and parking lot. Turn left to park in the lot, then walk across Panoramic Highway to the start of Pantoll Road. Across from the small dirt parking area, on the southwest side of Pantoll Road, is the signed trailhead for Coastal/Matt Davis Trail.

Is it a clear day in the San Francisco Bay Area? If so, then there is only one thing to do: lace up your hiking boots and head for this loop trail in Mount Tamalpais State Park. The Coastal, Cataract, and Old Mine Loop provides the best of all worlds—secluded forest groves laced with small, coursing streams, wide grasslands covered with lupine and poppies in the spring, and spectacular vistas of city and sea. Oh yeah, and don't forget to pack your lunch. Picnic spots are as abundant as deer on Mount Tamalpais.

Start your trip on the Coastal/Matt Davis Trail near Pantoll Ranger Station. After an initial glimpse at the ocean near the trail's start, you'll head into a dense mixed hardwood forest and remain there for just shy of a mile. The beauty is close at hand—thick moss growing like fur on the bay laurel trees, dense ferns clustered around seasonal streams, and dappled sunlight filtering through the canopy of leaves.

Just as your eyes grow accustomed to the low light of the forest, the trail suddenly opens out to wide, sloping grasslands and bright sunshine. In spring, the mountain's wildflowers burst into colorful display, spurred on by cooling fog and plentiful sunlight. The blue and gold of poppies and lupine will make you feel a rush of patriotism for California's state colors. Because you can see so far and wide down the grassy slopes of Mount Tamalpais, views are extraordinary.

The Pacific Ocean glitters in the distance. You may spot deer on a hillside a mile away, or a couple of miniature hikers having lunch on a rock, looking like pieces out of a model train set.

From your vantage point on Coastal Trail, the mountain slopes drop 1,500 feet to the ocean. The farther you walk, the wider your view becomes, until it finally stretches from the San Francisco skyline to the south to Stinson Beach and Bolinas in the north, then still farther north to the Point Reyes peninsula. If you ever wanted to explain to somebody how large the ocean is in relation to the size of the land, this would be the place to do it.

Don't miss following an unmarked spur trail on the left at 1.4 miles in. A short climb to a grassy knoll brings you to Coastal Trail's best view of the day, encompassing the entire Marin County coast. Soak in the scenery for as long as you please, then return to the main trail. It will soon fork; Matt Davis Trail heads downhill to Stinson Beach (see the story on pages 103-106). Take the right fork on Coastal Trail, continuing gently uphill.

Where Coastal Trail meets a wide fire road at 3.3 miles out, turn right and climb steeply uphill for a brief stretch. Look for a side trail cutting off the fire road to the left; this will deliver you to paved Ridgecrest Boulevard at its junction with Laurel Dell Fire Road. Cross the paved road (watch for cars), then take Laurel Dell Fire Road. The dirt and gravel road makes a gentle descent through

Coastal Trail, Mount Tamalpais

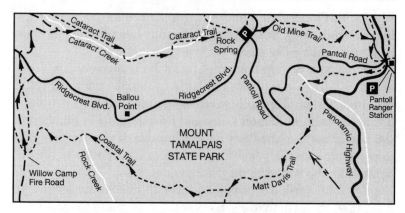

a mossy, shady bay forest to the edge of Cataract Creek. Watch for a right turnoff on Cataract Trail; a footbridge will carry you across the creek. If you miss it, you can stay on the fire road until it crosses the creek near Laurel Dell, then pick up Cataract Trail on its far side.

The next mile on Cataract Trail is as lovely as the first miles on Coastal Trail, but its scenery couldn't be more different. Cataract Trail parallels its pretty stream, passing within arm's length of the mossy trunks of bays and tanoaks in a dense green forest canopy. The trail opens out to a meadow near Rock Spring, then deposits you at the Rock Spring parking lot. Cross Ridgecrest Boulevard again and pick up Old Mine Trail on its far side, a few yards to the left. A brief, steep climb takes you uphill to stellar views of San Pablo Bay, the Richmond Bridge, and San Francisco. Perhaps this vista is so striking because the glittering, urban cityscape contrasts sharply with Cataract and Coastal trails' all-natural beauty. A few large boulders on a grassy knoll make a perfect viewing stop.

Follow Old Mine Trail back downhill for three-quarters of a mile to paved Old Stage Road. The path drops 500 feet through a series of steep switchbacks. Finally, turn right on Old Stage Road and walk back to your car at Pantoll Ranger Station.

Trip notes: A $5 day-use fee is charged per vehicle if you park at the paved parking lot at Pantoll Ranger Station. If you park legally in any pullout along the road, there is no fee. Leashed dogs are allowed on Cataract Trail only (Marin Municipal Water District land). Bikes are not allowed. A trail map is available at Pantoll Ranger Station for $1. For more information, contact Mount Tamalpais State Park, 801 Panoramic Highway, Mill Valley, CA 94941; (415) 388-2070 or (415) 893-1580.

37. BENSTEIN, MICKEY O'BRIEN, & CATARACT LOOP
Marin Municipal Water District

DISTANCE: 4.0 miles round-trip; 2 hours   **LEVEL:** Easy

ELEVATION CHANGE: 500 feet   **RATING:** ★ ★ ★

DIRECTIONS: From San Francisco, cross the Golden Gate Bridge and drive north on U.S. 101 for four miles. Take the Mill Valley/Stinson Beach/Highway 1 exit and continue straight for one mile to a stoplight at Shoreline Highway (Highway 1). Turn left on Shoreline Highway and drive 2.5 miles, then turn right on Panoramic Highway. Drive nine-tenths of a mile until you reach an intersection where you can go left, straight, or right. Take the middle road (straight), continuing on Panoramic Highway for 4.3 more miles to Pantoll Road. Turn right on Pantoll Road and drive 1.4 miles to its intersection with Ridgecrest Boulevard, where there is a large parking area called Rock Spring. Park there and take the signed Cataract Trail from the north side of the lot.

If you just want a quiet walk in the woods, maybe with a little picnicking or a nature lesson along the way, here's a trail loop that's just right. Lots of people come to Mount Tamalpais to see the tall coastal redwoods or take in the sweeping coastal views, but there's much to be said for a simple woodland hike offering a little exercise, some solitude, and the comforting sounds of the birds and your own breathing.

The plethora of cars parked at Rock Spring parking area on the weekends might concern you, but fear not. Rock Spring is a major hub of trails; most hikers have set out on other paths to the scenic lookout at O'Rourke's Bench or the historic Mountain Theater. On one weekend trip, the only people I saw on this trail were a group of senior hikers who looked to be in their 70s. They were speeding up Benstein Trail as if they were going to a fire, arguing all the way about what species of oriole they had just seen. They passed me near Potrero Meadow and I never caught up with them.

Start by walking north from the parking area, traveling on Cataract Trail until it splits—Cataract to the left and Benstein to the right. Take Benstein Trail northeast, heading immediately into a tanoak and Douglas fir forest where you'll likely be greeted by the drumming of woodpeckers.

Trail markers point you toward Potrero Meadow. Benstein Trail ascends steadily until it reaches a junction with Rock Spring and Lagunitas Fire Road. Take the fire road left for only a few dozen yards. Join Benstein Trail again where it veers off to the left, back on single-track.

Prepare for a sudden scenery change as you come out of the hardwoods and on to the rocky back side of this ridge. You'll enter a contrasting world of manzanita, chamise, small Sargent cypress trees, and serpentine rock. Serpentine, California's state rock, is formed when water mixes with peridotite. It's a pretty grayish-green on Mount Tamalpais, although in other areas it's mostly gray. Spend some time examining the foliage growing here; it consists of plants that require few nutrients and are often dwarfed in size, which is typical of a serpentine environment. The most fascinating flora are the miniature cypress trees, which mature when they are only a few feet tall. Ironically, two of the world's largest Sargent cypress trees—over 80 feet tall—grow near here on the Mickey O'Brien Trail.

Descending from this gravelly, exposed ridge, follow Benstein Trail north for a quarter mile until you reach Laurel Dell Fire Road.

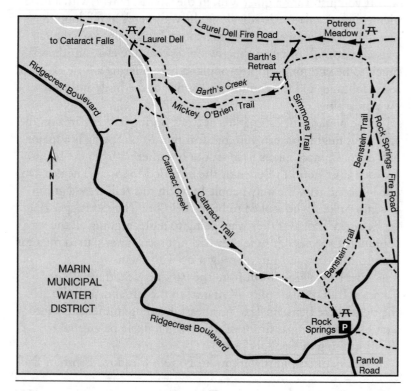

(A picnic area can be found across the road at Potrero Meadow if anyone in your group is getting hungry.) Turn left on the fire road and hike an eighth of a mile. You'll gain a short but spectacular view of Bon Tempe Lake and the Marin watershed to the north.

Turn left on another fire road at a trail sign for Barth's Retreat. Barth's Retreat is an old camp that was built by poet, musician, and hiker Emil Barth in the 1920s. He was an avid Mount Tamalpais trail builder. Turn right and cross a bridge, pass by yet another picnic area, then continue straight. You are now on Mickey O'Brien Trail heading west along Barth's Creek in a thick forest of oak, bay, and Douglas fir. This is one of the best sections of the loop, especially when the stream is running strong, creating an enchanting melody of water sounds. Mickey O'Brien Trail, named for the 1920s president of the Tamalpais Conservation Corps, leads you gently downhill toward Laurel Dell, a grassy meadow.

Just before the meadowy dell, Mickey O'Brien Trail ends at an intersection with Cataract Trail. The latter is your ticket back to Rock Spring. Turn left on Cataract; it's just over a mile to the parking lot. If you want to make a side trip to picnic at Laurel Dell, go right for 150 yards, have your lunch, then follow Cataract home.

In winter and spring, you can add on a visit to Cataract Falls from Laurel Dell. Just follow Cataract Trail northwest from the far end of the dell, then begin a steep descent through redwoods and Douglas firs. Watch for an intersection with High Marsh Trail on the right; continue straight and shortly you'll reach the uppermost cascade of Cataract Falls. Cataract Trail curves in tightly, bringing you right alongside the stream. Water tumbles over huge boulders as it rushes downhill. Pick a rock and watch the show. If you like, you can continue downhill along Cataract Trail, visiting as many of the trail's cascades as you wish. Remember that the return trip to Laurel Dell is all uphill. (For more details on Cataract Falls, see the story on pages 95-96.)

Trip notes: There is no fee to park at Rock Spring. Leashed dogs are allowed. Bikes are not allowed. For more information and a $2 map, contact Marin Municipal Water District at 220 Nellen Avenue, Corte Madera, CA 94925; (415) 945-1195. Or phone Sky Oaks Ranger Station at (415) 945-1181. You may also contact Mount Tamalpais State Park, 801 Panoramic Highway, Mill Valley, CA 94941; (415) 388-2070 or (415) 893-1580.

38. PANORAMIC, LOST TRAIL, & FERN CREEK LOOP
Muir Woods National Monument

DISTANCE: 3.4 miles round-trip; 1.5 hours   **LEVEL:** Easy

ELEVATION CHANGE: 800 feet   **RATING:** ★ ★ ★

DIRECTIONS: From San Francisco, cross the Golden Gate Bridge and drive north on U.S. 101 for four miles. Take the Mill Valley/Stinson Beach/Highway 1 exit and continue straight for one mile to a stoplight at Shoreline Highway (Highway 1). Turn left on Shoreline Highway and drive 2.5 miles, then turn right on Panoramic Highway. Drive nine-tenths of a mile and turn left on Muir Woods Road. Drive 1.5 miles to the Muir Woods parking area.

The redwoods at Muir Woods National Monument are true beauties. The foliage in the understory of the big redwoods—bays, tanoak, thimbleberry, sword ferns, and sorrel—is lush, green, and pretty year-round. Redwood Creek, which cuts through the center of the park, is a pristine, coursing stream.

No doubt about it, Muir Woods is a winner. Its only drawback is its popularity. This little tiny national monument, not much larger than a few city blocks, gets visited by more than one million people each year.

How do you hike in the park and see its lovely trees without getting run over by the crowds? Summer is the busiest time, of course, so it's best to avoid May to September all together. Weekends tend to be more crowded than weekdays, but weekdays bring school groups. (Thirty sixth-graders on a field trip can be pretty boisterous.) The best choice? Try to show up early in the morning, as in 7 A.M. when the park gates open. During the week, the school buses and tour buses don't usually arrive until 9 or 10 A.M. On the weekends, most visitors don't show up until mid-morning. An eight o'clock start any day of the week should give you at least a two-hour window of peace among the redwoods. Winter and early spring are the least crowded and also the loveliest seasons, when Redwood Creek runs full and high.

And don't worry about visiting on a rainy day; just pack along your rain gear. A redwood forest is the best place to hike in the rain.

You'll be partially protected by the big trees, and the drops of water on every fern, branch, and leaf only accentuate their beauty.

Start your trip from the entrance gate to Muir Woods near the small visitor center. The main trail is a wide, paved path that runs along the bottom of the canyon, passing the most impressive redwoods. You'll walk the entire length of this trail on your return. For now, bear right and in about 100 yards you'll reach a fork with Panoramic Trail. Once named "Ocean View Trail" although it has no ocean views, Panoramic Trail ascends the hillside to the right. Follow it and say good-bye to the pavement.

The path is completely forested, but the redwood trees are younger and smaller than in the canyon below and interspersed with many Douglas firs. Panoramic Trail climbs moderately and curves around the canyon until it reaches a junction with Lost Trail at 1.5 miles. Note this junction, then continue straight for 200 yards until Panoramic Trail emerges from the forest just below Panoramic Highway, a busy road. A large boulder rests on the hillside between the trail and the road; this is the best spot to obtain a long-distance vista. On a sunny day, it's a nice viewpoint, looking out over the forests of Muir Woods below.

When you've had your fill of sunshine, return to the shade of the woods and the previously noted junction. Turn right on Lost Trail, now heading downhill. Similar to Panoramic Trail, Lost Trail weaves through a young redwood, Douglas fir, and bay forest. Soon

Forests of ferns at Muir Woods

Blooming redwood sorrel

it descends more steeply on railroad-tie stairsteps, and in seven-tenths of a mile it connects with Fern Creek Trail. Fern Creek is a lovely seasonal tributary to Redwood Creek, the main stream that flows through Muir Woods' canyon. Fern Creek Trail follows Fern Creek's delightful course for a half mile, crossing it on two footbridges.

Near the end of Fern Creek Trail you pass a sign marking the border of Muir Woods National Monument. In a few more steps you're at the base of the Kent Memorial, a very large Douglas fir tree dedicated to the man who was responsible for the creation of this park.

There's a wonderful story about Congressman William Kent. He and his wife purchased this land and granted it to the federal government in 1905 under the condition that it be named for the naturalist John Muir. When President Theodore Roosevelt suggested the forest be named "Kent Woods" instead, Kent refused, saying he believed that naming the forest after himself was an implication that immortality could be bought, not earned.

"So many millions of better people have died forgotten," Kent wrote. "I have five good, husky boys that I am trying to bring up to a knowledge of democracy. If these boys cannot keep the name of Kent alive, I am willing it should be forgotten."

Roosevelt wrote back: "By George, you are right... Good for you, and for the five boys who are to keep the name of Kent alive. I have four boys who I hope will do the same thing by the name of Roosevelt."

Roosevelt officially created Muir Woods National Monument in 1908. The loop trail ends with a three-quarter mile walk from the Kent Memorial back up the main trail to your starting point. For more information on Muir Woods' main trail, see the next story.

Trip notes: There is a $2 entrance fee per adult. Children ages 16 and under enter free. Dogs and bikes are not allowed. A free park map is available at the entrance station. For more information, contact Muir Woods National Monument, Mill Valley, CA 94941; (415) 388-2595. Website: www.nps.gov/muwo

39. BOOTJACK, BEN JOHNSON, & HILLSIDE TRAIL LOOP

Muir Woods National Monument & Mount Tamalpais State Park

DISTANCE: 6.4 miles round-trip; 3 hours   **LEVEL:** Moderate

ELEVATION CHANGE: 1,100 feet   **RATING:** ★ ★ ★

DIRECTIONS: From San Francisco, cross the Golden Gate Bridge and drive north on U.S. 101 for four miles. Take the Mill Valley/Stinson Beach/Highway 1 exit and continue straight for one mile to a stoplight at Shoreline Highway (Highway 1). Turn left on Shoreline Highway and drive 2.5 miles, then turn right on Panoramic Highway. Drive nine-tenths of a mile and turn left on Muir Woods Road. Drive 1.5 miles to the Muir Woods parking area.

Muir Woods National Monument is filled with gems, like its virgin grove of coast redwoods and pristine Redwood Creek, which flows through the monument. But Muir Woods is small. If you want to hike any distance, you must leave the monument's borders and explore the adjoining lands of Mount Tamalpais State Park. This loop trail starts and ends in the monument and explores the best of it, then makes a brief tour of the equally fine redwood forest beyond its boundary.

The loop begins on the main trail in Muir Woods, a wide, paved path through the big trees that is usually packed with people. (For tips on how to avoid the Muir Woods crowds, see the previous story.) Follow the trail as it parallels Redwood Creek and relax in the knowledge that you will soon leave most visitors behind. (You know you're in a heavily visited urban park when you see signs stating, "Help keep the creek clean. Do not throw coins in the water.")

If you've visited the coast redwood forests in Redwood National Park and its neighboring state parks, you may be surprised to find that the redwoods in Muir Woods are not as big. Whereas the trees around Redwood National Park grow to 20 feet in diameter, the broadest tree in Muir Woods is only 13.5 feet in diameter. What the Muir Woods redwoods lack in girth, however, they make up for in setting: they thrive in a steep, lush, stream-filled canyon that appears almost mystical on a foggy or rainy day. The monument's highlights include the dense stands of ancient redwoods in the

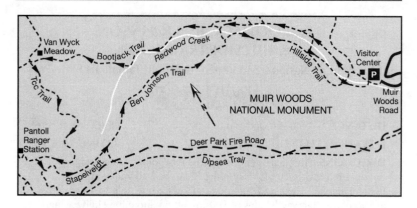

Cathedral Grove and Bohemian Grove. The latter has some of the tallest trees in the park at 250 feet.

A new section of the main trail was built in 1999. The park service removed a substantial length of pavement and installed a boardwalk made of recycled redwood. This helps to protect the big trees' fragile roots. The new trail was moved a few yards away from Redwood Creek to aid the fish who return to it each year to spawn. If you visit the park in winter, you may be lucky enough to spot some of the native wild population of steelhead trout or coho salmon. The fish are born in Redwood Creek, live out their adult lives in the Pacific Ocean, then return here to breed and die.

Continue down the main trail, passing the Fern Creek Trail and Camp Alice Eastwood Trail turnoffs. In a few more yards you reach the pavement's end at a junction with Bootjack Trail, which continues on a smooth dirt path along the stream to the right. You are now one mile from Muir Woods' entrance.

Bootjack Trail makes an easy to moderate ascent along Redwood Creek, passing a cornucopia of splashing cascades in winter. The trail stays close to the water's edge, making this a perfect rainy season hike for whitewater lovers. The forest is a dense mix of bigleaf maples, bays, and redwoods. Bootjack Trail steepens a bit, then travels up wooden stairsteps fashioned from old park signs, until it tops out at Van Wyck Meadow, 1.3 miles from Muir Woods. The postage stamp-sized meadow has a big boulder to sunbathe on and a brown sign stating "Van Wyck Meadow, population 3 stellar jays."

Enjoy this peaceful spot and its sunshine, then turn left on TCC Trail to head back into the woods. (The path is signed as TCC Trail to Stapelveldt Trail.) TCC Trail meanders on a nearly level course through young, slender Douglas firs for 1.4 miles. Most noticeable is the silence—for the first time on this loop hike, you're nowhere near a boisterous creek. Where you reach two junctions immediately following one another, bear left at both. You'll wind up on Stapelveldt Trail heading for Ben Johnson Trail in a half-mile.

Now you're back in a wetter forest again, featuring many graceful, mossy bay trees. At a junction with Ben Johnson Trail, you return to the redwoods. Many of these trees rival the size and beauty of those on the monument's main trail.

In the last mile of the trip, you have a choice: turn right to walk the paved canyon trail back to the park entrance, or turn left to walk Hillside Trail above the canyon. Hillside Trail deposits you at Bridge #2 on the paved trail, where you turn right and walk the last few yards back to your car.

Trip notes: There is a $2 entrance fee per adult. Children ages 16 and under enter free. Dogs and bikes are not allowed. A free park map is available at the entrance station. For more information, contact Muir Woods National Monument, Mill Valley, CA 94941; (415) 388-2595. Website: www.nps.gov/muwo

40. MUIR BEACH—COASTAL TRAIL
Golden Gate National Recreation Area

DISTANCE: 7.0 miles round-trip; 4 hours   **LEVEL:** Strenuous

ELEVATION CHANGE: 1,800 feet   **RATING:** ★ ★ ★

DIRECTIONS: From San Francisco, cross the Golden Gate Bridge and drive north on U.S. 101 for four miles. Take the Mill Valley/Stinson Beach/Highway 1 exit and continue straight for one mile to a stoplight at Shoreline Highway (Highway 1). Turn left on Shoreline Highway and drive 5.2 miles, then turn left on Pacific Way (by the Pelican Inn). Drive a half-mile on Pacific Way to the Muir Beach parking lot. The trail begins on the southwest side of the lot near the restrooms.

The Coastal Trail in the Marin Headlands runs along the bluffs from Muir Beach to Rodeo Beach, then heads inland around Point Bonita and meanders a while until it winds up at the Golden Gate Bridge. It's 11 miles one-way to hike the whole thing, but there's a better, shorter option for beach lovers. The stretch that stays closest to the ocean for the longest distance runs between Muir Beach and Tennessee Beach in southern Marin County. An out-and-back hike from the trailhead at Muir Beach provides a seven-mile round-trip with three beaches to visit and non-stop coastal views.

Know before you go: this is not a level, easy walk. Coastal Trail climbs, then descends, then climbs again, at times with a vengeance. An advantage to starting your trip at Muir Beach is that if you tire of the trail's continual ups and downs, you can always skip the final descent to Tennessee Valley Beach and the ensuing return climb. An abbreviated walk on the Coastal Trail is almost as good as the whole thing.

Start by locating the trail, which is on the southwest side of the Muir Beach parking lot, near the rest rooms. Walk across a footbridge over a marsh to reach the signed Coastal Trail. Take the wide fire road to the right and immediately make a steep, quick climb up a ridge. Follow the single-track spur to the right to reach the trail's first overlook point, where you can catch your breath and enjoy a fine view to the north of Muir Beach's picturesque, semi-circular cove and small community of homes.

Then regain the main path at a major junction of trails; you'll stay to the right along the coast. (For the next two miles, Coastal Trail is a single-track trail for hikers only. Mountain bikers aren't permitted; they must keep to the fire roads.)

Coastal Trail between Tennessee Valley and Muir Beach

Coastal Trail descends, offering fine views of the crashing surf below. Straight ahead to the south you can observe the line of ridges and valleys and pick out your final destination at Tennessee Cove. An intermediate destination is reached at two miles from the trail-head; watch for a spur trail leading to tiny, rocky Pirate's Cove. (Just before the spur, the main trail heads inland to curve around the cove's inlet stream.) Follow the short but steep spur path to what must be Marin County's smallest and most secluded beach. Rest up while you're there; the next half-mile is a steep ascent that gains 550 feet.

March your way uphill through the sweaty climb. A series of wooden stairsteps make the work a little easier. At the end of the ascent, you'll reach a junction of trails and a rewarding overlook point. Here, on a flat, high bluff, you're provided with a 360-degree panorama of the Pacific Ocean to the west, Tennessee Valley and its blue lagoon to the south, Bolinas and Point Reyes to the north, and the San Francisco skyline to the southwest. To the east are the lovely rolling hills of the Golden Gate National Recreation Area.

Consider your position carefully before continuing onward to Tennessee Valley. If you're tiring out, this high point makes an excellent turnaround. Most of your return trip will be downhill. If you have energy to burn, head steeply downhill on the wide dirt road to Tennessee Valley, then turn right on Tennessee Valley Trail and take a level, lovely stroll to the beach. You'll pass by a pretty lagoon and an abundance of coastal chaparral along the way. (For more information on Tennessee Beach, see the following story.) Enjoy your stay at this fine, black-sand pocket beach, then shore up your energy for the hilly return trip.

Note that your dog may accompany you on this hike right up to the point where Coastal Trail joins Tennessee Valley Trail. All canines must make a turnaround where the trails junction. Although dogs are allowed at Muir Beach, they are not permitted at Tennessee Valley Beach nor on its trail.

Trip notes: There is no fee. Dogs are allowed on Coastal Trail up to its junction with Tennessee Valley Trail. Bikes are allowed only on fire roads. A free map is available by contacting Golden Gate National Recreation Area, Building 1056, Fort Cronkhite, Sausalito, CA 94965; (415) 331-1540. Website: www.nps.gov/goga

41. TENNESSEE VALLEY TRAIL
Golden Gate National Recreation Area

DISTANCE: 4.0 miles round-trip; 2 hours   **LEVEL:** Easy

ELEVATION CHANGE: 150 feet   **RATING:** ★ ★ ★

DIRECTIONS: From San Francisco, cross the Golden Gate Bridge and drive north on U.S. 101 for four miles. Take the Mill Valley/Stinson Beach/Highway 1 exit and continue straight for six-tenths of a mile to Tennessee Valley Road on the left. Turn left and drive two miles to the trailhead.

The Tennessee Valley Trail is the most popular trail in the Golden Gate Recreation Area and probably the most heavily used trail in all of Marin County. But don't let the crowds scare you away. Time your trip for an early morning or a weekday and you'll enjoy a peaceful, easy walk to a postcard-quality beach.

Aside from the first-class scenery, the main reason for the crowds at Tennessee Valley is its proximity to the homes of thousands of San Francisco and Marin residents. Mount Tamalpais is only a few miles up the road from Tennessee Valley, but it's a steep, winding drive to get there. Tennessee Valley is in the flats, close to

Tennessee Valley Cove

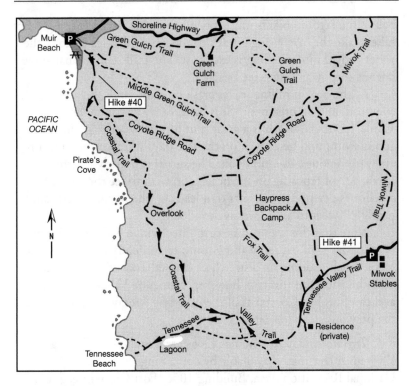

town and U.S. 101. Plus, Tennessee Valley Trail is open to bikers as well as hikers, and it's a popular route for runners and parents pushing baby strollers. Fortunately the route is wide enough so there's plenty of room for everybody. Trail conflicts are rare to nonexistent.

The trail begins as a paved route by Miwok Stables, where horses can be rented and riding lessons are held. Shortly the pavement forks left and the main trail continues straight as a wide dirt road. The mostly level path follows a creekbed between tall grassy ridges lined with coastal chaparral. Rabbits, deer, and bobcats are often seen in the early morning. Your destination is two miles away at Tennessee Cove, where a small, black sand beach is bracketed by high cliffs. This picturesque pocket beach is where the steamship *Tennessee* wrecked in dense fog on its way to San Francisco in 1853. The ship was carrying cargo, mail, and 600 passengers. Miraculously all lives were saved, although the rough surf soon tore the ship to pieces.

While the beach is the trail's prime attraction, a bird-filled, blue lagoon along the way is a close runner-up. The trail forks shortly before the lagoon; bikers must stay on the wide road to the right but hikers take the lovely single-track to the left, which leads along the water's edge. Birdwatching is excellent. The trails rejoin a half-mile later as they near Tennessee Beach.

At the beach, rolling waves crash on dark sands, pelicans soar overhead, and an offshore rock is battered by continual breakers. While Tennessee Beach is a great spot for surf-watching, don't think about swimming here, even on the rare days when the air and sun are warm enough to tempt you. The surf is extremely treacherous. If you tire of reposing on the beach and wish to see the world from a pelican's perspective, a short trail leads up the northwestern bluff nearly 200 feet to an impressive overlook.

Note that this trail can be combined with a walk on neighboring Coastal Trail, either heading south to Rodeo Beach or north to Muir Beach. Adding on a stretch of Coastal Trail will dramatically alter the nature of this trip, however. Tennessee Valley Trail is level and carefree, but Coastal Trail is marked by strenuous climbs. (See the previous story for details.)

Trip notes: There is no fee. Dogs are not allowed. Bikes are allowed. A free map is available by contacting the Golden Gate National Recreation Area, Building 1056, Fort Cronkhite, Sausalito, CA 94965; (415) 331-1540. Website: www.nps.gov/goga

42. LAGOON TRAIL
Golden Gate National Recreation Area

DISTANCE: 1.75 miles round-trip; 1 hour   **LEVEL:** Easy

ELEVATION CHANGE: Negligible   **RATING:** ★ ★ ★

DIRECTIONS: From San Francisco, cross the Golden Gate Bridge on U.S. 101 and take the first exit north of the bridge, Alexander Avenue. Turn left and loop back under the freeway, then turn right on Conzelman Road. (Coming southbound on U.S. 101, take the last Sausalito exit just before the Golden Gate Bridge.) Drive one mile, then turn right on McCullough Road and drive nine-tenths of a mile. Turn left on Bunker Road and drive two miles. (Follow the signs for the Marin Headlands Visitor Center.) Park at the visitor center and locate the Lagoon Trail marker near the rest rooms on the west side of the parking lot.

You have to look long and hard to find a hiking trail in the Marin Headlands that is nearly level. Or you can head directly for the Lagoon Trail at Rodeo Lagoon and spare yourself a lot of searching. The trail begins conveniently at the Marin Headlands Visitor Center, where you can get a few natural and cultural history lessons before heading out on the scenic, easy path.

From the northwestern edge of the parking lot, start walking directly toward the ocean and Rodeo Beach. A trail veers off to the right, but continue straight ahead, marching toward the sea. Hiking on a wide gravel path, you can hear the rhythm of the ocean waves and watch the birds in Rodeo Lagoon. This natural lagoon is separated from the ocean by a narrow strip of beach. Winter storm waves occasionally wash over the beach, resulting in a mixed freshwater and saltwater environment that makes Rodeo Lagoon a happy home for brown pelicans, snowy egrets, diving wood ducks, and other water birds. Red-winged blackbirds and other songbirds like it too. Hope you brought your binoculars.

For a brief stretch, the foliage alongside the trail is very dense and high, and you can't see far in any direction. Walk past a feeder stream where horsetail ferns grow in thick clusters. The trail begins to climb, rising 100 feet above the lagoon and opening up your views. Across the water, you can see the buildings of the Headlands

Footbridge across Rodeo Lagoon

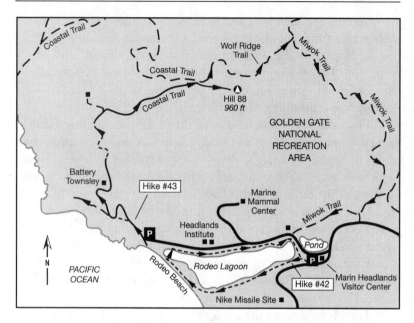

Institute and the Marine Mammal Center. The latter is a nonprofit
organization that rescues and rehabilitates injured marine animals.

Where the trail drops back down again, nearly at the edge of
Rodeo Beach, you are greeted by poppies, ice plant, and deep blue
lupine. Follow the sandy trail straight out to the beach, or climb up
on the bluffs on your left for a fine view of rocky sea stacks and the
coast to the south. Most prominent is Bird Island, a giant sea stack
that is only barely disconnected from the coast. Because of its sepa-
ration, Bird Island is inaccessible to ground predators such as foxes,
bobcats, raccoons, and people. It serves as a major rest stop for
seabirds—as many as 1,200 brown pelicans have been counted on
the island at one time. It's pure paradise for serious birdwatchers.

If you head straight for Rodeo Beach, you'll find it peopled by
a mixed collection of fishermen, surfers, dog walkers, birdwatchers,
and beach-lovers. When it's sunny on Rodeo Beach, it's often windy.
When it's foggy, it's usually still and peaceful. Look closely at the
tiny, colorful pebbles on the beach. Some are semiprecious stones
such as carnelians, jasper, and agates, but because this is a national
park, collecting them is prohibited. Swimming at the beach is not
recommended because of rip tides. The lagoon is also off-limits
for swimming.

To finish out your trip, you can loop back by exiting the beach on a wooden footbridge, then walking along the north side of the lagoon, paralleling the road. I'd recommend a turnaround instead; just reverse your steps and enjoy this path all over again.

Trip notes: There is no fee. Leashed dogs are allowed. Bikes are not allowed. The Marin Headlands Visitor Center is open daily from 9:30 A.M. to 4:30 P.M. A free map is available at the Marin Headlands Visitor Center or by contacting Golden Gate National Recreation Area, Building 1056, Fort Cronkhite, Sausalito, CA 94965; (415) 331-1540. Website: www.nps.gov/goga

43. COASTAL TRAIL & HILL 88 LOOP
Golden Gate National Recreation Area

DISTANCE: 5.5 miles round-trip; 3 hours   **LEVEL:** Moderate
ELEVATION CHANGE: 1,000 feet   **RATING:** ★ ★ ★
DIRECTIONS: From San Francisco, cross the Golden Gate Bridge on U.S. 101 and take the first exit north of the bridge, Alexander Avenue. Turn left and loop back under the freeway, then turn right on Conzelman Road. (Coming southbound on U.S. 101, take the last Sausalito exit just before the Golden Gate Bridge.) Drive one mile, then turn right on McCullough Road and drive nine-tenths of a mile. Turn left on Bunker Road and drive 2.4 miles to the end of the road at Rodeo Beach.

At one time the Coastal Trail at Rodeo Beach was a paved road, but over the years, weather and erosion have taken their toll. The trail has been rebuilt, rerouted, and reworked so many times that today the path is a patchwork: part paved road, part dirt road, part single-track, and part wooden stairsteps. But its destination remains the same. The Coastal Trail leads from Rodeo Beach to the top of mighty Hill 88 in the Marin Headlands, providing what many consider to be the finest views in the Golden Gate National Recreation Area—a park rife with memorable views.

Even better, once you reach the top you don't have to turn around and retrace your steps. A convenient 5.5-mile loop can be made by descending via Wolf Ridge Trail and Miwok Trail, then cruising alongside Rodeo Lagoon back to your car. On a clear day when the fog has vanished from the Golden Gate, this loop trip may be the best possible way to spend an afternoon.

One more incentive, if it's needed: Spring wildflowers along Wolf Ridge are exemplary. The April to June show includes grasslands peppered with colorful shooting stars, California poppies, and fringe cups.

The trip begins at the big parking lot by Rodeo Beach in the Marin Headlands. Start hiking on the gated, paved road that leads uphill along the coastal bluffs. A bonus is that you can bring your dog along on this trail; just be sure to keep him or her leashed. Bikes share sections of the route as well, but there's plenty of room for everybody.

Take the first left cutoff signed as Coastal Trail, only 100 yards up the road. This spur leads up a few easy switchbacks to an overlook perched a few hundred feet above the sea. Spectacular? Yes, it's spectacular. Consider it a preview of the vistas to come. A maze of paths lead along the ocean bluffs, but none of them are through-trails. Return to the pavement again and continue uphill, soon approaching Battery Townsley. One of several dismantled military installations in the Marin Headlands, Battery Townsley was built during World War II to protect the coast against a possible aerial attack. Townsley was the first battery on the Pacific Coast to fire a 16-inch projectile.

Explore the battery's old concrete structures, then climb some more. The clanging bell of an offshore fog signal provides background music for your walk. You'll leave the pavement near an obvious landslide (the paved road was washed out) then continue uphill on single-track trail and wooden stairsteps. Up, up, and up. Is this starting to feel like a workout? Yes, but the views inspire you all the way. It's a total of 2.3 miles and a 1,000-foot elevation gain from Rodeo Beach to the summit.

Finally you top out at the paved road again. A wide dirt road continues uphill to the west past more abandoned military buildings. It's tempting to follow it to the high hill right above you, but hold off: Hill 88 is even higher, and not far off. Stay to the right on the pavement, heading east. The grade mellows as you follow the backbone of narrow Wolf Ridge. Note the junction with Wolf Ridge Trail and Coastal Trail to Tennessee Valley on your left; you'll take Wolf Ridge Trail for the return leg of your loop.

For now, continue straight on the pavement for the final third of a mile to the summit of Hill 88. The junky, rusting bunkers and square, cinder block structures won't hold your attention. Instead

San Francisco Bay and Pacific coast view from Coastal Trail's Hill 88

it's the view... An enormous expanse of ocean and bay is visible, plus Mount Diablo to the east, Montara Mountain to the south, Mount Tamalpais to the northwest, Tennessee Valley to the west, and a multitude of landmarks in the city of San Francisco—Twin Peaks, Ocean Beach, the tall buildings of downtown, and so on. Hill 88's best viewpoint is an old cement gun placement facing south, which makes a perfect flat overlook with a metal railing.

After you've seen enough, retrace your steps down the pavement to the junction with Wolf Ridge Trail. Turn right and head steeply downhill for three-quarters of a mile. You'll gain views of Mount Tamalpais, Tennessee Valley, and pristine Gerbode Valley. As you admire the green valley floor, consider the fact that in the 1960s, developers planned a community of several thousand homes to be built in Gerbode Valley. Although the gateposts had already been set, dedicated conservationists fought the development plan and won.

At the next junction, turn right on Miwok Trail. Wolf Ridge Trail is open to hikers only, but you'll probably share wide, smooth Miwok Trail with mountain bikers. A mile and a half of downhill walking (with a near-guarantee of spotting deer, hawks, and other raptors) brings you to the base of Hill 88 and a junction of trails. Follow Miwok Trail for another four-tenths of a mile to its end at a large building across from Rodeo Lagoon. Cross Bunker Road to the lagoon's edge, then take the trail alongside it for a little more than a half mile back to Rodeo Beach.

Trip notes: There is no fee. Leashed dogs are allowed. Bikes are allowed on Coastal Trail and Miwok Trail, but not on Wolf Ridge Trail. The Marin Headlands Visitor Center is open daily from 9:30 A.M. to 4:30 P.M. A free map is available at the Marin Headlands Visitor Center or by contacting Golden Gate National Recreation Area, Building 1056, Fort Cronkhite, Sausalito, CA 94965; (415) 331-1540. Website: www.nps.gov/goga

44. POINT BONITA LIGHTHOUSE
Golden Gate National Recreation Area

DISTANCE: 1.0 mile round-trip; 1 hour   **LEVEL:** Easy

ELEVATION CHANGE: 100 feet   **RATING:** ★ ★ ★

DIRECTIONS: From San Francisco, cross the Golden Gate Bridge on U.S. 101 and take the first exit north of the bridge, Alexander Avenue. Turn left and loop back under the freeway, then turn right on Conzelman Road. (Coming southbound on U.S. 101, take the last Sausalito exit just before the Golden Gate Bridge.) Follow Conzelman Road all the way to its end (the road becomes one-way) at the Point Bonita Lighthouse parking area. (You can also reach the lighthouse from the Marin Headlands Visitor Center on Bunker Road; follow the brown signs for one mile.)

SPECIAL NOTE: The Point Bonita Lighthouse and its trail are open on Saturdays, Sundays, and Mondays from 12:30 to 3:30 P.M.

Okay, this isn't the Bay Area's longest hike. It's so short and easy, let's just call it a walk. But the trail to Point Bonita Lighthouse must be considered one of the Bay Area's most spectacular paths, if not for its unique destination and historical interest, then for its heart-stopping scenery.

A half-mile walk takes you from the Point Bonita trailhead along a thin backbone of land to the Marin Headlands' southern tip, where the Point Bonita Lighthouse shines its mighty beacon. As you walk this knife-thin ridge, the realization hits you that Point Bonita is really *out there*, as in just barely attached to the rest of the continent. It's a place unlike any other in the Bay Area.

Constructed in 1855, Point Bonita was the third lighthouse built on the West Coast, after the Alcatraz and Fort Point lighthouses. (Marin County's other famous lighthouse at Point Reyes was built in 1870.) Point Bonita's original glass lens has been in continuous use for nearly 150 years, shining a light that is seen for 18 miles out to sea. Prior to the lighthouse's construction, mariners frequently sailed right by San Francisco Bay without even noticing it, particularly in heavy fog. As settlers and gold seekers poured into the Golden Gate with the Gold Rush in 1848, a lighthouse was needed to make the port's entrance more visible.

Your trip begins with a glance at your calendar. The Point Bonita lighthouse and the trail that accesses it is open only on Saturdays, Sundays, and Mondays from 12:30 to 3:30 P.M., so you can't just show up whenever you feel like it. Next you should glance at the skies. Although the lighthouse is open to visitors in any weather except extreme high winds, it's best to save your trip for a clear day when the coast and bay vistas will be optimal.

Finally, you ought to borrow your great-aunt's convertible, because the drive to the lighthouse along Conzelman Road is one of the most spectacular in all of California. If you've never driven this remarkable road on the edge of the Marin Headlands, you're in for a treat. (You can also drive to the lighthouse via Bunker Road in the Marin Headlands, but it's nowhere near as thrilling.)

Point Bonita's lighthouse and suspension footbridge

Once you're at the trailhead, the trip is self-explanatory. The trail is wide, paved, and easy, with a slight downhill grade to the lighthouse. Views of the Golden Gate Bridge, San Francisco, and the immense blue bay are excellent to begin with, but just wait until you proceed along Point Bonita's curving tip of land that juts precipitously into the bay. The panorama just keeps expanding.

In your first few steps, you'll pass the worn metal rails of an abandoned lifesaving station. The station was established in 1899 to aid shipwrecked boats. Despite the warning beacon of the light-house, hundreds of vessels have been lost near the entrance to the Golden Gate. Long before the U.S. Coast Guard came into existence, the crews at this lifesaving station had the daring job of rescuing lives and property in treacherous seas. The "surfmen" (as they were called) would row out to sea in oarboats to search for shipwreck survivors. Their foreboding motto was "You have to go out, but you don't have to come in." Too often they didn't.

After walking less than a quarter mile you reach the trail's famous hand-dug tunnel, a six-foot-high, 50-foot-long hole bored through a pillow basalt formation. (The tunnel is the point where the Park Service closes off the trail when the lighthouse is closed.) Tall people have to duck when passing through; kids usually run back and forth a few times.

On the tunnel's far side, the trail continues along a thin back-bone of volcanic rock, then reaches a series of boardwalks and a mini-suspension bridge. Yes, it's just like the Golden Gate Bridge, but a lot smaller and white, not orange. The piece of land connect-ing Point Bonita to the coast is so minimal, and has been so badly worn by the ravages of waves and weather, that it's just shy of being disconnected. Point Bonita will eventually become an island, a rocky sea stack just off the coast.

Only five people at a time are permitted on the 40-yard-long suspension bridge; otherwise it gets a little tippy. If you have to wait a minute to get on, you're lucky. From the bridge's entrance the views of the Golden Gate and the lighthouse are perfectly framed. A lot of photo-snapping happens here.

Finally you arrive at Point Bonita's lighthouse. You can explore its lower floor, talk to the volunteers who staff it, and learn all kinds of facts about the hard life of a lighthouse keeper. Then again, you might just stand around on its deck and gaze in wonder at the crashing waves, black sand coves, and the magnificent Golden Gate.

Trip notes: There is no fee. Dogs and bikes are not allowed. The Marin Headlands Visitor Center is open daily from 9:30 A.M. to 4:30 P.M. A free map is available at the Marin Headlands Visitor Center or by contacting Golden Gate National Recreation Area, Building 1056, Fort Cronkhite, Sausalito, CA 94965; (415) 331-1540. Website: www.nps.gov/goga

45. PHYLLIS ELLMAN TRAIL
Ring Mountain Preserve

DISTANCE: 3.0 miles round-trip; 1.5 hours   **LEVEL:** Easy

ELEVATION CHANGE: 600 feet   **RATING:** ★ ★ ★

DIRECTIONS: From San Francisco, cross the Golden Gate Bridge and drive north on U.S. 101 for seven miles to Corte Madera. Take the Paradise Drive exit and head east for 1.6 miles (through a residential neighborhood). The preserve trailhead is on the right. Park in the gravel pullouts on the side of the road.

The Nature Conservancy's Ring Mountain Preserve is located smack in the middle of the Corte Madera suburbs, not far from Paradise Drive's paradise of shopping malls. But while all the surrounding development may seem discouraging, Ring Mountain Preserve is a little paradise of open space. It features lovely grassland wildflowers, fascinating rock outcrops, and outstanding views.

The Nature Conservancy acquired this hillside land tucked between neighborhood developments in order to protect the Tiburon mariposa lily, which grows nowhere else in the world. Six other species of Ring Mountain wildflowers grow in few other areas, landing them a spot on the rare plant list. These special flora share Ring Mountain with many more common wildflowers and grasses, as well as bay trees, live oaks, deer, grey fox, rabbits, quail, and songbirds. To see the preserve at its best, you must visit in spring when the grasslands are in bloom, and preferably on a clear day.

Phyllis Ellman Trail loops through the preserve. Take the left side of the loop first, saving the right side for your return. At the trailhead, things don't look all that promising, but just be patient. Ignore the neighboring houses and the busy road behind you, start climbing, and take your time—there's nowhere to go but up.

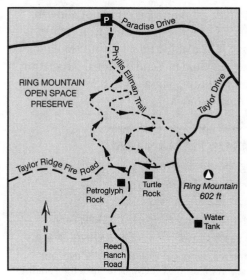

RING MOUNTAIN OPEN SPACE PRESERVE

Paradise Drive

Phyllis Ellman Trail

Taylor Drive

Taylor Ridge Fire Road

Petroglyph Rock

Turtle Rock

Ring Mountain 602 ft

Water Tank

Reed Ranch Road

N

As you ascend, be sure to turn around every few minutes to check out the view at your back. You gain elevation quickly, and with every few footsteps your vista will expand to include more of the North and East bays. Ring Mountain is situated directly across the bay from two easy landmarks: the Larkspur Ferry Terminal and San Quentin Prison. As you scan the horizon, you'll see the East and West Brothers Islands near Richmond, the East and West Marin Islands near San Rafael, Point San Pedro, the Richmond Bridge, and parts of the East Bay. The islands are perhaps the most intriguing sight. This is the only park in Marin where you can simultaneously see the Marin Islands, which are state-owned and unoccupied, and the East and West Brothers Islands, which feature a lighthouse and tiny inn.

As you hike, don't be confused by the numerous spur trails that interlace with the main trail. Stick to the most well defined path heading uphill and keep an eye on the numbered posts. You may want to take a few side trips to climb on the large rock outcrops that jut out from the hillside or to examine the wildflowers close-up. Look for sky lupine with clusters of dark blue flowers, blue-eyed grass, western larkspur, Douglas iris, light blue flax, pink onions, tarweed, yarrow, owl's clover, and the yellow spikes of false lupine. California poppies are the most prevalent bloomers. If you want to see the rare Tiburon mariposa lily, you must show up in late May, after many of the other wildflowers have finished their bloom. Even then, you must look carefully for this precious plant. Its mottled flowers are camouflaged against the surrounding grasses.

You'll be in open sunshine for most of this walk, but as you gain the ridge the trail passes through small groves of live oaks. The trees create a surprisingly dense canopy of branches and leaves, shading the sky as you pass through.

On top of Turtle Rock, Ring Mountain

Near the top of the ridge (at interpretive post number 11), the trail meets up with a wide fire road. You'll see a large water tank and a handful of immense houses to your left and a prominent serpentine outcrop straight ahead. This is Turtle Rock, although you may not recognize its moniker at first (the top of the rock resembles a turtle, but only when seen from the west). Climb on top of Turtle Rock for a fabulous view to the south of San Francisco, Angel Island, Alcatraz, Tiburon, and Sausalito. The whole of the East and North bays remain visible in the opposite direction. You can see both San Francisco Bay and San Pablo Bay at the same time.

After enjoying the view from the big rock overlook, head west (right) on the fire road for a short distance to a junction of trails near interpretive post number 12. Walk to the south for a few yards to examine Petroglyph Rock, another large serpentine outcrop. The rock was carved by Native Americans approximately 3,000 years ago. The carvings are oval in shape and quite deep. (Unfortunately the rock has been carved by vandals in more recent years.) Additional carvings are found on at least 30 other outcrops in the preserve. A midden on the lower part of the mountain suggests that Miwok Indians were living on Ring Mountain as early as 370 B.C.

Finally, return to the junction and take the signed Phyllis Ellman Trail back downhill for the return leg of your loop. The vistas should continue to inspire you all the way downhill.

Trip notes: There is no fee. Leashed dogs are allowed. Bikes are not allowed. For more information, contact Marin County Open Space District, 3501 Civic Center Drive, San Rafael, CA 94903; (415) 499-6387. Or contact The Nature Conservancy at (415) 435-6465 or (415) 777-0487.

46. PERIMETER TRAIL
Angel Island State Park

DISTANCE: 5.0 miles round-trip; 2.5 hours   **LEVEL:** Easy

ELEVATION CHANGE: 200 feet   **RATING:** ★ ★ ★

DIRECTIONS: Ferry service to Angel Island is available from Tiburon via the Tiburon Ferry, and from San Francisco, Oakland/Alameda, and Vallejo via the Blue & Gold Fleet. For departures from Tiburon, phone the Tiburon Ferry at (415) 435-2131. For the Blue & Gold Fleet, phone (415) 773-1188 for San Francisco departures, (510) 522-3300 for Oakland or Alameda departures, and (707) 64-FERRY for Vallejo departures.

The Perimeter Trail at Angel Island State Park may be the most spectacular easy hike in the entire San Francisco Bay Area. How easy? It's paved and nearly level, so you can push a baby stroller around the whole thing. How spectacular? The Bay Area has plenty of first-rate trails, but what sets this one apart is that it's on an island in the middle of the bay. The 360-degree views alone are reason enough to make the journey.

What comes as a surprise to first-time visitors is how fun it is just getting to Angel Island—walking up the ferry gangway, finding a spot on the boat's top deck or inside the lower deck, watching the mainland diminish as you pull away from the harbor, feeling the cool bay breeze, smelling the salt air... No matter how crowded the boat is, everybody is always smiling.

In about 20 minutes from Tiburon and 40 minutes from San Francisco or the East Bay, your ferry docks at Ayala Cove. Buy a map at the ferry landing and walk to your right, past the island's cafe and bike rental kiosk. The picnic area at Ayala Cove is usually packed with people, but you'll quickly leave them behind. Take the well-signed trail to the left of the picnic tables, which switchbacks gently uphill to join the main Perimeter Trail.

Perimeter Trail is a wide, paved road, although the pavement deteriorates to gravel and dirt in some places. Because the road loops around the island, you can head either right or left. If you go left, heading clockwise around the island, you will face most of the oncoming bicyclists, who usually ride in the opposite direction. (The trail is wide enough to easily handle all its users, but it helps when hikers see bikers coming.)

You'll have only one major hill to face on the southeast side of the island. The views will more than compensate. Heading clockwise, you begin with a panorama of Tiburon and its Mediterranean-looking waters, then the Richmond Bridge and the northern tip of San Pablo Bay. Far beyond are the hills of Napa and Sonoma counties. The panorama changes with every few steps. You have to keep analyzing and re-analyzing what you're seeing, because your perspective is so different from the center of San Francisco Bay than it is from its edges.

One of the best viewpoints is on the southeast side of the loop, at an open stretch where you glimpse the Bay Bridge and Golden Gate Bridge simultaneously, plus everything in between and on either side, including Alcatraz, which lies directly ahead. You're

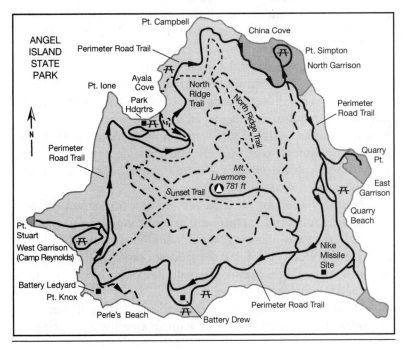

Perle's Beach on Angel Island

viewing the whole line of cities from Berkeley to San Francisco to Sausalito, a 180-degree scene.

Numerous historical side trips are possible on Perimeter Trail. Angel Island has a long and varied history as a military outpost, a Russian sea otter hunters' site, and an immigrant detention center. The visitor center near the picnic area at Ayala Cove has brochures and exhibits on the island's history. One recommended side trip is a visit to Camp Reynolds on the island's southwest side. Established in 1863, Camp Reynolds was built to protect the Bay Area from Confederate sympathizers during the American Civil War. A dozen years later it was used as a staging area for troops fighting various American Indian "wars" in the West. The camp remained in use by the military through World War II. You can walk its parade grounds and visit some of its remaining buildings, including a chapel, mule barn, hospital, and barracks.

Another important site is the old immigration station at China Cove, where Asian immigrants were detained for long, arduous periods in the years following World War I. This so-called "Ellis Island of the West" qualifies as the saddest chapter in Angel Island's history. During World War II, German, Italian, and Japanese prisoners of war were confined here.

My favorite side trip on Angel Island is the half-mile walk to Perle's Beach, a windy strip of sand with an amazing vista facing south toward Alcatraz and San Francisco. You'll find the turnoff for its dirt road at a spectacular overlook point above Battery Ledyard, where everyone stops on the roadside benches to admire the Golden Gate Bridge view. Another popular beach is Quarry Beach on the island's east side, which is larger, more protected from the wind, and better for sunbathing than Perle's Beach.

Keep in mind that the weather can be fickle at Angel Island and the fog can come in on a moment's notice. Come prepared with an extra jacket, even on sunny days. A pleasant bonus for day-hikers is that if you didn't bother to pack a lunch, you can buy one at the cafe near the boat dock. Their outside deck is inviting, but most likely you'll want to choose your own private picnic spot somewhere on the island.

Trip notes: From Tiburon, the ferry costs $7 for adults. From San Francisco, the ferry costs $11 for adults. The ferry crossing fee includes day-use of Angel Island State Park. Dogs are not allowed. Bikes are allowed on Perimeter Trail. A park map is available for $2 at the ferry landing on the island. For more information, contact Angel Island State Park at (415) 435-1915 or (415) 893-1580. For ferry schedules, phone the numbers listed under "directions" at the top of this story. Website: www.angelisland.org

47. NORTH RIDGE & SUNSET TRAIL LOOP
Angel Island State Park

DISTANCE: 4.5 miles round-trip; 2 hours   **LEVEL:** Easy
ELEVATION CHANGE: 780 feet   **RATING:** ★ ★ ★ ★
DIRECTIONS: Ferry service to Angel Island is available from Tiburon via the Tiburon Ferry, and from San Francisco, Oakland/Alameda, and Vallejo via the Blue & Gold Fleet. For departures from Tiburon, phone the Tiburon Ferry at (415) 435-2131. For the Blue & Gold Fleet, phone (415) 773-1188 for San Francisco departures, (510) 522-3300 for Oakland or Alameda departures, and (707) 64-FERRY for Vallejo departures.

You say you want to visit Angel Island but you can't bear to hike on pavement? You don't like sharing the trail with bikers and you want a hikers-only path? No problem. It just so happens there are two completely different ways to hike Angel Island. One way is walking the wide, paved Perimeter Trail as it circumnavigates the island. The other way is hiking the dirt, single-track North Ridge and Sunset Trail Loop to the island's highest point, the summit of Mount Livermore. For the Perimeter Trail, see the previous story. For the North Ridge and Sunset Trail Loop, read on.

The hardest part of this trip is in the first 10 minutes after you get off the boat. While everyone else disembarks and heads to the right toward Ayala Cove and the island's concession stands, you'll head the other way. North Ridge Trail starts on the north side of the ferry dock to the left of the restrooms. It begins with a quick, steep climb of more than 100 stairsteps, leading past a couple of well-placed picnic tables (with a great view) and then up to the paved Perimeter Road.

Cross the road, pant a few times, then pick up North Ridge Trail on its far side. Now the path is more like a trail and less like a staircase. The single-track is well graded and alternates through sunny chaparral-covered slopes and a shady, fern-filled canopy of live oaks. At just over one mile up the trail, the path traverses the northern flank of Mount Livermore, passing a surprising grove of non-native Monterey pines. Views widen as you climb, and Tiburon

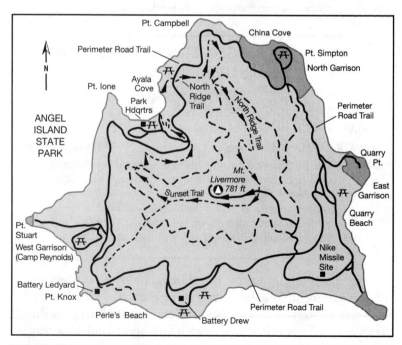

and Belvedere begin to fade into the distance.

Where North Ridge Trail junctions with the paved road to the summit, turn right and follow the pavement uphill. (Note the signed Sunset Trail across the road; this is the return leg of your loop.) A steep quarter-mile climb brings you to the hill's flat 781-foot summit, where you'll find a grouping of picnic tables and signs pointing out the landmarks of the bay. What landmarks? These and more: Berkeley, Mount Diablo, San Leandro, Alameda, Mission Peak (38 miles away), Mount Hamilton (56 miles away), Santa Clara, Mountain View, San Francisco's Telegraph Hill, Alcatraz Island, Montara Mountain, Twin Peaks, the Golden Gate Bridge, Mount Tamalpais, Tiburon, Belvedere, San Quentin Prison, and Mount St. Helena in Napa (57 miles away). Whew!

With a view like that, it's not surprising that Mount Livermore's picnic tables are in high demand on sunny weekend days. After you've lunched or just enjoyed the view, head back downhill on the paved road. Turn right on Sunset Trail, enjoying another half-mile of open views as you descend through the grasslands. The trail heads into a forest of oaks and bays, switchbacking gently downhill to another wide viewpoint and a crossing of Perimeter Road. You can follow the paved road back downhill to Ayala Cove, or take the forested single-track just to the right of it.

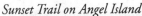

Sunset Trail on Angel Island

Views of Tiburon and Mount Tamalpais from Angel Island

Trip notes: From Tiburon, the ferry costs $7 for adults. From San Francisco, the ferry costs $11 for adults. The ferry crossing fee includes day-use of Angel Island State Park. Dogs are not allowed. Bikes are allowed on the island, but not on this loop. A park map is available for $2 at the ferry landing on the island. For more information, contact Angel Island State Park at (415) 435-1915 or (415) 893-1580. For ferry schedules, phone the numbers listed under "directions" at the top of this story. Website: www.angelisland.org

East Bay

48. BAY VIEW LOOP
Point Pinole Regional Shoreline

DISTANCE: 5.0 miles round-trip; 2.5 hours   **LEVEL:** Easy

ELEVATION CHANGE: Negligible   **RATING:** ★ ★ ★

DIRECTIONS: From Interstate 80 in Richmond, take the Hilltop Drive exit west. Turn right on San Pablo Avenue, then left on Richmond Parkway. Follow Richmond Parkway to the Giant Highway exit. Turn right and drive three quarters of a mile to the park entrance on the left.

Or, from U.S. 101 in Marin, take the San Rafael-Richmond Bridge east (Interstate 580), then take the first exit east of the bridge, signed for Castro Street and Richmond Parkway. Drive 4.3 miles on Richmond Parkway to the Giant Highway exit. Take the exit and drive a half-mile, then turn right on Giant Highway. Drive three-quarters of a mile to the park entrance on the left.

Point Pinole Regional Shoreline is a little park with a big heart, a place of tranquility not far from the urban bustle of the East Bay. Few visitors other than avid fishermen and dog walkers make the trip to the tip of Point Pinole, but those who do are surprised at how much their four-dollar park admission can buy. In addition to spectacular bay views, a fascinating history, and good pier fishing, the park offers volleyball courts, picnic areas, and more than 12 miles of winding dirt trails suitable for hiking or mountain biking.

Don't be put off by the drive in to the park. Point Pinole Regional Shoreline has some odd neighbors, including Chevron's oil refineries and a juvenile detention center. The Southern Pacific Railroad runs right alongside the park. But once you're inside the gates of Point Pinole, all is peaceful. On two weekend visits here, we found the place largely deserted except for a few hikers and bike riders. The ranger at the entrance kiosk told us that some people are discouraged by the park's Richmond address; others are put off by the four-dollar admission fee.

Start your hike on the main paved trail by the entrance kiosk. You'll notice a small mound planted with flowers and a plaque denoting the site of the Giant Powder Company from 1892 to 1960. When terrible explosions ruined its Berkeley and San Francisco factories, Giant Powder moved to remote Point Pinole to manufacture dynamite. Here they built a thriving company town and local railway.

Follow the paved road for 200 yards to a railroad bridge. Cross the bridge and take the signed trail on the left, Bay View Trail. The wide dirt trail skirts the edge of Point Pinole's peninsula and provides continual views of San Pablo Bay. To the southwest, you see plumes of gas and steam rising from Chevron's oil refineries. To the west, Mount Tamalpais looms over Marin County. In the foreground are miles of open bay water, interrupted only by the San Rafael-Richmond Bridge

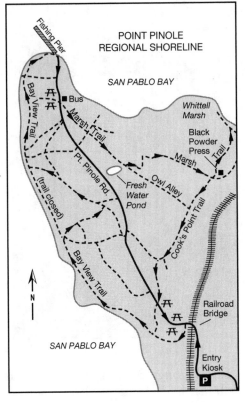

and the East and West Brothers Islands. A few duck blinds dot the shoreline. Seabirds gather on the mud flats during low tide.

Due to a trail closure, the path moves away from the bay and into a eucalyptus grove for a brief stretch, then returns to the meeting of land and sea. Just under two miles from the trailhead, the path curves around the tip of Point Pinole's peninsula to reach its quarter-mile-long fishing pier. Walk out to the pier's end, then sit and sniff the salty air while you admire the views of Mount Diablo on your right and Mount Tamalpais on your left. Look back toward shore and note the rugged coastal bluffs rising 100 feet above the bay. Point Pinole is the only place on this side of San Pablo Bay with shoreline cliffs; elsewhere the water is surrounded by flatlands.

The pier's plexiglas shelters provide protection for anglers and hikers when the wind howls. If you're interested in fishing, note that you don't need a license to pier fish here. For those with luck, the catch may include sturgeon, striped bass, and kingfish.

Snowy egret at Point Pinole

From the pier, follow the paved road 100 yards south to a wooden bus shelter. (Shuttle buses ride this paved route from the parking lot to the pier every hour from 7:30 A.M. to 2:30 P.M. For a buck, anglers who don't want to walk to the pier can catch a ride.) Beyond the bus shelter, take the signed Marsh Trail on the left. In just under a half-mile you'll see a small pond on your right; turn left by the pond to stay on Marsh Trail.

Now facing eastward, your perspective on the bay is totally different. The Carquinez Bridge appears, as well as Vallejo and Napa. A large salt marsh lined with pickleweed borders the trail. The wide, gentle waters of San Pablo Bay remain constant.

Where Marsh Trail junctions with Cook's Point Trail, you'll see an odd structure sheltering a large hunk of metal. It's a black powder press remaining from the days of Giant Powder Company. Head past it on Marsh Trail to the edge of the bay; you can make a short loop to the right along the shoreline if you wish. Birdwatching is excellent near the salt marsh.

The return leg of the loop is Cook's Point Trail. This path will lead you all the way back to the park's picnic areas. From there it's a short stroll over the railroad bridge and back to your car.

Trip notes: A $4 day-use fee is charged per vehicle. Leashed dogs are allowed except on the pier. Bikes are allowed. A free map is available at the entrance kiosk. For more information, contact East Bay Regional Park District, 2950 Peralta Oaks Court, P.O. Box 5381, Oakland, CA 94605-0381; (510) 237-6896, (510) 562-7275, or (510) 635-0135. Website: www.ebparks.org

49. TWO TRAILS at CARQUINEZ STRAIT
Carquinez Strait Regional Shoreline

DISTANCE: 1.0 to 3.0 miles round-trip; 1-2 hours   **LEVEL:** Easy

ELEVATION CHANGE: 150 feet   **RATING:** ★ ★ ★

DIRECTIONS: For the Crockett trailhead—From Interstate 80 in Richmond, drive north for 10 miles to the Crockett exit (just before the Carquinez Bridge). You'll exit on Pomona Street; head east. Pomona Street becomes Carquinez Drive just outside of Crockett. Drive two miles to the Bull Valley Staging Area on the left.

For the Martinez trailhead—From Highway 4 in Martinez, take the Alhambra Avenue exit and drive north through Martinez for two miles. Turn left on Marina Vista, drive two blocks, then turn right on Talbart Street, which becomes Carquinez Scenic Drive. Drive four tenths of a mile to the Carquinez Strait East Staging Area on the right. Begin hiking on the California Riding and Hiking Trail from the far end of the horse trailer parking lot.

The name "Carquinez Strait" sounds like someplace foreign and exotic. Although San Francisco Bay and San Pablo Bay are as familiar as the local freeways to most Bay Area residents, the waterway at Carquinez Strait is far less known. The northeastern arm of the conglomeration of waterways that constitute the bay and river delta, Carquinez Strait forms the narrow passageway between San Pablo and Suisun bays. It's the meeting place of the Sacramento and San Joaquin rivers, where they join together to flow to the Pacific Ocean through the Golden Gate.

The bluffs above Carquinez Strait are a wonderful place for an easy hike. Carquinez Strait Regional Shoreline encompasses 1,300 acres of land on the strait's south side. The park's main two parcels are located along Carquinez Scenic Drive near the cities of Crockett and Martinez. Both areas have fine trails to explore and plentiful scenery along the waterway. Unfortunately, they aren't contiguous, because the middle section of Carquinez Scenic Drive washed out in a landslide in 1982. So the people of Martinez have one slice of the bluffs above Carquinez Strait and the people of Crockett have a separate slice. Both are worth a visit.

To see the western area of the park, drive to the Bull Valley Staging Area near Crockett, just a few miles from the Carquinez

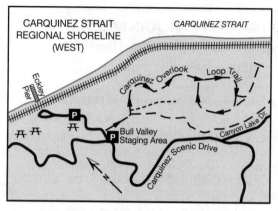

CARQUINEZ STRAIT REGIONAL SHORELINE (WEST)

CARQUINEZ STRAIT

Eckley Pier

Carquinez Overlook

Loop Trail

Bull Valley Staging Area

Canyon Lake Dr.

Carquinez Scenic Drive

N

Bridge. From the parking lot, take the trail at the cattle gate by the portable toilet. Head east along the grassy bluffs, which are littered with owl's clover every spring. The green hills lie in sharp contrast to the bright blue of the strait. You may hear the sound of a commuter train roaring past on the tracks that hug the shoreline, or the horn of a tugboat working the waterway. Part of the joy of this walk is watching the ships, large and small, journey in and out of the strait. You might see anything from a windsurfer to a freighter.

Where the wide double-track trail forks, bear left and walk through a planted eucalyptus grove until your view of the strait is unobstructed again. At a second junction, bear left again; the right fork is the return of a short loop. The far end of the trail is marked by a bench on a grassy knoll. It's well positioned for a wide view to the north, east, and south. Benicia State Recreation Area is visible

Carquinez Strait

across the strait, as well as the houses and businesses of the town of Benicia, but what captures your attention is the wide expanse of blue waterway.

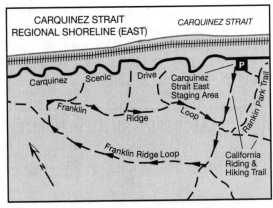

Consider the story of Carquinez Strait. Hundreds of thousands of king salmon once passed through here on their way to the Sacramento and San Joaquin rivers to spawn. Native Americans lived off their abundance for centuries. In the 1800s, white settlers set up commercial fishing operations and canneries along the strait. Salmon ran the economy of this area until the mid-twentieth century, when laws were passed that banned all commercial fishing east of the Carquinez Bridge. Although this was a great victory for the conservation movement and the future of fish populations, it made ghost towns of the once bustling communities along Carquinez Strait.

Beyond the bench and viewpoint, the trail loops back through a forest of eucalyptus. You might skip the loop and walk back the way you came; the views of the strait are worth a second look.

To see the eastern area of the park, drive to the Carquinez Strait East Staging Area in Martinez. Follow the California Riding and Hiking Trail from the far end of the equestrian parking lot (don't take the Rankin Park Trail from the left side of the lot). You'll head uphill through a shady ravine filled with oaks, bays, and eucalyptus. In a third of a mile, turn left and walk the two-mile Franklin Ridge Loop. You'll leave the trees in the canyon below; up on the ridge, native grasslands sway and dance in the breeze and raptors soar overhead. Lucky hikers may spot a bobcat or fox as it darts across the trail. From atop Franklin Ridge, you can see Mount Tamalpais to the west and Mount Diablo to the east, plus the grassy ridges of Briones and Las Trampas regional parks to the south. Combined with the long blue stretch of Carquinez Strait to the north, the overall effect is stunning. If you seek more views, walk a half-mile out-and-back along the California Riding and Hiking Trail from the east end of the Franklin Ridge Loop.

Trip notes: There is no fee. Leashed dogs and bikes are allowed. Free trail maps are available at the entrance kiosk. For more information, contact East Bay Regional Park District, 2950 Peralta Oaks Court, P.O. Box 5381, Oakland, CA 94605-0381; (510) 635-0135 or (510) 562-7275. Website: www.ebparks.org

50. SAN PABLO RIDGE & WILDCAT CREEK LOOP
Wildcat Canyon Regional Park

DISTANCE: 6.8 miles round-trip; 3 hours   **LEVEL:** Moderate

ELEVATION CHANGE: 1,200 feet   **RATING:** ★ ★ ★

DIRECTIONS: From Interstate 80 heading north in Richmond, take the Amador/Solano exit and drive three blocks east on Amador. Turn right on McBryde Avenue and drive a half-mile to the entrance to Wildcat Canyon Regional Park. (Bear left where the road forks.) The trail begins on the far side of the parking lot and is paved at the start. (Heading south on Interstate 80, take the McBryde Avenue exit and go east.)

Never judge a trail by its trailhead, sage hikers say. When you park your car at Wildcat Canyon Regional Park's Alvarado staging area, you'll think, "Aha, a forested hike through eucalyptus and oaks." But looks are deceiving at Wildcat Canyon. What begins as a tree-shaded, paved trail quickly becomes a dirt path through the grasslands that takes you up 1,000 feet for wide views of the San Francisco Bay Area.

Begin your hike by walking a half mile on Wildcat Creek Trail, an old paved road that begins on the east side of the parking lot. At the trail sign for Belgum Trail, turn left and begin climbing up the grassy hillside. The wide dirt path makes a moderate ascent, passing two stately palm trees that mark an old homestead. On the surrounding hills, you'll see nonnative purple thistles, which in autumn and winter bear dried, puffy pom-poms. They grow as tall as four feet high. Several slopes at Wildcat Canyon are covered with entire armies of them; their spine-tipped leaves provide thorough protection against grazing cattle. In spring, you'll see big yellow mule's ears and plenty of blue-eyed grass.

Keep looking over your right shoulder as you hike. In short order you'll gain enough elevation to be rewarded with wide-angle

A bouquet of thistles at Wildcat Canyon

views of the San Francisco Bay Area, from Vallejo to San Francisco and the southern East Bay. On a clear day, you can pick out all the famous landmarks: Bay Bridge, Transamerica Pyramid, Twin Peaks, Golden Gate Bridge, Angel Island, and so on. (When it comes to views, I've always preferred a sea of conifers to a sea of civilization. Still, this vista—truly an urban view—makes a lasting and memorable impression.)

In less than a mile, Belgum Trail meets up with a junction of several trails, both formal and informal. Bear left to stay on Belgum Trail (don't take the hard left on Clark-Boas Trail). After curving around the north side of a grassy hill, turn right on San Pablo Ridge Trail. The short climb that follows is memorably steep. But once you complete it, you've gained San Pablo Ridge and the rest of the walk is an easy cruise.

No matter how calm and warm it was when you started your hike, it's likely to be windy on top of the ridge. Numerous raptors and songbirds (including red-wing blackbirds) take advantage of the lofty breezes up here.

You just cruise along, stopping when you feel like it to enjoy the sights from your top-of-the-ridge perch. At a cattle gate, the trail turns from dirt to pavement. You're leaving San Pablo Ridge Trail and following Nimitz Way Trail, a paved path that is popular with bicyclists and hikers. (Most of them access the trail from Inspiration

Point in Tilden Regional Park.) The trail hugs the ridgetop, and the vistas keep changing with every footstep. There's San Pablo Reservoir and Briones Reservoir behind it, plus looming Mount Diablo, all on your left. Then there's San Francisco Bay, the Golden Gate Bridge, and Angel Island on your right. At every turn in the trail, over every hill, you get a slightly different twist on the view. The Richmond Bridge drops into sight, the Gold Coast comes into frame up ahead, then San Francisco disappears and the Brothers Islands come into view. Suddenly Napa and Carquinez show up to the north. And so it goes.

After three-quarters of a mile on paved Nimitz Way, turn right on Havey Canyon Trail. The path narrows as it descends, closely following a spring-fed stream. You'll leave the sunshine and wide open grasslands for a forest of willows, oaks, bay laurel, and a plethora of vines. The trail drops gently over the course of a mile and a half, never leaving the canopy of shade, until it bottoms out at Wildcat Creek Trail. Turn right to finish out your loop, walking a level mile and a half back to your car.

Trip notes: There is no fee. Leashed dogs and bikes are allowed. Free trail maps are available at the parking area. For more information, contact East Bay Regional Park District, 2950 Peralta Oaks Court, P.O. Box 5381, Oakland, CA 94605-0381; (510) 635-0135 or (510) 562-7275. Website: www.ebparks.org

51. WILDCAT PEAK & LAUREL CANYON LOOP
Tilden Regional Park

DISTANCE: 3.5 miles round-trip; 1.5 hours   **LEVEL:** Easy

ELEVATION CHANGE: 500 feet   **RATING:** ★ ★ ★

DIRECTIONS: From Interstate 580 in Berkeley, take the University Avenue exit and go east. Drive two miles to Oxford Street and turn left. Drive a half mile to Rose Street and turn right. Drive one block and turn left on Spruce Street. Drive 1.7 miles on Spruce Street. Immediately after crossing Grizzly Peak Boulevard, turn left on Cañon Drive. Drive a half-mile and turn left on Central Park Drive. Follow Central Park Drive for a quarter-mile to its end by the Tilden Nature Area and Environmental Education Center. The trail begins behind the education center.

Most people think of Tilden Park as a place to take the kids. The park has pony rides, a carousel, a miniature train, a swimming beach at Lake Anza, and lots of other diversions that keep children occupied and happy. But over on the northwest edge of the park lies the Tilden Nature Area, a very different part of Tilden Park. Here the only amenities are trail signs and the only diversions are the natural beauty and the views.

Start your trip at the Tilden Environmental Education Center at the northwest end of Central Park Drive. Take a look around this marvelous visitor center, then walk out its back door to access Laurel Canyon Trail. Its trailhead is located to the left of Little Farm and to the right of Jewel Lake Nature Trail. Oddly, Laurel Canyon Trail isn't signed with its name, but with a symbol: a narrow bay laurel leaf and a berry. You'll follow these iconographic trail markers through several junctions.

Start hiking gently uphill through a eucalyptus grove. The narrow, well built trail dips and rolls, gaining elevation very slowly. In the rainy season, Laurel Creek runs nearby, making pretty water music. You'll reach several junctions in the first half mile, but just keep following the laurel leaf symbols. The path departs the eucalyptus and enters a dense grove of canyon oaks and bay laurels. Leaves crunch underfoot as you tunnel your way through the forest. Where the trees open up, look up to your left and you'll spot your destination: Wildcat Peak.

A mile up the trail, take the trail fork signed to Nimitz Way. Where Laurel Canyon Trail tops out at a wide dirt road (Laurel Canyon Road), turn right and continue uphill for a short distance to Nimitz Way. This paved multi-use trail runs along the ridgetop from Inspiration Point in Tilden Regional Park to Wildcat Canyon Regional Park. It's one of the East Bay's greatest bicycle trails. Turn left and follow Nimitz Way for just under a half mile, then turn left on Wildcat Peak Trail. The dirt trail makes a half-mile climb to the summit of Wildcat Peak, elevation 1,250 feet. (This is the steepest section of the loop, but even so, it's quite easy.)

Wildcat Peak's summit vista is surprising. From the stone overlook platform on top, you can see all of San Pablo Reservoir, the edge of Briones Reservoir, and mighty Mount Diablo to the east. San Pablo Bay appears to the north. To the west, you gain a wide view of famous landmarks. San Francisco Bay sparkles in the sunlight. Mount Tamalpais, Angel Island, the Golden Gate Bridge, the

San Pablo Reservoir seen from Wildcat Peak

Richmond Bridge, the Bay Bridge, and downtown San Francisco are easily recognizable. You're directly across from Brooks Island, a large, flat island south of Richmond that was once owned by a private hunting club and is now managed by the East Bay Regional Park District.

Wildcat Peak's stone overlook is marked with a sign denoting the Rotary Peace Grove below, a living memorial of giant Sequoia trees dedicated to people who have worked for world peace. The grove was a joint project between the Rotary Club of Berkeley and the East Bay Regional Park District.

From Wildcat Peak, head back downhill on Wildcat Peak Trail (its trail signs are marked with a rounded peak). The path descends open, grassy slopes. When you reach Sylvan Trail (marked with three trees), turn left. Follow Sylvan Trail through a eucalyptus grove back to the visitor center.

Trip notes: There is no fee. Dogs and bikes are not allowed. A free map is available at the visitor center. For more information, contact Tilden Regional Park at (510) 544-2711. Or contact East Bay Regional Park District, 2950 Peralta Oaks Court, P.O. Box 5381, Oakland, CA 94605-0381; (510) 635-0135 or (510) 562-7275. Website: www.ebparks.org

52. BRIONES LOOP TOUR
Briones Regional Park

DISTANCE: 7.0 miles round-trip; 4 hours **LEVEL:** Moderate

ELEVATION CHANGE: 1,400 feet **RATING:** ★ ★

DIRECTIONS: From Highway 4 in Martinez, take the Alhambra Avenue exit. Turn south on Alhambra Avenue, drive a half mile and bear right on Alhambra Valley Road. Drive 1.2 miles, then turn right to stay on Alhambra Valley Road. In about 75 yards, turn left on Briones Road and continue 1.5 miles to the trailhead.

Briones Regional Park is nearly 6,000 acres of grasslands and oaks that was once part of Rancho San Felipe, a Spanish land grant. In the mid 1800s, it was an important fruit growing region. Today it's the grassy home of grazing cows and frequently visited by hikers, mountain bikers, dog walkers, and horseback riders.

I wouldn't want to be accused of overselling Briones. Its sunny exposure, wide dirt roads, and large expanse of open grasslands are perhaps better suited to bikers and equestrians than to hikers. But on a breezy spring day when the wildflowers are blooming and the grasslands are glowing green, well, it wouldn't be hard to wax poetic about the place. And considering the fact that Briones is bordered on three sides by freeways—Highway 4, Interstate 680, and Highway 24—it's a miracle that this giant open space even exists. For residents of Martinez, Concord, Pleasant Hill, Walnut Creek, and Lafayette, Briones is only a stone's throw away and a welcome vacation from urban life.

Briones has three main staging areas—Bear Creek, Alhambra Creek, and Lafayette Ridge—but this loop hike starts at a less developed trailhead at the end of Briones Road. As the crow flies, it's only about a mile from the Alhambra Creek Staging Area, but it's much higher in elevation. Your car does some of the climbing for you. Also, no fee is charged at the Briones Road trailhead.

Start your hike on Old Briones Road, a gated dirt road that leads from the parking area. The initial stretch heads through a dense grove of canyon oaks. In autumn, their leaves turn bright gold and capture the low afternoon sun. In just over a half-mile of gentle climbing, you'll reach a hiker's gate and leave the trees behind.

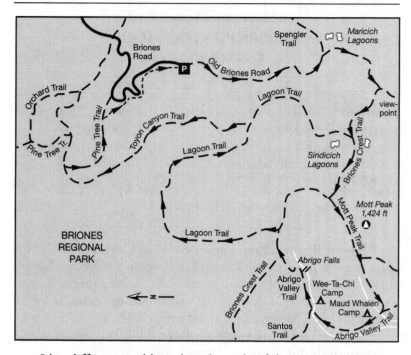

It's a different world on the other side of the gate—wide open expanses of grasslands with an occasional cluster of cows adding variety to the scene. At a junction with Spengler Trail, bear right to stay on Old Briones Road. You'll pass two small ponds, whimsically named "Maricich Lagoons." They are naturally occurring vernal pools. A third of a mile farther brings you to another junction; bear right on Briones Crest Trail. (You might consider going straight uphill for 100 yards to a gate with a lovely view of the valley below.)

Briones Crest Trail leads you past Sindicich Lagoons—two more vernal pools, one on either side of the trail. As the dirt road begins to climb, you gain views to the north of Carquinez Strait, Suisun Bay, San Pablo Bay, and the Benicia Martinez Bridge. The industrial waterfront of Martinez lies in the foreground. Hey, what are all those ships lined up down there? That's the Mothball Fleet—old military ships that have been put out to pasture, and Jacques Cousteau's *Glomar Explorer* sitting all by itself between the last Navy ship and the bridge. Also in sight are the oil refineries along Contra Costa County's shoreline, often referred to as the Oil Coast.

At 1.5 miles, Briones Crest Trail junctions with Mott Peak Trail. Bear left, descend a bit, then leave the trail and hike uphill to the summit of Mott Peak, elevation 1,424 feet. (It's not the high hill lined with a fence; it's the one beside it to the west.) A climb to Mott Peak's grassy summit provides you with a 360-degree vista. In addition to views of Suisun Bay, Carquinez Strait, and smaller waterways to the north, the panorama includes miles of open parkland to the south and west, framed by the distant outline of Mount Tamalpais. Ever-present Mount Diablo towers over the eastern scenery, which includes the suburbs of Concord and Walnut Creek.

Mott Peak isn't the highest point in the park; Briones Peak is 60 feet higher. But Mott Peak is a balder summit and offers a better view. It was named for William Penn Mott, champion of parks. During Mott's long career, he worked as the general manager of the East Bay Regional Park District, then as director of California State Parks, and finally as director of the National Park Service.

When you've seen enough, return to Mott Peak Trail and head west, meeting up with Abrigo Valley Trail in a half-mile. In winter, the cheerful presence of Abrigo Creek is a welcome sight. Turn right and pass two campgrounds, Maud Whalen and Wee-Ta-Chi. Pay

Briones Regional Park

close attention to the creek just beyond Wee-Ta-Chi Camp. Look and listen carefully and you may spot Abrigo Falls dropping 15 feet over a rock face into a narrow, cave-like canyon. The waterfall is nearly hidden, and if the stream isn't flowing strong, it can be difficult to spot. It's located at the point where the trail makes a short, steep climb. (Where the trail makes a hairpin turn to the left and moves away from the creek, you've passed it.)

Continue another quarter mile to Abrigo Valley Trail's junction with Briones Crest Trail; bear right and then left shortly thereafter on Lagoon Trail. Follow Lagoon Trail for 1.2 miles, looping around to Toyon Canyon Trail. You'll enter a live oak forest, a nice change of pace from the sunshine and grasslands. Turn left on Toyon Canyon Trail and continue gently downhill for one mile, then turn right on Pine Tree Trail. You'll have to climb a bit to finish out the loop. When you see the paved road you drove in on, follow the single-track trail that parallels it back to the parking area and your car.

Trip notes: There is no fee at the Briones Road trailhead. Leashed dogs and bikes are allowed. Free trail maps are available at the entrance kiosk. For more information, contact East Bay Regional Park District, 2950 Peralta Oaks Court, P.O. Box 5381, Oakland, CA 94605-0381; (510) 635-0135 or (510) 562-7275. Website: www.ebparks.org

53. HUCKLEBERRY PATH
Huckleberry Botanic Regional Preserve

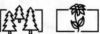

DISTANCE: 1.7 miles round-trip; 1 hour   **LEVEL:** Easy

ELEVATION CHANGE: 400 feet   **RATING:** ★ ★ ★

DIRECTIONS: From Highway 24 near Orinda, take the Fish Ranch Road exit immediately east of the Caldecott Tunnel. (You'll need to be in the right lane as you exit the tunnel.) Drive one mile northwest on Fish Ranch Road to Grizzly Peak Boulevard. Turn left and drive 2.4 miles to Skyline Boulevard. Turn left and drive a half mile to the park entrance on the left (past Sibley Volcanic Regional Preserve).

Alternatively, from Interstate 580 in Oakland, take the 35th Avenue exit and turn north. Drive 2.4 miles (35th Avenue will become Redwood Road). Turn left on Skyline Boulevard and drive 5.2 miles to the preserve. (Skyline Boulevard makes a sharp right turn after the first half mile.)

Rare manzanitas grow at Huckleberry Regional Preserve

Trailheads along Skyline Boulevard in the East Bay hills are about as common as the million-dollar houses clinging to steep hillsides. Home to several regional parks and a large section of the 31-mile East Bay Skyline National Trail, the Skyline Boulevard area is a weekend recreationist's paradise. Mountain bikers, dog walkers, runners, hikers—everybody finds a trail to suit their desires.

This being the case, your chance of finding solitude anywhere in these parks on a Saturday or Sunday is next to nil. Parking lots usually fill up before noon at Sibley Volcanic Regional Preserve and Skyline Gate at Redwood Regional Park. Late arrivals must squeeze into pullouts along the road.

But one park on Skyline Boulevard presents a greater chance for peace and quiet (plus a parking space): Huckleberry Botanic Regional Preserve. Unlike its neighboring parks, Huckleberry is designated for hikers only. No bikes, horses, or dogs are allowed; this reduces the number of comers dramatically. Even joggers are discouraged. People come here because they are serious about one thing—nature.

The park is home to a large number of native plants that are extremely rare in the East Bay, plus some that are extremely rare, period. Even hikers who know nothing about botany will appreciate one obvious fact: Unlike most of the East Bay Regional Parks, there aren't any eucalyptus trees here! (No matter what your opinions are about nonnative flora, you must agree that eucalyptus is ubiquitous in the East Bay.)

Another feature distinctly absent from Huckleberry Preserve is wide dirt roads. The park's main trail is called simply Huckleberry Path, and it's a well built, narrow, meandering footpath that weaves its way through dense foliage. A self-guided trail brochure is available for free at the trailhead; it corresponds to numbered posts along the path. Unless you're a botanist by trade, carrying a brochure will greatly enhance your experience at the preserve.

Huckleberry Path is a loop with a total distance of only 1.7 miles. (To hike the loop in the proper direction, bear left at the first junction.) You can easily tack on another three-fourths of a mile to the far end of the loop, where the trail connects with a trailhead at Pinehurst Road. Or, since part of the Huckleberry Path is the East Bay Skyline National Trail, you can add on a trip northward to Sibley Preserve (about two miles) or southward to Redwood Regional Park (one mile).

Take your pick of the add-on trails or simply choose to linger within the boundaries of Huckleberry. Stay for a while at the sunny, manzanita-lined overlook by interpretive post number 6, where the view of Mount Diablo is inspiring. Or take time to study or photograph the preserve's rare plants, such as western leatherwood (look for leathery branches and bright yellow flowers from December to March), and tall pallid manzanita with its delicate, pink, bell-like blossoms. Or perhaps best of all, time your trip so you can sample the preserve's namesake huckleberries, which fruit in late summer and early fall.

Any season is a good time to visit this preserve. The trail is completely shaded by long-limbed bay laurels plus some madrones and oaks, so it remains cool even in the heat of summer. Plentiful sword and wood ferns "green up" and come to life after winter rains. Spring wildflowers are always worth a special visit; look for purple Douglas iris in the early months and orange bush monkeyflower as summer approaches.

Trip notes: There is no fee. Dogs and bikes are not allowed. Free trail maps are available at the entrance kiosk. For more information, contact East Bay Regional Park District, 2950 Peralta Oaks Court, P.O. Box 5381, Oakland, CA 94605-0381; (510) 635-0135 or (510) 562-7275. Website: www.ebparks.org

54. STREAM TRAIL & WEST RIDGE TRAIL LOOP
Redwood Regional Park

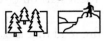

DISTANCE: 4.8 miles round-trip; 2.5 hours   **LEVEL:** Easy

ELEVATION CHANGE: 700 feet   **RATING:** ★ ★ ★

DIRECTIONS: From Interstate 580 in Oakland, take the 35th Avenue exit and turn north. Drive 2.4 miles (35th Avenue will become Redwood Road). Turn left on Skyline Boulevard and drive 3.7 miles to the Skyline Gate Staging Area. (Skyline Boulevard makes a sharp right turn after the first half mile.) The staging area is located at the intersection of Skyline and Pine Hills Drive.

They don't call this place Redwood Regional Park for nothing. The dark, shaggy-barked trees grow more than 100 feet tall and their shady canopy covers a vast expanse of the park. A walk among these lofty trees is the perfect antidote to too much time spent in Emeryville office buildings or on East Bay freeways.

The redwoods aren't first-growth. Rather, they are the second-generation offspring of the original trees that once towered over this canyon. Between 1840 and 1860, logging companies constructed lumber mills and mill workers built shantytowns in what is now Redwood Regional Park. They logged the virgin redwoods to provide lumber for the growing cities of San Francisco and San Jose. In 20 years, all the giant trees in a five-square-mile area were felled.

Some botanists believe this grove's original redwoods may have been the largest the world has ever known. The massive trees were used as navigational guides by ships sailing into San Francisco Bay before the construction of lighthouses. Located high on a ridge 16 miles from the Golden Gate, the redwoods were prominent enough to steer sailors away from Blossom Rock, submerged in the bay between Alcatraz and San Francisco. (The actual "landmark trees" were located in what is now Roberts Regional Park, next door to Redwood Park. Their site is denoted by a state historic plaque.)

The redwoods aren't the only prizes of Redwood Regional Park. Redwood Creek, which bisects the park, is home to rainbow trout that are descendants of the original, pure strain of rainbows—the ones the species is named after. In addition, the park is bordered by two high ridges to the east and west. Both offer expansive views.

Start your trip at the Skyline Gate Staging Area on Skyline Boulevard. Three trails lead from the parking lot—East Ridge, Stream, and West Ridge. You'll start on Stream Trail and return on West Ridge Trail.

Stream Trail, a wide fire road that is closed to bikes, makes a quick drop from the trailhead. The first three-quarters of a mile are a mellow, pretty descent through a mixed forest of oaks, madrones, ferns, and huckleberries, punctuated by occasional tall eucalyptus. Farther downhill you enter a redwood grove and remain under the spell of the big trees for a long, dreamy stretch. In the rainy season, the sight and sound of splashing Redwood Creek enlivens the dark canyon. A split-rail fence lines the streambank; it's an attempt to keep people, dogs, and horses away from the fragile riparian habitat.

At 1.5 miles, you'll pass two camping and picnicking areas in a row—Mill Site on the left and Fern Hut on the right. (The camps' stone buildings were built by the Works Progress Administration in the 1930s.) A few feet past Fern Hut is the right turnoff for Fern Trail. Follow it steeply uphill. A half mile of heavy breathing will bring you to West Ridge Trail; turn right again.

Second-growth redwoods in Redwood Park

What's this, sunshine? Yes indeed. After a long stretch of shaded greenery, the trail opens out on sunny West Ridge. Hike northwest, climbing a bit more. An interesting side trip is possible a half mile out on the ridge. Take the right fork, then the left fork immediately following, to hike up to the top of Redwood Peak, elevation 1,619 feet. As you might guess from its name, you won't get much of a summit view. The redwoods hide most everything except for a glimpse northeast toward Moraga and San Leandro Reservoir. But the peak is littered with interesting sandstone boulders. Under the canopy of redwoods, the rocks make fine seats for lunch or quiet contemplation.

Backtrack to West Ridge Trail. Heading northwest, you'll pass the edge of the archery range in Roberts Recreation Area. (At this book's press time, West Ridge Trail was rerouted for a half mile in this area due to construction at the new Chabot Observatory. The construction should be completed, and the trail back in place, by the end of 2000.) The path climbs a bit farther to a eucalyptus grove, then suddenly a surprising vista of Oakland, San Francisco, and the bay appears. Depending on the day's visibility, this can be a breathtaking sight. The tall buildings of Oakland and San Francisco appear amazingly close. The bay's bridges look like delightful miniatures in some kid's train set. Turn around and check out the opposite view—to the east is ever-prominent Mount Diablo at 3,849 feet.

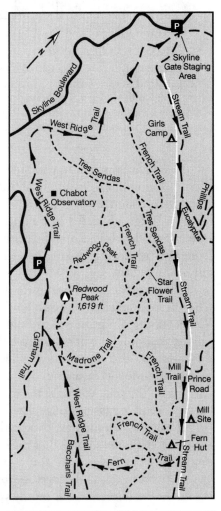

Continue on West Ridge Trail to finish out the loop. It's an easy cruise of just over a mile back to Skyline Gate through a shady forest of bay laurel, madrones, and Monterey pines. Watch for more peek-a-boo views of monolithic Mount Diablo through the trees.

Trip notes: There is no fee. Leashed dogs are allowed. Bikes are allowed on West Ridge Trail. A free park map is available at the Skyline Gate Staging Area. For more information, contact East Bay Regional Park District, 2950 Peralta Oaks Court, P.O. Box 5381, Oakland, CA 94605-0381; (510) 635-0135 or (510) 562-7275. Website: www.ebparks.org

55. ROCKY RIDGE & DEVIL'S HOLE LOOP
Las Trampas Regional Wilderness

DISTANCE: 6.8 miles round-trip; 3.5 hours   **LEVEL:** Moderate
ELEVATION CHANGE: 1,200 feet   **RATING:** ★ ★ ★
DIRECTIONS: From Interstate 680 south of Danville, take the Crow Canyon Road exit west. Drive 1.3 miles to Bollinger Canyon Road, then turn right (north). Drive 4.5 miles on Bollinger Canyon Road to its end at the main parking area at Las Trampas Regional Wilderness. (Go past the stables and the Little Hills Picnic Ranch.)

If you have some energy to burn, Las Trampas is a great place to tromp around. Quite simply, all trails at Las Trampas go up. The park is comprises of two parallel ridges—Rocky Ridge and Las Trampas Ridge—bisected by Bollinger Creek. The park road and its many trailheads lie along the creek canyon, which means that no matter where you start hiking, sooner or later you'll have to climb one of the ridges.

But no matter; the rewards for doing so are great. An excellent 6.8-mile loop hike can be taken on the park's western ridge, Rocky Ridge. Starting from the end of Bollinger Canyon Road at the main staging area, you hike uphill on paved Rocky Ridge Road. Don't let the pavement discourage you; you'll leave it shortly. The ascent is a bit steep, but if you turn around to catch your breath about a quarter-mile up the trail, you'll see the summit of Mount Diablo poking up over the park's eastern ridge, Las Trampas.

A half mile up the trail, two single-track trails meet up with the paved trail, one shortly after the other. Take the upper trail, signed as Rocky Ridge Trail. You've climbed to nearly 2,000 feet in elevation. From this high ridgetop, you can faintly hear the distant rumble of the interstate, but mostly your ears are filled with the whistling of wind in the rye grass. Bald Rocky Ridge is covered with grasslands, while parallel Las Trampas Ridge is lined with chaparral and bay laurel. In spring, Rocky Ridge's grasslands are littered with ubiquitous poppies, blue-eyed grass, and brodiaea. The ridgetop winds are fierce, but the grassland flowers are tenacious. Like the willow tree, they have learned to bend in the breeze. Bright yellow mule's ears and purple non-native thistles add to the show.

At the next junction, take Upper Trail. (A gate on your right leads through East Bay Municipal Utility District lands; the area can only be hiked with a permit.) Follow Upper Trail south along the ridge. On your left, you look down at the park's stables, buildings, and road. To your right is a barbed wire fence. But have patience; in a few minutes the fence disappears and you gain far-reaching views to the west and south. The large water body in the foreground is Upper San Leandro Reservoir. Your vista takes in the East Bay and extends down the Peninsula. To the west, views expand across San Francisco Bay to Mount Tamalpais in Marin.

A few scattered bay laurel trees grow along the top of the ridge, their lower limbs wrapped tightly around sandstone rocks. The closer you look at them, the more impossible it becomes to tell if the trees grew over the rocks or if the rocks grew out of the trees.

Take the right turnoff for Sycamore Trail downhill and then up again toward the huge rock outcrop a quarter mile away. As you approach it, leave the trail and scramble up the formation to explore its wind-sculpted caves. Exercise caution; the outcrop is jealously guarded by clumps of poison oak and bay laurel. Note the rock's many varieties of colorful lichen in bright shades of orange, green, and gray. With some careful maneuvering, you can climb all the way to its summit, where you are provided with far-reaching views, a headstrong wind, and a great place for lunch. All you can see from here is wild land—no buildings, roads, or anything "civilized."

Continue on Sycamore Trail (it is often quite narrow and overgrown with grasses) for another mile to Devil's Hole on Cull Creek. Set in a box canyon, Devil's Hole's rock-lined cascades are a lovely sight after a period of rain. Sycamore, bay laurel, and live oaks shade the stream. Then take signed Devil's Hole Trail steeply back uphill to Upper Trail. Hike southward on Upper Trail for another third of a mile; views range to the south toward Livermore. Keep watching on your right for what appears to be a low rock wall. Look closely at its rocks and you'll see clamshells embedded in them, proof positive that this area was once undersea. (This also explains the sandstone on top of the ridge.)

You can loop back on Elderberry Trail, the most direct route back to the parking area. But cows graze along this trail, and if that insults your wilderness sensibilities, you can backtrack on Upper Trail for a half mile to single-track Cuesta Trail. Then take Cuesta Trail back downhill to paved Rocky Ridge Road. Spring wildflowers are excellent in the grasslands surrounding Cuesta Trail.

Rocky Ridge, Las Trampas Regional Wilderness

Trip notes: There is no fee. Leashed dogs are allowed. Bikes are allowed on fire roads only. A free map is available at the visitor center. For more information, contact East Bay Regional Park District, 2950 Peralta Oaks Court, P.O. Box 5381, Oakland, CA 94605-0381; (510) 635-0135 or (510) 562-7275. Website: www.ebparks.org

56. ROSE HILL CEMETERY LOOP
Black Diamond Mines Regional Preserve

DISTANCE: 2.5 miles round-trip; 1 hour   **LEVEL:** Easy

ELEVATION CHANGE: 400 feet   **RATING:** ★ ★

DIRECTIONS: From Highway 4 in Antioch, take the Somersville Road exit south. Drive 3.8 miles south on Somersville Road to the end of the road and the trailhead. (You'll pass the park entrance kiosk at 3.0 miles, then continue another three-quarters of a mile to the trailhead.)

From 1860 to 1906, the Mount Diablo Coal Field was the largest coal mining district in California. Located near present-day Antioch in what is now Black Diamond Mines Regional Preserve, this productive coal field on the northern side of Mount Diablo prompted the digging of 12 major mines and the growth of five townships. Nearly four million tons of coal were extracted from the earth in less than 50 years. Much of this mining history, and a large acreage of rolling grassland hills and chaparral-clad slopes, is preserved at Black Diamond Mines.

A good introduction to the park can be gained by hiking the Nortonville Trail to a preserved pioneer cemetery, then looping back on Black Diamond Trail, Manhattan Canyon Trail, and Chaparral Trail for a sampling of the region's native flora.

From the parking lot at the end of Somersville Road, begin hiking on Nortonville Trail, a wide paved road that's an extension of the road you drive in on. Head toward the picnic area, then bear right at the fork just before it. The trail is a wide dirt road leading uphill to Rose Hill Cemetery. You'll pass by the townsite of Somersville, once a thriving mining town but now just a large clearing along the trail.

Leave the trail to explore inside the cemetery's fence. You'll note that most of the graves are from the late 1800s, and most of the dead are Welsh. Although the Mount Diablo miners and their families came from all over the world, Rose Hill Cemetery was a "Protestants-only" graveyard. Some of the epitaphs are still visible, like this one: "Tis God lifts our comforts high or sinks them in the grave. He gives and when he takes away, he takes but what he gave."

When you've explored enough, exit the cemetery on its far side and rejoin the dirt road, continuing your uphill climb through wide open grasslands. The native grasses bloom in spring with annual wildflowers such as owl's clover and brodiaea.

Turn left on Black Diamond Trail and note the views you're gaining to the north of Suisun Bay. Piles of mine tailings are visible along the hillsides. Where the trail starts to descend, watch for a single-track path on the left signed "to Manhattan Canyon Trail." (Take the second cutoff, not the first.) This narrow trail makes several tight, steep switchbacks downhill until it junctions with Chaparral Loop Trail. Turn right on Chaparral Loop, a steep roller-coastering trail with a few uphill stretches that will raise your heart rate. You stroll among the good company of manzanita and monkeyflower. A few coulter pines make an appearance here; they are at the northernmost edge of their range.

1880s headstone at Rose Hill Cemetery

At a junction with Ridge Trail, consider a short out-and-back (and uphill) jaunt to gain some excellent views of Mount Diablo. Take any of the short spurs off the Ridge Trail to reach the best viewpoints. To the north, you have more wide views of Carquinez Strait and Suisun Bay, and you can look back west to the graveyard on the hill. With a stiff breeze blowing through the ridge's pines, this could be an excellent place for a picnic.

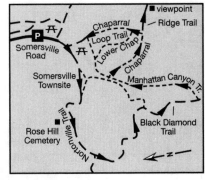

If you visit Black Diamond Mines on a weekend day, you must pay a visit to the Greathouse Visitor Center, which is built into a mine tunnel. It's located just 100 feet uphill from the picnic area near the trailhead. If you're seeking some good exercise and a longer exploration in Black Diamond Mines Regional Preserve, see the following trail description.

Trip notes: A $4 day-use fee is charged per vehicle. Leashed dogs are allowed. Bikes are allowed on fire roads only. A free map is available at the entrance kiosk. For more information, contact Black Diamond Mines at (925) 757-2620, or contact East Bay Regional Park District, 2950 Peralta Oaks Court, P.O. Box 5381, Oakland, CA 94605-0381; (510) 635-0135 or (510) 562-7275. Website: www.ebparks.org

57. STEWARTVILLE & RIDGE TRAIL LOOP
Black Diamond Mines Regional Preserve

DISTANCE: 7.0 miles round-trip; 3.5 hours   **LEVEL:** Moderate

ELEVATION CHANGE: 1,500 feet   **RATING:** ★ ★ ★

DIRECTIONS: From Highway 4 in Antioch, take the Somersville Road exit south. Drive 3.8 miles south on Somersville Road to the end of the road and the trailhead. (You'll pass the park entrance kiosk at 3.0 miles, then continue another three-quarters of a mile to the trailhead.)

Black Diamond Mines Regional Preserve is a strange mix of elements—manmade history combined with natural history, wild green hills juxtaposed with industrial complexes north of the park, rare species of plants commingled with nonnative flora planted by late 1800s settlers. The 3,700-acre park has many moods and puts

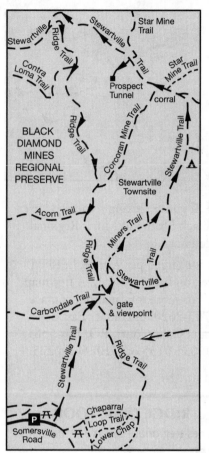

on different faces in changing seasons and weather conditions. This seven-mile loop reveals some of its highlights and adds in some good exercise to the bargain.

Begin your trip at the trailhead at the end of Somersville Road. Take the paved road from the gate at the parking lot, walk about 50 yards, then turn left on signed Stewartville Trail. Named for one of the coal mining towns that thrived in this area in the late 1800s, Stewartville Trail is a wide dirt road that climbs moderately and steadily uphill. As you hike through open grasslands, you'll pass some nonnative trees that the miners planted—pepper, eucalyptus, almond, and locust. The almond trees produce fragrant flowers in the spring.

A half mile climb brings you to a cattle gate at a high point on Stewartville Trail. Go through the gate and admire the deep, green, grassy valley below you. The good news is that you're going to hike into that pretty valley; the bad news is that you'll have to climb back out of it. On the far side of the gate, turn right to stay on Stewartville Trail. (The return of your loop is Ridge Trail, on your left.) Mount Diablo looms large to the south.

As you start to descend, watch for the single-track cutoff for Miners Trail; bear left on this trail and leave the wide roads behind. Miners Trail is a narrow, well built footpath that descends along the shoulder of the canyon wall, cutting across its steep slope. It leads through a surprising grove of gnarled gray pines and coulter pines. (Black Diamond Mines Preserve is noted as the northernmost location of coulter pines, black sage, desert olive, and dudleya.)

Where Miners Trail touches down to the valley floor, continue straight ahead to rejoin Stewartville Trail. Down in this valley, you'll hear nothing but wind and the sound of your own breathing. The wide clearing on your left is part of the original townsite of Stewartville, although nothing is left of its buildings.

Bear left on wide Stewartville Trail. In a half mile you'll pass Stewartville Backpack Camp, a hike-in camp that can be reserved by individuals or groups. You can hike, bike, or ride your horse into the camp. At a junction with single-track Star Mine Trail, consider adding on a 1.5-mile loop trip to see the closed-off tunnel of Star Mine, one of the last active coal mines in the area. (The loop will bring you back to Stewartville Trail.) Or continue straight ahead for a quarter mile, passing an outcropping of colorful boulders that is lined with swallow's nests, to the left turnoff for Prospect Tunnel.

The tunnel's spur trail leads a few hundred yards to an obvious opening in the hillside. You can explore about 150 feet into the mine shaft before you reach a steel gate. The air inside its sandstone walls is a little musty, but always cool. Tall people will have to duck their heads. Usually there is enough daylight to guide your way, but a flashlight is helpful. The shaft was driven in the 1860s by miners in search of coal or "black diamonds."

Back on the main path, follow Stewartville Trail for nearly a mile farther, climbing gently, then make a sharp left turn on Ridge

Stewartville Trail at Black Diamond Mines

Trail. You're leaving the valley now and beginning the steep ascent back to the trailhead. Ridge Trail rollercoasters along, dipping down occasionally but more often rising steeply. The climb is eased by the sudden appearance of views to the north of Carquinez Strait, Suisun Bay, Pittsburg, and Antioch.

When at last Ridge Trail returns you to the gate at Stewartville Trail, consider a rest on the bench by the gate. Once again you can admire the green valley below. Then it's an easy half-mile stroll back down Stewartville Trail to the trailhead.

Trip notes: A $4 day-use fee is charged per vehicle. Leashed dogs are allowed. Bikes are allowed on fire roads only. A free map is available at the entrance kiosk. For more information, contact Black Diamond Mines at (925) 757-2620, or contact East Bay Regional Park District, 2950 Peralta Oaks Court, P.O. Box 5381, Oakland, CA 94605-0381; (510) 635-0135 or (510) 562-7275. Website: www.ebparks.org

58. MOUNT DIABLO LOOP
Mount Diablo State Park

DISTANCE: 9.0 miles round-trip; 4.5 hours   **LEVEL:** Strenuous

ELEVATION CHANGE: 2,200 feet   **RATING:** ★ ★ ★

DIRECTIONS: From Interstate 680 at Danville, take the Diablo Road exit and head east. Follow Diablo Road for 2.9 miles (you must turn right at 0.7 miles to stay on Diablo Road). At a stop sign at Mount Diablo Scenic Boulevard, turn left. Drive 3.7 miles on Mount Diablo Scenic Boulevard (it becomes South Gate Road) to the park's southern entrance station. Continue for another 7.3 miles to the summit of Mount Diablo. After visiting the summit, drive back down South Gate Road for 2.5 miles to Juniper Campground and Laurel Nook Picnic Area. Park outside the campground in the wide turnout along the road, then walk through the camp to pick up Mitchell Canyon Trail/Deer Flat Road at its far end, near site #23.

Alternatively, from Interstate 680 in Walnut Creek, take the Treat Road exit and go east for 1.2 miles. Turn right on Bancroft Road, which crosses Ygnacio Valley Road and becomes Walnut Avenue. Drive 1.6 miles on Walnut Avenue, then turn right on Oak Grove Road. Turn left immediately on North Gate Road and drive 12 miles to Mount Diablo's summit.

Most everybody thinks about making a trip to 3,849-foot Mount Diablo from time to time. After all, you see it from just about everywhere in the Bay Area. It's not the tallest mountain around San Francisco Bay (Mount Hamilton near San Jose is 360 feet taller), it just has a way of making its presence known, looming in the background of the lives of millions of East Bay residents.

When your time to visit Mount Diablo arrives, the first thing you should do is drive up to the summit and see what it's like to look at the greater Bay Area from Mount Diablo, rather than vice versa. Park as close to the top as possible, walk around the parking lot, and check out the 360-degree vista. On the clearest days, you can see all the way to the Sierra Nevada and Mount Lassen.

After being thoroughly wowed by the summit view, you'll be inspired to hike this nine-mile loop around the peak, which adds in two side trips to equally inspiring Eagle Peak and North Peak. The route includes substantial ups and downs, but you'll be rewarded with fine views and a variety of mountain flora.

Drive back downhill to Juniper Campground, park outside the camp, and walk through it to access Mitchell Canyon Trail/Deer Flat Road. Head out on the wide fire road and enjoy immediate

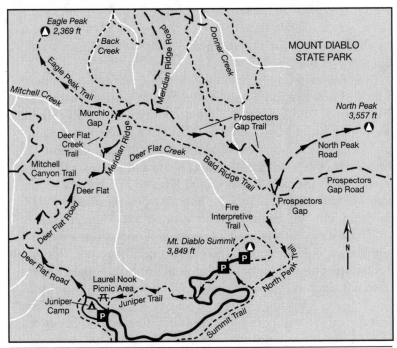

vistas to the west. On good days, San Francisco is clearly visible. With luck, you're hiking in spring, when the grassland wildflowers explode in color. Poppies and lupine headline the show. As you circumnavigate the mountain through a variety of terrain, different flowers will show themselves. Lucky hikers will spot Mount Diablo fairy lanterns, which grow nowhere else in the world. They have yellow, waxy-looking, nodding heads on stalks about five inches high. More prevalent are bright yellow marguerites, purple hooker's onions (brodiaea), purple fields of clarkia, red larkspur, and delicate mariposa lilies. If you visit after the March-to-May flower season has passed, you'll still have California laurel, magnificent oaks, and gray pines to keep you company along the trail.

Bear right at the road's first junction, three-quarters of a mile out. The descent steepens and in another three-quarters of a mile, you reach oak-shaded Deer Flat. It's marked by a junction where Mitchell Canyon Trail heads off to the left. In springtime, look for patches of light blue bird's eye gilia at Deer Flat.

Keep heading downhill on Deer Flat Road, entering a canyon filled with ceanothus and bay trees. Cross tiny Deer Flat Creek, then reach a junction with single-track Deer Flat Trail, a narrow path that exhibits an interesting array of serpentine outcrops and flora. Take the single-track or stay on the fire road; both trails join again at Murchio Gap. (Your downhill stint has ended; you'll be climbing for the next few miles.)

At Murchio Gap, hike out-and-back for one mile to the northwest to 2,369-foot Eagle Peak. The trail leads along the narrow backbone of Bald Ridge with steep dropoffs on both sides and fine views all the way. Many hikers consider this stretch to be the best part of the entire loop. From Eagle Peak's rocky summit, most impressive are the vistas of the Sacramento and San Joaquin Delta, Honker Bay, and Suisun Bay. Mount Diablo's North Peak, which you will soon visit, appears as an imposing pinnacle. Leave a note in the summit register, then retrace your steps to Murchio Gap.

At the gap, take your pick between following the fire road or single-track Bald Ridge Trail (on the far side of the road). Both trails make their way to Prospectors Gap near North Peak. Bald Ridge Trail has many steep up and down sections with loose, rocky soil, so if you aren't wearing your best hiking boots, stay on the fire road. But the narrow trail does pass some fascinating serpentine outcrops and dense groves of manzanita. Just above the distinct saddle at Prospectors Gap, you gain an interesting view of the rock quarries north of the park, the bays and delta, and the towns of Antioch and Pittsburg. At the gap, you have open views to the east and west.

If you have the energy, take the fire road from Prospectors Gap out-and-back for three-quarters of a mile to North Peak. Mount Diablo has two summits, the main one with the paved road to the top and North Peak, which is 292 feet shorter at 3,557 feet. If it's a clear

Wildflowers frame Mount Diablo's vistas

day, North Peak is your best bet for catching a glimpse of the Sierra.

Then follow single-track North Peak Trail to the right, along the rocky eastern slope of Mount Diablo. This is a particularly good area for spring wildflowers, including the rare Mount Diablo fairy lantern. The trail weaves in and out of chaparral and grasslands, interspersed with scraggly-looking gray pines. Views extend south-west to the windmills in Livermore and east to the Central Valley. You pass directly below the large rock outcrop called Devil's Pulpit on Mount Diablo's summit.

Where North Peak Trail ends at the paved park road, take Summit Trail uphill to the Lower Summit parking lot, then follow Juniper Trail downhill for one mile back to your car. Or, if you're tired of climbing by the time you reach the park road, just follow the road downhill for a mile.

There is only one important thing to remember about visiting

Mount Diablo: never hike in the blazing afternoon heat of summer. The best seasons to visit are winter, when you may be surprised to find snow on the summit; or spring, when the grasses are green and the wildflowers put on their show. Mount Diablo's sunsets, sunrises, and moon rises are spectacular in any season.

Trip notes: A $5 day-use fee is charged per vehicle. Dogs are not allowed. Bikes are allowed only on fire roads. A park map is available at the entrance station or summit visitor center for $1. (A more detailed map is available for $5.) For more information, contact Mount Diablo State Park, 96 Mitchell Canyon Road, Clayton, CA 94517; (925) 837-2525 or (925) 837-0904. Website: www.mdia.org

59. ROCK CITY & WALL POINT SUMMIT
Mount Diablo State Park

DISTANCE: 3.5 miles round-trip; 1.5 hours   **LEVEL:** Easy

ELEVATION CHANGE: 500 feet   **RATING:** ★ ★ ★

DIRECTIONS: From Interstate 680 at Danville, take the Diablo Road exit and head east. Follow Diablo Road for 2.9 miles (you must turn right at 0.7 miles to stay on Diablo Road). At a stop sign at Mount Diablo Scenic Boulevard, turn left. Drive 3.7 miles on Mount Diablo Scenic Boulevard (it becomes South Gate Road) to the park's southern entrance station. Continue eight-tenths of a mile farther to the Rock City parking area on the left, signed as Rock City/Live Oak. Park in any of the main picnic area parking lots, and begin hiking at the sign for Big Rock, Sentinel Rock, and Wind Caves.

If you're a kid or a kid at heart, you're going to love Rock City in Mount Diablo State Park. Set among clusters of tall manzanita, gray pines, madrones, and live oaks, Rock City is a jumble of eroded sandstone outcroppings that form a playground for hikers and rock climbers.

Rock City was formed 40 or 50 million years ago during the Eocene period, when Mount Diablo was buried under a great sea. Eventually the waters receded and the sand left behind hardened into a ridge of rocks along the slopes of Mount Diablo. This rocky ridge has been weathered and eroded by centuries of wind and rain, creating odd-shaped boulders with small caves and Swiss cheese-style holes. They're fun to look at and easy to photograph.

Rock City's boulders ignite the imagination. It isn't long before you notice that one rock resembles a barking sea lion, another looks like an elephant, and still another imitates a hippopotamus. Many paths wind over and around the sculpted rock formations, so you can have fun exploring without having to follow a set trail.

Most visitors find their way to Sentinel Rock, a tall pinnacle of sandstone with stairsteps leading to its summit. Because the rock's dropoffs are quite steep, the park has installed steel cables along the stairsteps and at the summit. No, it's not Half Dome, but it's a fun climb to the top, and the views of live oaks and gray pines in the valley below is quite lovely. Sentinel Rock is located about a quarter-mile from the main Rock City parking lot, heading in a northwest direction through numerous other wind-sculpted boulders. Another quarter mile beyond Sentinel Rock are the Wind Caves, a ridge of tan colored rocks riddled with holes and caverns.

If find yourself feeling annoyed at the hundreds of names and initials carved into the soft sandstone, take heart. This sandstone is so soft, the graffiti is worn off in a few decades.

Hikers who yearn to walk farther than the short paths in Rock City can set out on Wall Point Trail for a three-mile round-trip to the summit of Wall Point. You'll see Wall Point Trail from various

On top of Sentinel Rock at Rock City

points in Rock City; it's the wide fire road leading northwest (on your right as you head to Sentinel Rock). If you follow the spider web of paths heading west from Sentinel Rock, you'll eventually end up on one that connects to the fire road. If you don't find your way, just head back to the Rock City parking lot, then walk 100 yards north on the main park road. Across from the ranger's residence, on the west side of the road, is the start of Wall Point Trail.

The trail starts out mostly level and offers lovely views of Sentinel Rock, Rock City, and "real" cities to the west far beyond. In just under a mile you reach a saddle with a view over Dan Cook Canyon to the south. A half mile of climbing leads to the road's high point near the peak of bald Wall Point. Take the short spur trail on the left to the top for a panoramic view. (Watch out for poison oak around Wall Point.) Birders, bring your binoculars. Wall Point is considered to be one of the best birding spots on the mountain.

Trip notes: A $5 day-use fee is charged per vehicle. Dogs are allowed only in the Rock City picnic area. Bikes are allowed only on fire roads. A park map is available at the entrance station or summit visitor center for $1. (A more detailed map is available for $5.) For more information, contact Mount Diablo State Park, 96 Mitchell Canyon Road, Clayton, CA 94517; (925) 837-2525 or (925) 837-0904. Website: www.mdia.org

60. BACK & DONNER CANYON LOOP
Mount Diablo State Park

DISTANCE: 7.0 miles round-trip; 3.5 hours **LEVEL:** Moderate

ELEVATION CHANGE: 1,100 feet **RATING:** ★ ★ ★

DIRECTIONS: From Interstate 680 heading north in Walnut Creek, take the Ygnacio Valley Road exit. Drive east on Ygnacio Valley Road for 7.5 miles to Clayton Road. Turn right on Clayton Road and drive 2.9 miles (it becomes Marsh Creek Road, but don't turn right at the sign for Marsh Creek Road) to Regency Drive. Turn right and drive a half-mile to the end of the road and the trailhead.

Or, from Interstate 680 heading south in Walnut Creek, take the Treat Boulevard Road exit and go east. In one mile, turn right on Bancroft Road. In another mile, turn left on Ygnacio Valley Road and drive five miles to Clayton Road. Continue as above.

Waterfalls on Mount Diablo? It may seem hard to believe, but a trip to Clayton in the rainy season and a hike along the back side of this rugged, arid mountain reveals half a dozen gushing cascades. Scattered along the hillsides on two forks of Donner Creek, the falls drop in a canyon that is notoriously dry, steep, and hot as Hades most of the year. Pick the right day, soon after a good rain, and it's water, water everywhere.

Luckily, even if the falls aren't flowing, a hike through Mount Diablo's Back and Donner canyons is a pleasure. A visit on any day except for the hottest days of summer is a fine way to get to know the mountain more intimately. Unlike many of Mount Diablo's trails, this seven-mile loop follows single-track paths most of the way, weaving in and out of the mountain's deep northern canyons. Diablo's fascinating geology and vegetation are close at hand.

The trailhead is located at the end of Regency Drive, a suburban neighborhood in Clayton. (You don't have to pay the state park day-use fee here.) Walk down to Donner Creek beyond the street barrier and through the gated park boundary. Take the fire road on the right signed as Back Creek Road. (You can also follow its neighboring single-track trail, which soon rejoins Back Creek Road.)

Although the hike begins in grasslands and oaks, it won't stay that way for long. In a half mile, Back Creek Road meets up with its namesake stream, and shortly thereafter the road narrows to single-track. As soon as the trail drops down to proper hiking width, the vegetation closes in. Back Creek Trail climbs gently but steadily amid eroded rock formations and dense stands of sage, toyon, yerba santa, and monkeyflower, heading due south toward the mountain's summit. Watch for an abandoned mine tunnel, only a few feet deep, on the left side of the trail.

At the point where the canyon divides, turn left on Meridian Point Trail and climb more steeply through chaparral until the path tops out at Meridian Point. From the high overlook at this junction with Meridian Ridge Road, you gain a wide view of the town of Clayton and a glimpse at Suisun Bay to the northwest.

Follow Meridian Ridge Road downhill for a quarter mile to single-track Middle Trail. Turn right on Middle Trail; you've left Back Canyon and are now entering Donner Canyon. Look carefully and you'll see evidence of the 1977 fire that ravaged these slopes. New manzanita bushes have quickly grown up and replaced their burned predecessors. The steep buttress of Mount Diablo's North Peak towers above at 3,557 feet.

Watch for the left turnoff for Falls Trail, then follow this rough, narrower trail for 1.25 miles as it winds along the steep slopes of Donner Creek. Whereas Back Creek is only a small stream, Donner Creek can become a wide torrent during the rainy season. Where the loop trail reaches its southernmost point and starts to curve to the northeast, you'll cross a fork of Donner Creek and start seeing waterfalls. Most are about 20 feet high, although one impressive 30-foot freefall drops over jagged, red-brown rock. The trail stays about 100 feet distant from the cascades, so you won't get to admire them up close. You do get the extraordinary experience of seeing as many as five waterfalls at once in a very small area.

Note the occasional gray pines along Falls Trail; their cones are extremely dense and can weigh up to four pounds. Among the eroding rock formations you'll find scattered juniper trees bearing bright blue winter berries.

Where Falls Trail crosses the eastern fork of Donner Creek, the cascades are left behind. Watch out for steep dropoffs as you hike downhill out of Donner Canyon, enjoying more northward views of Clayton and Suisun Bay.

At Falls Trail's end, turn left on Cardinet Oaks Road. You'll make five knee-jarring, steep switchbacks downhill, cross Donner Creek again, then turn right on Donner Canyon Road at Cardinet Junction. To finish out your hike, you can follow Donner Canyon Road all the way back to the trailhead, but a better option is to turn right on single-track Hetherington Loop Trail. This narrow path tunnels through bay laurel trees and skirts Donner Creek, eventually returning you to Donner Canyon

Road. Then it's a level stroll through pastoral oaks, buckeyes, and grasslands back to the Regency Drive trailhead.

Trip notes: There is no fee at the Regency Drive trailhead. Dogs are not allowed. Bikes are allowed only on fire roads. A park map is available at the main park entrance stations or visitor center for $1. (A more detailed map is available for $5.) For more information, contact Mount Diablo State Park, 96 Mitchell Canyon Road, Clayton, CA 94517; (925) 837-2525 or (925) 837-0904. Website: www.mdia.org

61. ROUND VALLEY LOOP
Round Valley Regional Preserve

DISTANCE: 6.0 miles round-trip; 3 hours   **LEVEL:** Easy

ELEVATION CHANGE: 200 feet   **RATING:** ★ ★ ★

DIRECTIONS: From Interstate 580 in Livermore, take the Vasco Road exit and drive north for 14 miles. Turn left (west) on Camino Diablo Road and drive 2.1 miles. Camino Diablo Road becomes Marsh Creek Road; continue 1.6 miles to the Round Valley parking area on the left.

Alternatively, from Interstate 680 heading north in Walnut Creek, take the Ygnacio Valley Road exit and drive east for 7.5 miles to Clayton Road. Turn right on Clayton Road. In the town of Clayton, Clayton Road becomes Marsh Creek Road; continue east past Morgan Territory Road and Deer Valley Road to the Round Valley parking area on the right. (It's about 12 miles from Clayton.)

If you ever start to feel like the East Bay is too crowded, too congested, or has too much concrete, take a trip a little farther east to the back side of Mount Diablo. Here, on the far eastern edge of the Bay Area, just before the bay's geography converges with that of the San Joaquin Valley, are wide open spaces, spring wildflowers, and stately valley oaks.

Welcome to Round Valley Regional Preserve, one of the newest additions to the East Bay Regional Park system. It's the 2,000-acre home of nesting golden eagles, burrowing owls, chubby ground squirrels, and the endangered San Joaquin kit fox. In spring, the grassy hills of Round Valley turn a brilliant green and are sprinkled with grassland wildflowers. The small miracle of Round Valley

Creek flows with unmodulated passion until late spring or early summer, when it drops to meager pools along the streambed. In midsummer, temperatures at Round Valley can soar to more than 100 degrees, so be sure to plan your visit for the cooler months.

From the preserve's staging area, the trail starts out with a long bridge over Marsh Creek. At the far side of the bridge, turn right on Miwok Trail. Immediately you face the only two sizeable hills of the day. Hike up and over them, then relax—the remaining miles in the preserve are almost completely level.

In its first half-mile, wide Miwok Trail meets up with Round Valley Creek. If you've timed your trip for winter or spring, the stream will be running cool and clear alongside you for much of your hike.

You'll notice the remains of old ranching equipment along the dirt trail. This land was farmed by the Murphy family from 1873 until 1988 when it was donated to the East Bay Regional Parks.

Round Valley Regional Preserve

Prior to the Murphys' ownership, the Round Valley area was home to Native Americans, who probably used the land as a meeting and trading place between San Joaquin valley tribes and East Bay hill tribes.

You're bound to see dozens of chubby ground squirrels scurrying around the grasses and popping in and out of their burrows. These plentiful squirrels are one of the chief reasons that golden eagles nest in Round Valley. They're a critical part of the food chain. The squirrels' burrow holes double as homes for other animals such as burrowing owls.

Lucky hikers may spot an endangered San Joaquin kit fox. The tiny foxes are at the northern edge of their range in Round Valley. For the few remaining foxes, this land is rare and valuable habitat that could aid in the survival of their species.

Stay on Miwok Trail throughout the length of the preserve—almost three miles—then turn right on Murphy's Meadow Trail. In one mile, turn right again, remaining on Murphy's Meadow Trail and looping back on the far side of Round Valley Creek. When you reach a junction with Fox Trail in just under a mile, look for a good place to cross the creek (there is no formal trail). Miwok Trail is just on the other side, about 100 feet away. Cross the stream carefully, then rejoin Miwok Trail and turn left to head back to the trailhead.

Trip notes: There is no fee. Dogs are not allowed. Bikes are allowed. Free maps are available at the trailhead parking area. For more information, contact East Bay Regional Park District, 2950 Peralta Oaks Court, P.O. Box 5381, Oakland, CA 94605-0381; (510) 635-0135 or (510) 562-7275. Website: www.ebparks.org

62. MORGAN TERRITORY LOOP
Morgan Territory Regional Preserve

DISTANCE: 7.0 miles round-trip; 3.5 hours   **LEVEL:** Moderate

ELEVATION CHANGE: 1,200 feet   **RATING:** ★ ★ ★

DIRECTIONS: From Interstate 580 in Livermore, take the North Livermore Avenue exit and turn left (north). Drive north for four miles, then turn right on Morgan Territory Road. Drive 5.6 miles to the entrance to Morgan Territory Preserve on the right. (The road is narrow and steep.)

Or, from Interstate 680 heading north in Walnut Creek, take the Ygnacio Valley Road exit and drive east for 7.5 miles to Clayton Road. Turn right on Clayton Road. In the town of Clayton, Clayton Road becomes Marsh Creek Road; continue east for about five miles and turn right (south) on Morgan Territory Road. Drive 9.5 miles to the entrance to Morgan Territory Preserve on the left.

Morgan Territory—even the name sounds wild, like a holdover from the Old West. If you're wondering if anything wild could still exist in Contra Costa County, wonder no more. Come to Morgan Territory and rediscover the wild East Bay.

The drive to the trailhead is a trip in itself. First make sure you are traveling in the cooler months of the year, because the open hills around Livermore bake in the summer. (If you're visiting in the warm season, make sure it is *very* early in the morning.) Follow narrow, winding Morgan Territory Road north of Livermore to the preserve's main trailhead. Try not to get so wowed by the views that you drive right off the curvy road. Watch for cars coming the opposite way; the road is so narrow that usually somebody has to pull over to let the other guy pass.

At the trailhead parking lot, you've climbed to 1,900 feet in elevation. (Okay, so your car has done the work.) You're greeted by grassy hillsides and usually a fair breeze. Pick up a free trail map and follow Volvon Trail uphill and through a cattle gate. This first climb allows for no warmup, but fear not, the trail mellows at the top.

After a half-mile on Volvon Trail, bear right on Blue Oak Trail and prepare yourself for a few glimpses of the San Joaquin Valley far to the east. When you aren't facing east, you have great views of Mount Diablo to the west. (Now that's a change—seeing Mount Diablo in the *west*.) The dirt road rolls gently up and down small hills. The ruts and holes underfoot are caused by the trampling feet of cattle. You'll probably see a few bovines somewhere along the path. If you're lucky, you'll see a few deer as well, or maybe a coyote.

True to its name, Blue Oak Trail features some magnificent oak trees, interspersed with rocks coated with colorful lichens. Dozens of spots invite you to throw down your day-pack, wander among the trees, and spread out a picnic. This is especially true if you're visiting during the wildflower bloom. More than 90 flower species blossom along Morgan Territory's grassy hillsides, creating an unforgettable sight in good wildflower years. The most common flowers are California poppies, brodiaea, blue-eyed grass, mariposa lilies, elegant clarkia, and larkspur.

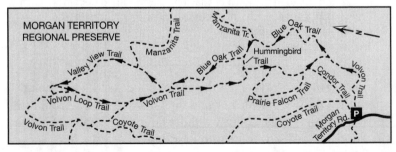

East Bay

Grasslands and oaks at Morgan Territory Regional Preserve

Stay on Blue Oak Trail for 1.3 miles until you reach a cattle gate at a portable toilet. Go through the cattle gate and turn right on Valley View Trail. (The path straight ahead will be the return of your loop.) A rather quick and steep descent on Valley View Trail leads you to remarkable views to the east of the San Joaquin Valley. On the clearest days, the snow-capped High Sierra can be seen far beyond, more than 100 miles away. Mount Diablo shows its face to the west, and Mount St. Helena in Napa appears to the north. After relishing the vista, turn right on Volvon Loop Trail to start your return, climbing back uphill to the cattle gate. From there you have an easy hike on Volvon Trail all the way back to the trailhead and parking lot.

A couple of tips to make your hike at Morgan Territory ideal: One, pick a cool day. Two, make sure you take one of the park's free trail maps so you can negotiate your way through numerous junctions. And three, carry plenty of water and a suitable picnic to spread out under the shade of the biggest oak you can find.

Trip notes: There is no fee. Leashed dogs and bikes are allowed. Free trail maps are available at the trailhead. For more information, contact East Bay Regional Park District, 2950 Peralta Oaks Court, P.O. Box 5381, Oakland, CA 94605-0381; (510) 635-0135 or (510) 562-7275. Website: www.ebparks.org

63. COGSWELL MARSH TRAIL
Hayward Regional Shoreline

DISTANCE: 3.6 miles round-trip; 1.5 hours   **LEVEL:** Easy

ELEVATION CHANGE: Negligible   **RATING:** ★ ★

DIRECTIONS: From Interstate 880 in Hayward, take the Highway 92 exit west. Drive 1.7 miles and take the Clawiter Road exit. Cross Clawiter Road and turn left immediately on Breakwater Road. Drive one mile on Breakwater Road to the Hayward Regional Shoreline interpretive center.

Hayward Regional Shoreline is a place to consider two things: wetlands and birds. Both require more than a casual glance, and as you hike around the bay shore's 3.6 miles of perfectly level, gravel trails, you'll have ample opportunity for slow, careful study.

Start your trip with a visit to the excellent interpretive center at the trailhead, then take the wide dirt trail from the building's back side. The path skirts along a freshwater marsh until it reaches the shoreline of San Francisco Bay. Although Highway 92 and the San Mateo Bridge are close by at the trail's start, they are quickly left behind as the path heads northward. The San Francisco skyline can be seen across the water to the northwest.

As you walk, consider the wetlands around San Francisco Bay. We've built houses, factories, and roads around most of the bay's perimeter; concrete rip-rap lines much of the rest. Thousands of acres of bay marshes have been diked, drained, filled, dredged, and destroyed to build salt mines, make room for airports and highways, or create huge ports.

But despite the damage that's been done to them, the bay's wetlands are still the best friend the Bay Area could have. The many streams and waterways at the bay's edge hold millions of gallons of water, protecting us from flood damage during harsh winter storms. Much of the fish and shellfish we eat spends a part of their lives in the bay's wetland areas. In addition, at least one third of the nation's rare and endangered species are dependent on wetland areas such as those around the bay for nesting, feeding, or growing habitat. Without these wetlands, some endangered species would face extinction.

The coastal mud flats around San Francisco Bay have been reduced to ten percent of their original size. The bay's salt marshes have been reduced to fifteen percent of their original size. Although many people think these flat, mucky areas are suitable only for land fill, mud flats and salt marshes are among the most nutrient-rich and productive habitats on earth.

That's why some forward-thinking people got together in the 1970s to rebuild Hayward Shoreline. The area was dramatically altered in the 1850s when dikes and levees were built to increase salt production. In the process, a huge expanse of wetlands became dry land. Only a generation ago, environmental engineers redesigned and reclaimed 400 acres of freshwater, brackish water, and saltwater marshes in one of the largest marsh restoration projects on the West Coast. Through careful science, humans tried to reconstruct what Mother Nature had originally made.

The effort is paying off. For starters, Hayward Regional Shoreline is now crawling with birds. Even the most novice birdwatcher strolling along the levees will soon notice many distinct and varied species on the waterways. Tall, elegant great egrets share the mud flats with their smaller cousins, the snowy egret. Black-necked stilts race around on their remarkably long, thin, pink-red legs. Avocets use their distinctive curved bills to scoop through the nutrient-rich waters. Migrating ducks line the freshwater ponds and waterways. Other commonly seen species are terns, willets, cormorants, sandpipers, and pelicans.

Footbridge at Cogswell Marsh, Hayward Regional Shoreline

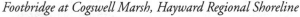

After 1.2 miles of easy walking, with no trail junctions to distract you from your bird and wetland studies, you reach a fork in the trail. Bear left and cross the long footbridge. A short distance farther is a bench with a fine view of the water. Loop back on the trail to the right, which travels through restored Cogswell Marsh.

Trip notes: There is no fee. Dogs are not allowed. Bikes are allowed. A free map is available at the trailhead. For more information, contact East Bay Regional Park District, 2950 Peralta Oaks Court, P.O. Box 5381, Oakland, CA 94605-0381; (510) 635-0135 or (510) 562-7275. Website: www.ebparks.org

64. BAY VIEW & RED HILL LOOP
Coyote Hills Regional Park

DISTANCE: 4.8 miles round-trip; 2.5 hours   **LEVEL:** Easy

ELEVATION CHANGE: 200 feet   **RATING:** ★ ★ ★

DIRECTIONS: From Interstate 880 in Newark, take Highway 84 west for two miles. Take the Paseo Padre Parkway exit, turn right (north) and drive one mile to Patterson Ranch Road. Turn left and drive 1.5 miles to the visitor center parking lot at Coyote Hills.

If you ever have occasion to drive across the Dumbarton Bridge from the South Bay to the East Bay, a few things will catch your attention... like the huge electrical towers that straddle the water and the dismantled, decaying railroad bridge that parallels Dumbarton. The bay itself seems impossibly huge and blue in contrast to the density of the cities and freeways that surround it. But urban-weary eyes come to rest on the soft green knolls of Coyote Hills Regional Park. Situated on your left as you head east across the bay, the park's tule marshes, creeks, and acres of grassland hills beckon you to pull off the freeway and explore.

A 1,000-acre patch of open space along the edge of San Francisco Bay, Coyote Hills was the homeland of Ohlone Indians for more than 2,000 years. The Indians fished bay waters for food and cut willow branches along the creeks to build their homes. Today the park is a wildlife sanctuary, both a permanent home and a temporary rest stop for thousands of resident and migratory birds.

Coyote Hills Regional Park

Binoculars are an excellent accessory for this trail, but many of the birds are so close that you don't even need them. On one short walk at Coyote Hills, we watched a great egret stalk and catch a field mouse 20 yards from us, then fly off with it in his beak. Moments later a peregrine falcon soared overhead, shortly followed by a red-tailed hawk swooping and floating over the grasslands.

In winter, great egrets and snowy egrets displaying exquisite white plumage are as common as human visitors to the park. Two of the largest egret nesting colonies in Northern California are located in neighboring San Francisco Bay National Wildlife Refuge. Their numbers are plentiful at Coyote Hills.

The park has a paved multi-use trail lateraling its hillsides, allowing hikers, baby stroller-pushers, wheelchair users, and bikers access to breathtaking bay and marsh views. But hikers who prefer earthen paths to pavement won't be disappointed. Red Hill Trail climbs to the top of the park's grassy hills for panoramic views and a close-up look at some odd rock formations—outcrops of reddish-gold chert that were once part of the ocean floor.

It's a park for wandering, with or without a formal plan. Start your trip at the Coyote Hills Visitor Center, which is open daily except Mondays and has some interesting displays on the natural and cultural history of the area. Then follow the gated, paved road, Bay View Trail, heading north from the visitor center parking lot.

Leave the pavement in 100 yards as you turn left on wide Nike Trail, heading toward the bay. In a quarter-mile, turn right on Red Hill Trail to begin a 2.3-mile loop on Red Hill and Bay View trails. Hike up and over a grassy hill, then drop back down to the water's edge. Rejoin paved Bay View Trail and stroll southward along the bay, only 50 feet above the water's edge. After a full mile of nonstop views, you'll round Glider Hill and see the turnoff for Soaproot Trail. Turn left on Soaproot, then left again on Red Hill Trail to finish out your loop. As you hike to the top of Red Hill, consider the fact that when San Francisco Bay's waters were higher (before dikes were built in the late 1800s), Red Hill and its neighboring hills were islands.

After exploring Red Hill and its red-colored rock formations, return to the junction with Nike Trail and retrace your steps to the visitor center parking lot. Then head off in the opposite direction, walking 50 yards south on the road you drove in on. Watch for a wooden boardwalk crossing the tule-lined marsh on your left. Follow the boardwalk through a labyrinth of tules, cattails, and sedges. (Children love this maze-like walk.) Where the marsh opens up, birdwatching for ducks and other waterfowl is excellent. The path leads to an Ohlone Indian shellmound. The largest of four shellmounds in the park, this debris pile provides archaeological proof that Indians inhabited this area for at least 2,200 years.

Boardwalk through the tule marsh at Coyote Hills Regional Park

Trip notes: A $4 day-use fee is charged per vehicle. Leashed dogs are allowed except in the marsh area. Bikes are allowed. A free map is available at the entrance kiosk or visitor center. For more information, contact East Bay Regional Park District, 2950 Peralta Oaks Court, P.O. Box 5381, Oakland, CA 94605-0381; (510) 635-0135 or (510) 562-7275. Website: www.ebparks.org

65. MISSION PEAK
Mission Peak Regional Preserve

DISTANCE: 6.6 miles round-trip; 3.5 hours   **LEVEL:** Strenuous
ELEVATION CHANGE: 2,000 feet   **RATING:** ★ ★ ★ ★
DIRECTIONS: From Interstate 880 in Fremont, take the Warren Avenue/ Mission Boulevard exit and drive east 1.5 miles. Turn right on Stanford Avenue and drive a half mile to the trailhead parking area.

Alternatively, from Interstate 680 in Fremont, take the Durham Road exit and drive east for one mile. Turn right on Mission Boulevard, drive three-quarters of a mile, then turn left on Stanford Avenue. Drive a half mile to the trailhead parking area.

The grassy slopes of 2,517-foot Mission Peak are a prerequisite hike for outdoor lovers in Alameda County. On any sunny weekend day with good visibility, hundreds of East and South Bay residents make the pilgrimage to Mission Peak's summit. At the top, they enjoy first-rate views of the South Bay, the northern Santa Cruz Mountains, the Peninsula, San Francisco, and even the summits of the Sierra Nevada. Along the way, they are entertained by colorful hang gliders and paragliders taking off from Mission Peak's slopes, then soaring with the thermals high overhead.

The trail to Mission Peak is a wide, exposed fire road, so be sure to wear your sunscreen. Also, forget hiking on hot days. Some of the grades are quite steep, and with its shadeless slopes, the peak can bake in summer. Although the trail has a reputation for being a butt-kicker, it's only three miles to the summit from the main Fremont trailhead, and even children can make the trip in cool weather. Just remember to bring along plenty of water and snacks, and take your time.

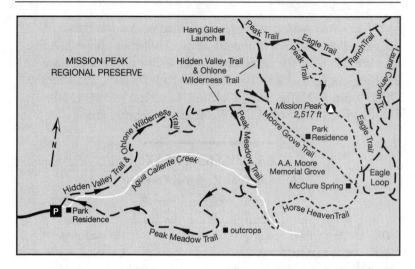

One way to make the trip easier is to stay on the trail. Mission Peak Regional Preserve is lined with well marked fire roads, including a section of the 31-mile Ohlone Wilderness Trail. But these roads diverge into a spider web of use trails, most which cut the switchbacks and head straight up the mountain. If you ignore the use trails and stay on the wide, signed, multi-use path, you'll enjoy a much more pleasant grade up the mountain.

From the trailhead, start by taking the left fork, which is signed as Hidden Valley Trail and Ohlone Wilderness Trail. Almost immediately you'll spot a parallel use trail on your left; it will meet up with the main trail in less than a mile at a rocky outcrop with a wide view of the South Bay. Many people just walk up to this viewpoint and then turn around. You'll stay on the wide fire road, sweating through a few steep stretches for the first 1.5 miles. The view gets wider and more impressive with every twist and turn. The Coyote Hills are a standout; they are the only landmarks in the foreground with any elevation. The rest of the South Bay is remarkably flat.

At a junction with Ohlone Wilderness Trail marker #2, note the right fork for Peak Meadow Trail. You'll follow this on your return. For now, bear left to stay on Hidden Valley Trail/Ohlone Wilderness Trail and enjoy an easier grade. The road enters into a grassy meadow directly below Mission Peak's fractured and rocky summit. Scattered rocks are evidence of ancient landslides.

The road winds around the northwest side of the mountain. At a cattle gate, turn right and follow Peak Trail, another wide fire road. Views are of Mount Diablo and the wildlands of Sunol and Pleasanton Ridge. The hang glider launch site is just downhill to your left; you'll see it as you rise up the summit flank.

In a quarter mile, reach a second junction where Peak Trail bears right and makes the final steep summit climb. The last quarter mile is a rocky single-track path; it leads to a metal post lined with pipes that serve as sight scopes. Look through them and note all the landmarks. To the north is Mount Diablo, Pleasanton Ridge, Livermore, San Antonio Reservoir, and Sunol Regional Wilderness. To the west is Mount Tamalpais, San Francisco, Redwood City, the Dumbarton Bridge, and Coyote Hills. To the south is Mount Loma Prieta and the Santa Cruz Mountains. To the east is Santa Clara County, Mount Hamilton, Lick Observatory, and Rose Peak in the Ohlone Wilderness. On the clearest days, you can make out the snowy peaks of the Sierra Nevada, far to the east. While you are admiring all this majesty, it's not uncommon to see a hang glider or paraglider fly by at eye level.

For your return trip, head back downhill the way you came. Before turning left at the cattle gate for Hidden Valley/Ohlone Wilderness Trail, continue straight ahead for a few hundred feet to the hang glider launch site. It's fascinating to watch these colorful, delicate human birds take off and soar overhead. Then take Hidden Valley/Ohlone Wilderness Trail back downhill to marker #2. Turn

Summit of Mission Peak

left on Peak Meadow Trail, a less-traveled fire road. This path almost guarantees solitude for the rest of your trip, plus it provides a pleasant stint through the oak-forested canyon of Agua Caliente Creek. Don't miss a side trip to the rock outcrops one mile down Peak Meadow Trail (on your left). The view to the south from these rocks is almost as good as Mission Peak's summit view.

Note that some people choose to hike to Mission Peak from a trailhead at Ohlone College in Fremont. Although the grade is somewhat less steep from this direction, the trailhead isn't easy to locate among the campus buildings and the first part of the trail is overrun by grazing cattle.

Trip notes: There is no fee. Leashed dogs and bikes are allowed. A free map is available at the trailhead. For more information, contact East Bay Regional Park District, 2950 Peralta Oaks Court, P.O. Box 5381, Oakland, CA 94605-0381; (510) 635-0135 or (510) 562-7275. Website: www.ebparks.org

66. SUNOL LOOP TOUR
Sunol Regional Wilderness

DISTANCE: 6.0 miles round-trip; 3 hours   **LEVEL:** Moderate
ELEVATION CHANGE: 1,700 feet   **RATING:** ★ ★ ★
DIRECTIONS: From Interstate 680 south of Pleasanton, take the Highway 84/Calaveras Road exit. Turn left on Calaveras Road and drive south 4.2 miles. Turn left on Geary Road and drive 1.7 miles to the park entrance. Continue another quarter-mile to the entrance kiosk, then drive 100 yards past the visitor center to the parking lot across from the horse rental area. The trail begins on the left side of the rest rooms at the footbridge.

A trip to Sunol is a trip to the country. Unlike many other East Bay parks, Sunol isn't bordered by neighborhoods or major thoroughfares. You can't reach it any other way than by driving slowly on a narrow, country road. When you hike the grassy, oak-studded hills of Sunol, all you see are more grassy, oak-studded hills, and an occasional glimpse at shimmering Calaveras Reservoir. Sunol is bordered by San Francisco Water District lands to the north and south and Ohlone Regional Wilderness to the east. It is protected land surrounded by protected land. And that's what makes it good.

The following hike is a six-mile loop tour of Sunol that reveals many of the park's best features. It is steep in places, so come prepared for a hike that feels like a bit more than six miles. (Plenty of water and a few snacks will get you through it easily.) You should also check the temperature: Sunol is lovely in fall, winter, and spring, but it's often too hot on summer days.

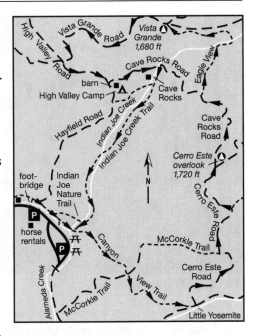

From the parking lot just east of the ranger station and visitor center, begin your hike by crossing the long footbridge over Alameda Creek. This is Alameda County's largest stream, and it can swell to 30 feet wide after winter rains. On the far side of the footbridge, turn right for Canyon View Trail and pass two trail junctions in the next few hundred yards. You're following one leg of Indian Joe Nature Trail, but don't turn left where the nature trail leads uphill. Instead, keep hiking eastward with Alameda Creek on your right. At a third junction (signed with a post in the middle of the path marked "Ohlone Wilderness Regional Trail") bear left and head uphill and away from the creek. Shortly you reach a clearly marked fork and the start of your loop, where Indian Joe Creek Trail veers left and Canyon View Trail continues straight ahead. This mess of junctions in the first quarter mile is annoying, but thankfully, you've reached the last of it.

Follow narrow Canyon View Trail as it rollercoasters up and down through grassy hillsides and oak woodland. Springtime brings an excellent display of flowers along the path. Most impressive are the huge yellow blooms of mule's ears, but you'll also find plentiful California poppies, elegant clarkia, mariposa lilies, owl's clover, brodiaea, and gilia. Birding is excellent throughout Sunol; the park is renowned for its yellow-billed magpies and acorn woodpeckers.

Boulder-choked stream at Little Yosemite

As you progress, you'll gain views to your right of Alameda Creek's steep, miniature canyon. One pleasant mile of strolling through the grasslands will bring you to Canyon View Trail's junction with Cerro Este Road and wide Camp Ohlone Road. Cross the latter to pay a visit to Little Yosemite, a narrow gorge on Alameda Creek that is choked with car-sized boulders. Little Yosemite would be best explored by taking off your shoes, but sadly, no swimming or water contact is allowed. The creek is on San Francisco Water District land. However, you may scramble down to the water's edge, sit on a rock, and admire Alameda Creek's clear green pools. Watch for the small trout that dart through the stream and listen to the music of tumbling waterfalls.

From Little Yosemite, prepare for a serious climb over the next mile on Cerro Este Road. Sticky monkeyflower and purple nightshade line the road's steep banks. The shadeless ascent on the fire road may seem uninspiring, but turn around occasionally as you climb and you'll glimpse fine views of Calaveras Reservoir to the south. The only downer in the vista is Camp Ohlone Road, which looks too much like a paved street, even though it's a gravel road.

Your ascent ends at Cerro Este Overlook, a grassy knoll at 1,720 feet in elevation that is signed by a large stone marker. Catch your breath and enjoy the wide views of the park and Calaveras Reservoir, then bear left on Cave Rocks Road. You have an easy half-mile walk before turning right on single-track Eagle View Trail, which winds along the slope of Sunol's high ridge. A gentle ascent through chaparral and sage over the course of a mile will bring you to Vista Grande Overlook at a junction with Vista Grande Road. This high point (1,680 feet) is actually 40 feet lower than Cerro Este, but the view is even more impressive because of the ridge's steep dropoffs. A gnarled oak tree and another stone marker denote the spot. This might be your best bet for a lunch break.

Turn west on Vista Grande Road and descend rather steeply along the ridgeline. A few curves and twists bring you down to High Valley Road; turn left and walk toward the huge barn you've been seeing from above. The barn is the site of High Valley Camp, a hike-in campground for groups. Bear left to stay on the road north of the barn and walk a half-mile to the right turnoff for Indian Joe Creek Trail. (This single-track trail was not signed on our visit; watch for it immediately after crossing a stream canyon.)

Follow Indian Joe Creek Trail all the way downhill and back to the start of your loop. Be sure to go slow and enjoy this last leg of the trail, one of its prettiest stretches. A highlight is Cave Rocks, a quarter-mile down the path, where huge fractured basalt boulders provide a playground for rock climbers and ambitious hikers. Other highlights are the crunching noise of autumn leaves underfoot and the springtime sounds of bird songs and the gurgling of Indian Joe Creek. In any season, this narrow footpath is the perfect finish to your day-hike at Sunol.

View of Maguire Peaks from Vista Grande Road

Trip notes: A $4 day-use fee is charged per vehicle. Leashed dogs are allowed. Bikes are allowed only on fire roads. A free map is available at the entrance kiosk. For more information, contact East Bay Regional Park District, 2950 Peralta Oaks Court, P.O. Box 5381, Oakland, CA 94605-0381; (510) 635-0135 or (510) 562-7275. Website: www.ebparks.org

67. MAGUIRE PEAKS LOOP
Sunol Regional Wilderness

DISTANCE: 5.5 miles round-trip; 3 hours   **LEVEL:** Moderate

ELEVATION CHANGE: 800 feet   **RATING:** ★ ★ ★

DIRECTIONS: From Interstate 680 south of Pleasanton, take the Highway 84/Calaveras Road exit. Turn left on Calaveras Road and drive south 4.2 miles. Turn left on Geary Road and drive 1.7 miles to the park entrance. Pay your entrance fee at the kiosk, then turn around and drive back out Geary Road for a quarter mile to Welch Creek Road. (Welch Creek Road is narrow and easy to miss; look for it on your right as you drive north on Geary Road.) Drive seven-tenths of a mile on Welch Creek Road to the trailhead on the left, at the cattle gate. Park in the pullout along the road.

As you drive south on Interstate 680 near Pleasanton, you can't help noticing the odd-shaped Maguire Peaks slanting outward from the round, grassy hills. The two side-by-side peaks aren't conical, like most peaks, or even rounded. Instead they're fin-shaped, like two obtuse triangles. Their summits point sideways, then upward. After a little while staring at these odd little mountains, you may find yourself longing to explore them.

You can hike to the peaks from the main Sunol Regional Wilderness entrance on Geary Road, but a shorter option is to start from the trailhead in the Sunol "backcountry" along Welch Creek Road. If the main part of Sunol is too developed for your tastes, you'll love the Welch Creek area. You won't find picnic areas, horse rentals, or a visitor center there; in fact, you won't even find a parking lot. Welch Creek Road is an incredibly narrow, single-lane road with only a few tiny pullouts for cars. Leave yours by the 0.72 mile marker and take the single-track Lower Maguire Peaks Trail from the cattle gate.

The first stretch of trail travels up a creek canyon that is so lush and shady that it harbors huge yellow banana slugs. Ferns and wildflowers line the forest floor; the branches of bay laurels and oaks form a dense canopy overhead. The Lower Maguire Peaks Trail is well built and quaintly signed with rusted arrow markers.

Soon you climb out of the lovely canyon into a more open area of oaks and grasslands. At a trail junction, two paths lead uphill to meet up with an old ranch road. Take either one and join wide Maguire Peaks Road, which circumnavi-

View from Maguire Peaks Loop

gates the two peaks. Go left on the road to make a clockwise circle.

Those who don't like hiking on dirt roads will find this one to be an exception. It's pleasantly overgrown by low grasses and it hasn't been rutted, eroded, or overrun by cows. It makes easy and pleasant walking. Heading west through open grasslands, you'll climb a bit to gain the Maguire Peaks' ridgeline. The sloping hills are peppered with occasional oaks and bay laurels, but for the most part, you're out in the sunshine. If you're fortunate enough to visit on a day when the wind blows, you'll be convinced that the grasses are alive. They tumble, roll, and travel with the wind like migrating creatures. In spring, check for wildflowers. We saw orange monkey-flower, paintbrush, larkspur, blue-eyed grass, mariposa lilies, and blue dicks, as well as huge yellow mule's ears.

When you crest the western ridge of Maguire Peaks, you're rewarded with views of huge San Antonio Reservoir to the north and the city of Pleasanton beyond, framed by Mount Diablo. After all the solitude you've had and the wild land you've been traversing, the sight of civilization is surprising. Head for a rocky outcrop on the ridge's high point where you'll find the widest views and the best picnic spot. Keep your eyes on the skies. Hawk sightings and even eagle sightings are fairly common around Maguire Peaks.

When you've seen enough, continue on your stroll around the perimeter of Maguire Peaks. It's tempting to make an ascent to the top, but you'll have to blaze your own trail to do so. (Beware of rattlesnakes, especially in springtime.) The summits of the peaks are lined with wind-sculpted basalt rock.

The peaks' east side is more vegetated than the west, particularly with large oaks and bay laurel. Poison hemlock grows 12 feet high in places. Too many nonnative thistles are evidence of the ranching that has taken place here. As in many East Bay parks, cows graze on Maguire Peaks. Fortunately, the area isn't overrun with them.

A long downhill returns you to the start of your loop. Turn left to regain the single-track trail back to your car.

An insider's tip: Maguire Peaks Loop is one of the nicest trails in the East Bay for a sunset hike. Just remember to bring a flashlight in case it gets dark before you get back to your car.

Trip notes: A $4 day-use fee is charged per vehicle. Leashed dogs are allowed. Bikes are not allowed. A free map is available at the park entrance kiosk. For more information, contact East Bay Regional Park District, 2950 Peralta Oaks Court, P.O. Box 5381, Oakland, CA 94605-0381; (510) 635-0135 or (510) 562-7275. Website: www.ebparks.org

68. MURIETTA FALLS TRAIL
Ohlone Regional Wilderness

DISTANCE: 12.0 miles round-trip; 7 hours   **LEVEL:** Strenuous

ELEVATION CHANGE: 3,500 feet   **RATING:** ★ ★ ★

DIRECTIONS: From Interstate 580 in Livermore, take the North Livermore Avenue exit and turn right (south). Drive south through the town of Livermore for 3.5 miles (North Livermore Avenue becomes Tesla Road) and turn right on Mines Road. Drive 3.5 miles on Mines Road to its junction with Del Valle Road. Continue straight at the fork, now on Del Valle Road.

Drive 3.2 miles to the entrance kiosk at Del Valle Regional Park. Purchase a wilderness permit at the entrance kiosk, then continue three quarters of a mile to the dam and cross it. Turn right and drive a half mile to the Lichen Bark Picnic Area. Take the trail signed as Ohlone Trail.

Everybody loves a waterfall, but do you love waterfalls enough to be willing to grunt out a 3,500-foot elevation change? Think it over. If your answer is yes, you're heading for a fine adventure in Ohlone Regional Wilderness, culminating in a visit to 100-foot Murietta Falls.

If your answer is "not sure," the first half-hour on this trail will be challenging enough to make up your mind, one way or the other.

Ohlone Regional Wilderness is one of the Bay Area's special places. No public roads lead through it or even near it. You have to hike to reach its boundary, starting either from Sunol Regional Wilderness to the west or Del Valle Regional Park to the north. To be more specific, you have to hike uphill.

In the same vein, Murietta Falls is one of the Bay Area's most special waterfalls. That's partly because it's much taller than other local falls and partly because it's hard enough to reach that most people never make the trip. The difficulty doesn't just lie in the trail's many steep ups and downs, its sunny exposure, and its 12-mile-long roundtrip distance. The real difficulty is that the waterfall has an extremely short season and must be seen immediately following a period of rain. More than a few hikers have made the long trip to Murietta and then been disappointed to find only a trickle of water. March is often the best month to see the fall flowing, but it depends on the current year's rain pattern. Depending on when the rains come, Murietta's top flow could happen anywhere from January to April. Keep your eyes on the skies.

One thing to remember: this trail is absolutely not suitable for a warm or hot day. It offers very little shade and a ton of climbing.

A single element makes the trip easy. The trail is remarkably well signed. Just pay attention at all junctions and keep following the red markers for Ohlone Wilderness Trail in the first five miles. Also, you must purchase a wilderness permit in order to hike on the Ohlone Wilderness Trail. With your permit you get a free map, which comes in quite handy.

The trail starts by climbing and stays that way for 2.4 miles. (Don't forget to stop and sign in at the wilderness register one mile in.) There are only a very few spots where the wide dirt road levels off. Otherwise, it's up, up, up all the way to the top of Rocky Ridge, a 1,670-foot gain from the trailhead. Then all of a sudden you start an incredibly steep descent—steep enough so that you'll wish you'd brought your trekking poles. You drop 530 feet in about a half mile. The good news is that you're heading for water; you can hear its welcoming sound. The wide fire road narrows to single-track for the first time all day as you descend into the beautiful stream canyon of Williams Gulch. The sound of the cascading creek is so refreshing

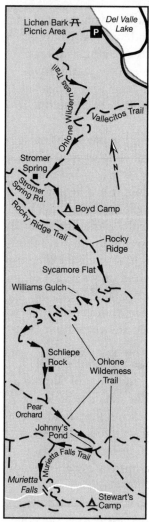

and inviting that you may suddenly remember why you are doing this hike after all. The half-mile stretch of path that cuts through the stream canyon is pure, refreshing pleasure.

You might as well enjoy it, because next you're going to climb out of the canyon in a 1,200-foot ascent. The single-track trail is surprisingly well graded with some good switchbacks, however, so this climb isn't nearly as bad as some of the dirt road stretches. The path is fairly well shaded. Prolific miner's lettuce and pink shooting stars grow alongside it.

You'll get a hint that you're nearing the falls when you start to notice rock outcrops along the trail. For the first four miles, you see mostly grasslands and massive oak trees, some with diameters that rival the size of giant redwoods. (The only exception to the oak savannah terrain is in riparian Williams Gulch.) But suddenly large rock outcrops start to pop up out of nowhere. One of these, on the left side of the trail, is signed as Schliepe Rock, with no explanation.

The trail also levels out substantially as you near the falls. At this 3,000-foot elevation, you'll gain some wonderful views to the north and west. (On our trip, we were amazed to see snow on the high ridges around us, and even a few lingering white patches right along the trail.)

Murietta Falls

Seven-tenths of a mile beyond Schliepe Rock you'll reach Johnny's Pond. Just beyond the small pond turn right at the sign for Murietta Falls (signpost 35). Hike a quarter mile farther, then turn left and start paying close attention to your surroundings. In just under a half mile, you'll reach a hairpin turn in the road. If you've timed your trip well, you'll note a few streams of water crossing the road. Leave the trail and follow the main stream downhill to your right; it will deliver you to the brink of the falls in a few hundred feet.

A good use trail makes a steep descent to the base of the falls. Follow it carefully—you've come this far, you might as well get the full effect. The waterfall's cliff, an incredible rocky precipice with a 100-foot drop, is composed of greenstone basalt. At its base is a wide, round, shallow pool. Many good picnicking spots are found nearby. If you made it this far, you deserve to eat well. Pull out that turkey and avocado sandwich.

Birdwatchers, take note: The trailside oak savannah is home to many residents and migratory birds. I counted more western bluebirds on this walk than I had seen in my entire life previously.

Trip notes: A $4 day-use fee is charged per vehicle from October to March ($5 from April to September). Hikers on the Ohlone Wilderness Trail must purchase a $2 wilderness permit, which includes a detailed trail map. (You may purchase a permit in advance by mail at the address below, or on the day of your hike at the park entrance station.) Leashed dogs are allowed. Bikes are not allowed. For more information, contact East Bay Regional Park District, 2950 Peralta Oaks Court, P.O. Box 5381, Oakland, CA 94605-0381; (510) 635-0135 or (510) 562-7275. Website: www.ebparks.org

Peninsula
&
South Bay

69. LAND'S END COASTAL TRAIL
Golden Gate National Recreation Area

DISTANCE: 3.5 miles round-trip; 2 hours   **LEVEL:** Easy

ELEVATION CHANGE: 250 feet   **RATING:** ★ ★ ★

DIRECTIONS: In San Francisco, head west on Geary Boulevard to 48th Avenue, where Geary becomes Point Lobos Avenue. Continue on Point Lobos Avenue for a half block to the Merrie Way parking lot on the right, just above Louis' Restaurant. The trail leads from the north side of the parking lot.

What is the wildest place in San Francisco? While some might argue for the South of Market nightclubs or the new wave industries of Media Gulch, I vote for the Land's End Coastal Trail. It's hard to believe you can find a city trail that feels this natural and remote, featuring million-dollar views of crashing surf, offshore outcrops, the Golden Gate Bridge, and the Marin Headlands. But here it is.

The trail begins near Ocean Beach and winds its way north and east along the ocean bluffs to China and Baker beaches. (It also runs south along Ocean Beach to Sloat Boulevard, but this section is paved and heavily used by tourists, rollerbladers, bicyclists, and beach bums of all kinds. While it's an enjoyable stroll, it's not really a hike.) In its entirety, Coastal Trail is 11 miles long, although not all of it is contiguous and some of it follows city streets. This 3.5-mile round-trip follows the most "wilderness-like" section of it from the Merrie Way parking lot above the Cliff House to 32nd Avenue and El Camino del Mar. It's guaranteed that at least for a minute you'll forget you're in a major metropolitan area.

The ocean views from the parking lot are a satisfying first impression. As you lace up your hiking boots, watch for a Golden Gate-bound freighter or the spout of a gray whale, and lend an ear to the chorus of barking sea lions. Then take the trail from the north end of the lot that dips into a canopy of cypress trees. Immediately you'll spot a couple spur paths on the left; these lead a few hundred feet to ocean overlooks—perfect spots for sunset watching. Take the right fork to connect to the wide main trail, which is the remains of the roadbed for Adolph Sutro's 1888 steam train.

Sutro was a San Francisco entrepreneur who wanted to make

his Cliff House Restaurant and adjoining bathhouse more accessible to working class folks. He built the railroad and charged people only a nickel to ride. Unfortunately, numerous landslides made maintaining the railway too expensive, and in 1925 it was closed down.

Today, the former rail trail offers postcard views of the Golden Gate Bridge, Marin Headlands, Pacific Ocean, and San Francisco Bay. The trail is lined with windswept cypress trees, which have taken on odd, stiff forms as if they've been hair-sprayed into shape. If you look closely at the ocean waters below the trail, you might spot the remains of several Golden Gate shipwrecks. Point Lobos and Mile Rock, two submerged rocks, have taken many casualties off Land's End. Today both rocks are marked with buoy signals.

A half mile in you'll see a right fork, where a gated road heads uphill to the Palace of the Legion of Honor art museum. Continue straight on the main path. In another 50 yards is a narrow trail on the left marked with a "leashed dog" symbol. Follow this stair-stepped path steeply downhill for a quarter-mile to Mile Rock Beach, named after the red and white fog signal in the middle of the bay. The small beach is strewn with driftwood and rounded rocks and is popular with sunbathers. On summer weekends, be prepared for an anatomy lesson: not everyone wears clothes here. From Mile Rock Beach you can take side trails east and west along the bluffs, but use caution. The soil is continually eroding and the paths are just "use" trails, not official trails.

Back on the main trail, you'll reach a fence at Painted Rock Cliff and a section of trail leading uphill and designated for hikers only. Ascend the stairsteps into a grove of eucalyptus, then continue

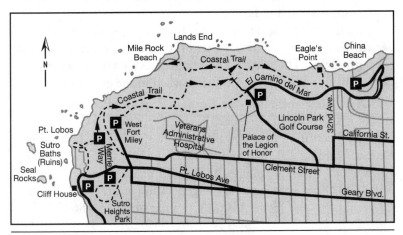

Land's End Coastal Trail

on a narrower trail as it curves along the edge of ocean bluffs, offering more Golden Gate views. Trailside anise grows 10 feet tall and the coastal scrub is aromatic after winter rains.

The trail winds up at Eagle's Point, a spectacular overlook near 32nd Avenue and across from Lincoln Park Golf Course. Follow its winding staircase down the bluffs for the best views of the day.

When you return to the Merrie Way parking lot, consider a walk on the abandoned rail trail into Sutro Heights Park. A short path loops around the remains of Sutro's estate. To access it, walk through the Merrie Way lot and cross Point Lobos Avenue. (It's about 100 yards uphill.) Be sure to stop at the loop's far end, just below a rock parapet that was built in 1880 as a viewing platform. From here, you are directly above the Cliff House, looking out toward the Farallon Islands.

Another excellent side trip leads from the west side of the Merrie Way parking lot, down a set of stairs to the concrete ruins of the Sutro Baths. The saltwater bathhouse was a popular San Francisco attraction until 1966, when it burned to the ground.

Trip notes: There is no fee. Leashed dogs are allowed. Bikes are allowed on part of the Coastal Trail. A free map of Golden Gate National Recreation Area is available by contacting GGNRA, Fort Mason, Building 201, San Francisco, CA 94123; (415) 556-0560. For more information, phone the Presidio Visitor Center at (415) 561-4323 or the Fort Funston Ranger Station at (415) 239-2366. Or phone the Cliff House Visitor Center at (415) 556-8642.

70. ALCATRAZ ISLAND'S AGAVE TRAIL
Golden Gate National Recreation Area

DISTANCE: 1.0 mile round-trip; 1 hour   **LEVEL:** Easy

ELEVATION CHANGE: 100 feet   **RATING:** ★ ★ ★ ★

DIRECTIONS: Alcatraz Island can be accessed via the Blue & Gold Fleet from Pier 41 in San Francisco (Fisherman's Wharf). Pier 41 is located near the corner of Jefferson and Powell streets. Parking is available in fee lots nearby. See "trip notes" on page 213 for ferry information.

SPECIAL NOTE: The Agave Trail is only open from late September to mid-February, when bird nesting season begins. The rest of Alcatraz Island is open year-round.

Everyone who has ever been to San Francisco knows about Alcatraz Island, but very few people know about Alcatraz Island's Agave Trail.

Agave? Isn't that the tall, funny looking plant that's the key ingredient in tequila? Yes, the very same.

The agaves were planted on Alcatraz Island by prison guards and their families in the 1930s and 1940s. Although Alcatraz was little more than a big, barren rock in the middle of the bay, the people who called it home were determined to grow gardens and make the place hospitable. So while the prisoners paced in their jail cells, the guards and their families formed a gardening association, imported topsoil from Angel Island and exotic plants from just about everywhere, and set out to make the island grow. The agaves and other ornamental flora took root and quickly took over. Today they frame the island's incomparable views of San Francisco and the Golden Gate.

You can visit Alcatraz and its famous prison any day of the year, but if you want to walk the short Agave Trail, you must show up between late September and mid-February. The rest of the year the trail is closed to protect nesting birds. Colonies of black-crowned night herons build their nests in trees and bushes around the island each spring. In summer, the prison's concrete parade ground is filled with the nests and chicks of western gulls, making this one of the largest western gull nesting sites on the West Coast. The birds build more than 450 nests on Alcatraz each year.

The timing of the trail's open season works out beautifully, because autumn and winter often provide the clearest, fog-free days on the bay. Also, the summer tourist crowds are nonexistent, so it's easy to get a seat on an Alcatraz ferry (except around Thanksgiving and Christmas). On late fall and winter weekdays, you can usually just show up at Pier 41 and get on the next boat. Not so the rest of the year.

Keep in mind that this trip is more like a walk than a hike. You won't need your two-hundred-dollar hiking boots, but you will need your camera and plenty of film. The scenery is incredible.

After an easy and scenic boat ride across San Francisco Bay, you disembark at the landing on the east side of the island. Most everybody heads to the right and up the hill to tour the prison. You head left instead, passing some picnic tables and a gated chain link fence. On the fence's far side is a sign marking the Agave Trail.

The path's first stretch is level, concrete, and wheelchair accessible. It allows you to stroll only a few feet from the water's edge, watching as boats sail by and seagulls fly overhead. Gentle lapping waves spill onto the walkway. Views of downtown San Francisco and the Bay Bridge are unforgettable. As you curve around to the south side of the island, you'll pass the large sign seen on your ferry ride, warning that "persons procuring or concealing escape of prisoners are subject to prosecution and imprisonment."

Alcatraz Island's Agave Trail

Agave Trail leads along the base of a steep hillside covered with agave plants. Their strange shapes make marvelous outlines against the bright blue sky. At the end of the trail's level stretch, you can see some of Alcatraz' rocky tidepools. A rare occurrence in San Francisco Bay, these tidepools were formed from manmade rubble created by years of blasting and building on the island. Although you can't access the tidepools, at low tide you can lean over the railing and glimpse anemones glittering in the sun.

Beautiful flagstone stairsteps lead uphill to the prison's parade grounds, which were once ringed by the houses of guards and their families. The demolished building remains are found in huge rubble piles scattered across the open concrete yard. The National Park Service tore down the houses in 1971 and the rubble piles quickly became homes for burrowing owls, night herons, deer mice, and salamanders.

From the parade grounds, your view expands to take in all of the Golden Gate Bridge and parts of the Marin Headlands. San Francisco shines to the south. If you can pull yourself away from the scenery, walk across the parade grounds and along the north side of the barracks to join the main paved trail leading to the cellhouse. There are several buildings to explore and many more views of the bay and mainland to see.

One more tip: If you've never done it before, be sure to buy a headset and take the self-guiding audio tour of Alcatraz prison. The tour features the voices of actual prisoners and prison guards, and it brings your prison tour to life.

Trip notes: The ferry fee is $8.75 per adult for daytime cruises and $19.75 per adult for evening cruises. (Children's and seniors' tickets are discounted.) A self-guided audio tour of the prison can be purchased for a small fee. Tickets for Alcatraz can be purchased in advance by phoning the Blue and Gold Fleet at (415) 705-5555, or on the Internet at www.telesails.com. Advance tickets are strongly recommended in the summer months and during holiday periods. Dogs and bikes are not allowed. A map of Alcatraz Island is available for $1 at the ferry landing. For more information, contact Golden Gate National Recreation Area, Fort Mason, Building 201, San Francisco, CA 94123; (415) 705-1045, (415) 561-4323, or (415) 556-0560. Website: nps.gov/alcatraz

71. SUMMIT LOOP TRAIL
San Bruno Mountain State & County Park

DISTANCE: 3.1 miles round-trip; 1.5 hours   **LEVEL:** Easy

ELEVATION CHANGE: 725 feet   **RATING:** ★ ★ ★ ★

DIRECTIONS: From U.S. 101 south of San Francisco, take the Brisbane/Cow Palace exit and drive 1.8 miles on Bayshore Boulevard, past downtown Brisbane. Turn left on Guadalupe Canyon Parkway and drive 2.3 miles to the park entrance. Turn right and drive past the entrance kiosk, then loop back underneath the road to the parking area and trailhead on the far side.

San Bruno Mountain is located a few miles off U.S. 101 in South San Francisco and Interstate 280 in Daly City. More specifically, it's situated about 1,200 feet above the Cow Palace, that huge entertainment arena that houses everything from monster truck shows to well-bred cat competitions. The bald, grassy mountain overlooks 3Com Park and the business complexes on U.S. 101. Does this seem like an unlikely place for a nature preserve? You bet. But San Bruno Mountain is full of surprises.

The Summit Loop Trail takes you on a tour of the mountain, providing a mix of city and bay views. Hikers who show up in spring will find the hillsides brimming with wildflowers. Some of them serve a critical role: San Bruno Mountain is prime habitat for the endangered mission blue butterfly. Three kinds of native lupine grow here that are crucial to the development of the butterfly's larva. The mission blue butterfly exists only on San Bruno Mountain and in the Golden Gate National Recreation Area.

San Bruno Mountain is also home to the rare San Bruno elfin, another endangered butterfly, as well as endangered plants including Montara manzanita (found nowhere else in the world) and Franciscan wallflower. The 2,700-acre park is carefully managed with a habitat conservation plan to protect the precious species. A legal agreement between the public and local developers, the plan limits the amount and type of building that can be done on San Bruno Mountain's slopes. Although developers have contested the conservation plan in court, it has always been upheld.

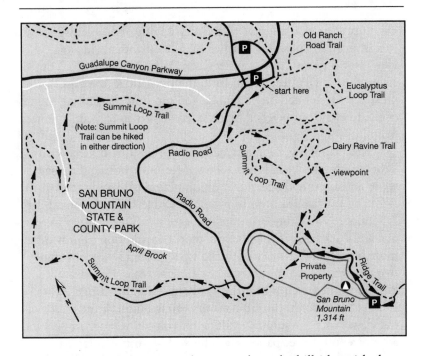

Meanwhile, hikers are welcome to share the hillsides with the butterflies and wildflowers. Start your trip at the trailhead on the south side of Guadalupe Canyon Parkway. Check out the San Bruno Mountain Botanical Garden, a native plant garden maintained by park volunteers, then begin hiking at the signboard. Bear right for Summit Loop Trail. In 100 yards, you'll reach a second junction; this is where you choose which leg of the loop to follow uphill. A right turn will lead you across the paved summit road and counterclockwise for the easiest grade. A left turn will take you on the shortest route to the summit, still with a very mild grade.

The shorter route will earn you dramatic views almost immediately. In just a few minutes of climbing, South San Francisco and San Francisco Bay appear. Mount Diablo looms large in the background. The panorama keeps changing with every switchback up the slope. Vistas are unobstructed because San Bruno Mountain is almost entirely grasslands, with just a few stands of eucalyptus and some low-growing chaparral. Although native grasslands have become increasingly rare in the Bay Area due to grazing and the introduction of nonnative species, San Bruno Mountain is home to more than 20 species.

Just beyond a junction with Dairy Ravine Trail, a left spur leads to a strategically positioned bench on a knoll with a wide-angle view. North to south you can see Twin Peaks, San Francisco's downtown, the Cow Palace, 3Com Park, the Bay Bridge, the East Bay hills, and Oyster and Sierra points. You can hear the rushing sound of the freeway, but perched high on this oasis you feel oddly remote from it.

Keep climbing, soon approaching the antenna-covered summit. Where Ridge Trail heads left, follow it for more outstanding bay views and a scenic final stretch. At a junction with a fire road, turn right and walk the last few steps uphill. Ridge Trail continues for 2.5 miles to San Bruno Mountain's East Peak. This makes a fine out-and-back hike, if you're in the mood. In addition to providing more incomparable views of the Bay, Ridge Trail is bordered by two unusual manzanita species: the endemic coastal manzanita and kinnikinnick, which is near the southern edge of its range.

At the summit, the radio towers barely diminish the drama of the view. From the summit parking lot you can wander around and admire a 360-degree panorama. This will be your first look at the coast; you'll enjoy more western views on the return leg of the loop.

When you've seen enough, head downhill on the paved road for a quarter mile to where Summit Loop Trail crosses the pavement. Bear left, taking the signed trail on the right side of a gated

South San Francisco and San Francisco Bay from San Bruno Mountain

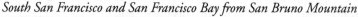

road. Enjoy more ocean vistas, plus glimpses of Mount Tamalpais and the Marin Headlands to the north. If you're hiking in spring, the park's best displays of wildflowers are found on this western slope. Look for lupine, poppies, Douglas iris, goldfields, pennyroyal, and owl's clover, among many others. More unusual species include broadleaf stonecrop and wild pansy. You'll be accompanied by wildflowers and ocean views all the way back downhill.

Trip notes: A $4 day-use fee is charged per vehicle. Dogs and bikes are not allowed on Summit Loop Trail. Bikes are allowed on the paved summit road. Free park maps are available at the entrance kiosk. For more information, contact San Bruno Mountain State and County Park, 555 Guadalupe Canyon Parkway, Brisbane, CA 94005; (650) 992-6770.

72. THREE TRAILS to SWEENEY RIDGE
Golden Gate National Recreation Area

DISTANCE: 4.0 or 5.0 miles round-trip; 2-3 hours   **LEVEL:** Moderate

ELEVATION CHANGE: 750 feet or 1,000 feet   **RATING:** ★ ★ ★

DIRECTIONS: For the Sneath Lane trailhead—From Interstate 280 in San Bruno, take the Sneath Lane/San Bruno Avenue exit and bear right. At the stoplight, turn left (west) on Sneath Lane. Drive 1.9 miles to the trailhead parking area.

For the Skyline College trailhead—From Interstate 280 in San Bruno, take the Westborough exit and turn right (west). Drive 1.4 miles, then turn left on Skyline Boulevard. Drive six-tenths of a mile, then turn right on College Drive. Drive a half mile. At the stop sign, turn left, drive a quarter mile, then turn left at the sign for Parking Lot 2. The trailhead is located on the back side of the parking lot.

For the Pacifica trailhead—From Highway 1 in Pacifica, turn east into Shell Dance Nursery (north of Reina del Mar Avenue and south of Sharp Park Road). Drive past the nursery buildings to the parking area at the end of the dirt road.

Has the fog vanished from San Francisco? Good. Is it morning? Good. These are the two crucial elements for a trip to Sweeney Ridge and the San Francisco Bay Discovery Site. Why? Zero fog is imperative in order to fully appreciate the stupendous views from the top of the ridge. Morning is the critical time to hike because if

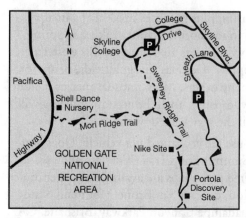

the weather is clear, by midday the wind is probably going to howl. Pick a still, sunny morning (most likely to occur in spring or fall) and you're set for a great hiking trip.

You have three good trail choices. The paved route from Sneath Lane in San Bruno is open to hikers, bikers, and dogs, and it offers views of San Andreas Lake and the prominent landmarks of South San Francisco and the northern peninsula. The path from Skyline College is a dirt trail, closed to bikes but open to dogs and hikers, that offers views of the ocean and Pacifica coast. The trail from Shell Dance Nursery in Pacifica is a bit longer and steeper than the others—five miles round-trip instead of four miles, and a 1,000-foot elevation gain instead of 750 feet. It's open to hikers, bikers, and dogs, and it also offers beautiful coastal views.

All three trails lead to the same result: an incredible 360-degree panorama from the top of Sweeney Ridge. This vista takes in the Pacific coastline and San Francisco Bay as well as the land mass to the east, north, and south. It was here, at the 1,200-foot summit on top of Sweeney Ridge, that Gaspar de Portola and the Portola Expedition discovered San Francisco Bay on November 4, 1769. A stone monument commemorates their discovery. Alongside it is a second monument in memory of Carl Patrick McCarthy, who "personally brought 11,863 visitors to this discovery site" and was instrumental in obtaining protective status for Sweeney Ridge. Carved on the granite marker are the outlines of all the major landmarks you can see from this spot, including Montara Mountain, Mount Tamalpais, Mount Diablo, Mount Hamilton, Point Reyes, Point San Pedro, and the Farallon Islands.

If you opt for the Sneath Lane paved trail, it's a simple deal. The trail begins at a gate at the parking area and slowly winds its way uphill. About two thirds of the way up you'll see a yellow line painted on the trail. That's the "fog line" designed to aid bikers and hikers when visibility is bad. Once you reach the fog line, the trail enters its steepest stretch, but the views of the peninsula more than compensate. At the top of the ridge, you'll find a major junction of trails. This is where you gain wide westward views to add to your collection of eastern views. Straight ahead is a wooden bench that overlooks the coast. Go left for a few yards to see the Portola monument. Then take the paved ridge trail to the right, which stays level and easy for a half mile, passes a big water tower, and ends at the abandoned buildings of an old Nike missile site.

If you opt for the trail from Skyline College, the trail begins from the back side of Parking Lot 2 and makes a brief, steep ascent uphill to join an old gravel road. Turn right on the road and enjoy a mellower grade and immediate coastal views. Mount Tamalpais appears to the north. In less than a mile, you'll reach an abandoned military bunker, a reminder of Sweeney Ridge's role in protecting San Francisco from possible military invasion during World War II. Because of the bunker's strategic high point, it has an excellent view of South San Francisco, the South Bay, the Pacific coast, and Mount Diablo to the east.

From the bunker, the trail drops steeply, soon joining a long series of stairsteps leading down into a ravine. If you look to your right, you'll see where the trail is heading—right back up the stairsteps on the far side. It's a mini-workout for your cardiovascular system.

On top of Sweeney Ridge

The trail tops out at the abandoned Nike missile site buildings, where the view is fine enough. But take a stroll along the paved, level ridge trail for a half mile to see the stone monument to Portola and check out the even better views from there.

If you choose to take the route from Pacifica, start at the gate behind Shell Dance Nursery. Take Mori Ridge Trail, an old dirt road, uphill for almost two miles. The trail leads through open grasslands and coastal scrub with nearly nonstop views of Mount Tamalpais, Montara Mountain, and the Pacific Ocean. Occasional Monterey pines provide a chance for shade. When Mori Ridge Trail meets up with Sweeney Ridge Trail (the path from Skyline College), turn right for the last half mile to the Nike missile site. Continue along the paved trail to the Portola monument.

Trip notes: There is no fee. Leashed dogs are allowed. Bikes are allowed on all trails except the route from Skyline College. A free map of Golden Gate National Recreation Area is available by contacting GGNRA, Fort Mason, Building 201, San Francisco, CA 94123; (415) 556-0560. For more information, phone the Presidio Visitor Center at (415) 561-4323 or the Fort Funston Ranger Station at (415) 239-2366.

73. MONTARA MOUNTAIN SUMMIT
McNee Ranch State Park

DISTANCE: 7.5 miles round-trip; 4 hours   **LEVEL:** Strenuous
ELEVATION CHANGE: 2,200 feet   **RATING:** ★ ★ ★
DIRECTIONS: From Half Moon Bay, drive north on Highway 1 for 10 miles to just north of Montara State Beach and the Chart House Restaurant and just south of Devil's Slide. The trailhead is marked by a yellow metal gate on the east side of the highway. There is parking for about six cars. If this lot is full, you can park farther south at Montara State Beach.

There are two routes to Montara Mountain's summit: the doggy route and the no-doggy route. Both trails are excellent and the summit vista is sublime no matter how you get there.

The no-dogs-allowed trail begins in Pacifica's San Pedro Valley County Park and is the preferred choice for hikers who love single-track. You won't face any mountain bikers on this path (except in the last three-quarters of a mile to the summit, where the two trails join), but you can't bring your dog, either. Details on this trail can be found in the following story, Brooks Falls Loop.

The dogs-allowed route, which begins in McNee Ranch State Park on Highway 1 just north of Montara, is an old paved road and a wide fire road that is open to hikers, bikers, equestrians, and dogs. It offers beautiful coastal views as it winds up the west side of the mountain. An advantage is that you don't have to hike all the way to the summit to gain a vista; the scenery is good for most of the trip. If you do go to the top, you can take an alternate route back down the mountain, making a nice semi-loop.

From the Highway 1 trailhead at undeveloped McNee Ranch State Park, begin hiking on the single-track trail just to the left of the gated road, Gray Whale Cove Trail. The first half-mile rises out of a cypress-lined canyon to gain lovely ocean views to the north, including the crashing surf and tall cliffs of Gray Whale Cove. At an unsigned junction, go right and join an old paved road, Old San Pedro Mountain Road. (If you prefer, you can just follow the gated road from the trailhead, then bear left on Old San Pedro Mountain Road by the ranger's residence.)

The road's broken pavement is being rapidly encroached by 10-foot-high pampas grass, coyote brush, and other coastal flora. For the next half-mile, you'll lose your coastal views as you traipse through a canyon, but this is the trail's only viewless stretch. Meanwhile, watch for bike riders flying downhill. You'll have plenty of time to see and hear them coming and get out of their way.

The road/trail is extremely well graded. A few benches are in place at strategic resting points. At 1.8 miles, as you pause to catch your breath and admire the ocean views, note a left spur trail signed "no bikes." That's where you'll loop back on your return. One hundred yards past the spur trail the old pavement veers off to the left; continue uphill to the right on a good dirt road. This is officially Montara Mountain Road; you'll follow it all the way to the summit.

Shortly the wide road enters its steepest stretch, which lasts for a half-mile. It takes you high up on a ridge, where you can see Pillar Point Harbor and the Half Moon Bay airport on your right and the boxy houses of Pacifica on your left. The road is lined with ceanothus, coffeeberry, and scrub oaks. At three miles, you'll pass the single-track trail coming in from San Pedro Valley County Park. Both routes share the final three-quarters of a mile to the summit.

Coast views from Montara Mountain

Now that you've gained some elevation, the coastal scrub and pampas grass are replaced by chinquapin and manzanita covered with lichen and moss. Tiny ferns grow in crags among the rock. These are a tribute to the amount of fog that Montara Mountain sees.

As you near the top, you'll find the chassis of an old, rusted car, a small sandstone cave, and a spur trail leading west to a slightly lower summit. Straight ahead lie the main two peaks of Montara Mountain, littered with microwave towers. Head for the north peak, which is the higher of the two at 1,898 feet.

What can you see from the top? To the east it's the famous sign on U.S. 101 proclaiming "South San Francisco the Industrial City," the Dumbarton Bridge, San Francisco Bay, plus Mount Diablo in the background. To the west it's the wild Pacific coast all the way north to San Francisco and south to Pescadero. The Santa Cruz Mountains rise to the southeast. Mount Tamalpais looms high above the tall skyline of San Francisco. It's a breathtaking panorama.

If you want to get away from the summit's antennas, head for the lower peak to the west that you passed (by the sandstone cave). This bald summit makes a fine picnic spot, although its views are only to the west.

Your trip back downhill is a treat, with nonstop coastal views in front of you, not at your back. If you want to skip the long spell on pavement, remember to watch for the alternate return route. When you leave the dirt road and join the old paved road, follow it for 100 yards to the single-track trail on your right. This path has a few extremely steep downhill pitches, so exercise some caution. When the path meets up with Gray Whale Cove Trail paralleling the coast and the highway, take the right fork for a level quarter-mile to a fine overlook with two benches. The ocean is so loud here that you can't hear the cars on the highway directly below.

Then backtrack on Gray Whale Cove Trail and follow the edge of the coast all the way back to your starting point.

Trip notes: There is no fee. Leashed dogs and bikes are allowed. A map of San Mateo Coast State Parks and Beaches, which includes McNee Ranch, is available for $1 from the address below. For more information, contact California State Parks, Bay Area District, 250 Executive Park Boulevard, Suite 4900, San Francisco, CA 94135; (415) 330-6300. Or call Montara State Beach at (650) 726-8819.

74. BROOKS FALLS LOOP
San Pedro Valley County Park

DISTANCE: 3.0 miles round-trip; 1.5 hours   **LEVEL:** Easy

ELEVATION CHANGE: 500 feet   **RATING:** ★ ★ ★

DIRECTIONS: From Highway 1 in Pacifica, turn east (left) on Linda Mar Boulevard. Follow Linda Mar Boulevard for two miles until it deadends at Oddstad Boulevard. Turn right and drive 50 yards to the park entrance on the left. Park in the upper parking lot (to the right of the visitor center as you drive in). Montara Mountain Trail is located next to the rest rooms.

The first time you drive to San Pedro Valley County Park you may think you have the wrong directions. You head down Highway 1 into Pacifica, then turn off at a shopping center with three different fast-food chains. The place doesn't look much like a nature preserve.

But have patience, because you need only drive another couple miles before leaving the city's entrapments behind. In a few minutes on the trail, you'll head up and away from the parking lots, noise, and traffic lights and enter a vastly different world.

If you're hiking in the rainy season, another surprise awaits. By hiking the Brooks Creek Trail in winter or spring, you have a chance

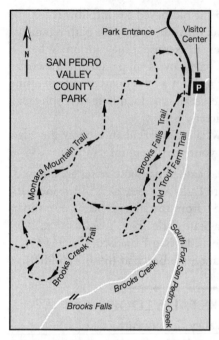

to see one of the Bay Area's prettiest waterfalls—Brooks Falls, a tall, narrow cascade of water that plunges 175 feet in three tiers. From a distance, it looks like one of the majestic tropical waterfalls of Hawaii.

Locate the trailhead for Montara Mountain Trail by the restrooms in San Pedro Valley County Park. A few feet beyond the trailhead, the trail splits: Montara Mountain Trail heads right and Brooks Falls Trail heads left. Go left and gently uphill through a dense grove of eucalyptus. At trail junctions, small signs direct you "to Waterfall Viewing Area." Bear right at two forks, now following Brooks Creek Trail, and keep heading uphill. The well-graded path soon emerges from the trees to open views of the canyon amid coastal sage scrub, ceanothus, and monkeyflower.

Twenty minutes of well-graded climbing delivers your first glimpse of the waterfall, far off in the canyon on your left. Look for a narrow plume of water cascading down the mountainside. Unfortunately, no trails lead to the base of the waterfall; you can only view it from a distance. The best viewpoint is at a conveniently placed bench right along the trail. After a hard rain, you can hear and see the water crashing down the canyon slopes a quarter-mile away. If you want photographs, bring your telephoto lens.

From the manzanita-lined overlook, continue uphill on Brooks Creek Trail, gaining more views of Brooks Falls. The trail tops out on a ridge with an overlook of Pacifica and the ocean to the west and the Marin Headlands to the north. On the clearest days, even the Farallon Islands show up. Montara Mountain Trail takes off from here; to the left and two miles farther is the summit of Montara Mountain (see the previous story). For a three-mile loop, turn right on Montara Mountain Trail and start to descend. You'll drop

500 feet in elevation through more stands of eucalyptus to reach the trailhead and parking area. If you happen to live in Pacifica, you might be able to pick out your house from the suburbs below as you descend.

Keep in mind that Brooks Falls is a seasonal waterfall. This loop trip makes a pleasant hike year-round, but you can view the falls only in the rainy season. If you want to explore more of the park, an excellent four-mile loop can be walked on Hazelnut Trail and Weiler Ranch Road, starting from behind the visitor center.

Trip notes: A $4 day-use fee is charged per vehicle. Dogs and bikes are not allowed on this trail. Bikes are allowed on other trails in the park. Free maps are available at the trailhead or visitor center. For more information, contact San Pedro Valley County Park, 600 Oddstad Boulevard, Pacifica, CA 94044; (650) 355-8289.

75. TIDEPOOL WALK
Fitzgerald Marine Reserve

DISTANCE: Up to 5.0 miles round-trip; 1-2 hours   **LEVEL:** Easy
ELEVATION CHANGE: Negligible   **RATING:** ★ ★ ★ ★
DIRECTIONS: From Half Moon Bay, drive north on Highway 1 for six miles to Moss Beach. Turn left (west) on California Street at the sign for Fitzgerald Marine Reserve. Drive one mile to the reserve parking lot.

There is no trail at Fitzgerald Marine Reserve. When you visit, you may hike a few miles or only a few yards. But no matter how much or how little distance you cover, it's probably going to be the slowest walk of your life.

That's because Fitzgerald Marine Reserve is hands-down the best place in the San Francisco Bay Area to go tidepool hunting. You'll walk at a snail's pace along the rocky reefs, moving inch by inch and keeping a careful eye out for slippery rocks and sneaking waves. With your head bent down, you'll discover colorful sea creatures that are revealed by the departing tide. You may see mussels, crabs, abalones, barnacles, starfish, anemones, snails, and limpets. If you're lucky, you might spot an octopus or a sea urchin.

Fitzgerald Marine Reserve is part of the Monterey Bay National

Fitzgerald Marine Reserve

Marine Sanctuary, the largest marine sanctuary in the United States, which runs along the coast from Marin County to San Simeon. This entire area is federally protected from activities such as oil drilling that would irreparably harm the ecosystem. Within this sanctuary lies a broad, rocky, intertidal reef that runs from Point Montara to Pillar Point. It's one of the largest intertidal reefs in California, and that's the *raison d'être* for the Fitzgerald Marine Reserve.

During the lowest tides of the year, which occur most often in late fall and winter, as much as 30 acres of tidepools are revealed at Fitzgerald Marine Reserve. More than 200 species of marine animals and 150 species of plants are available for observation. This means that nobody walks away disappointed; it's virtually impossible not to ogle an urchin or stare down a starfish. The reserve is a huge hit with children; they love to watch tiny sea creatures scurrying along the bottoms of clear pools. Every kid wants to be the first in their family to spot a limpet or a sculpin or find the prettiest periwinkle. If you have children with you, remember to tell them they may look at and gently touch the creatures, but they may not pick them up or take them out of their environment. Because this is a marine reserve, every rock, plant, shell, and marine animal is protected by law.

To optimize your trip, you must take one step: check the tide chart in the newspaper so that you plan your visit during a low tide, or even better, during a minus tide. With proper planning, you can walk the farthest and see the most.

From the parking lot, a wide trail parallels an ocean-bound creek down to the rocky beach. Head to your left toward Pillar Point in Half Moon Bay, 2.5 miles distant. When the tide is out, you can easily cover this distance, if you don't get too distracted in the first few hundred feet.

As you walk, notice the four central zones of a tidepool area. The first is the low intertidal zone, which is underwater 90 percent of the time, so you get to see its inhabitants only during the lowest tides of the year. This is where the most interesting creatures are: eels, octopus, sea hares, brittle stars, giant keyhole limpets, sculpins, and bat stars. The second area is the middle intertidal zone, which is underwater only 50 percent of the time, so it's in between the low and high tide line. This area has the creatures we usually associate with tide pools: sea stars or starfish, purple sea urchins, sea anemones, gooseneck barnacles, red algae, and mussels.

In the high intertidal zone (underwater only 10 percent of the time), you'll see common acorn barnacles, shore crabs, black tegulas, and hermit crabs. These creatures can live out of water for long periods of time. The final tidepool region is the splash zone, where you'll find rough limpets, snails, and periwinkles.

Sea urchins are uncovered at low tide

Armed with all this knowledge, wander as you wish among the rocks and pools. Or, if you'd prefer to go with a pro, sign up for one of the free night tidepool tours at the reserve. Rangers offer these tours just after dark during fall and winter, when tides are extremely low and you can easily observe nighttime activity on the reefs.

Trip notes: There is no fee. Dogs and bikes are not allowed. For more information, contact Fitzgerald Marine Reserve, P.O. Box 451, Moss Beach, CA 94038; (650) 728-3584.

76. PURISIMA GRAND LOOP
Purisima Creek Redwoods Open Space Preserve

DISTANCE: 10.0 miles round-trip; 5.5 hours   **LEVEL:** Strenuous
ELEVATION CHANGE: 1,600 feet   **RATING:** ★ ★ ★
DIRECTIONS: From San Francisco, drive south on Interstate 280 for 19 miles to the Highway 92 west exit. Go west on Highway 92 for 2.7 miles, then turn left (south) on Highway 35 (Skyline Boulevard). Drive 4.3 miles to the Purisima Creek Redwoods Open Space Preserve parking area on the right, just past a small store.

Purisima Creek Redwoods Open Space Preserve is a hiker's heaven. With breathtaking ocean views, towering redwood and fir trees, a year-round creek, and plentiful wildlife and wildflowers, the preserve shows off some of the best features of the Santa Cruz Mountains. Purisima delivers on its Spanish name—it's pristine.

You can access the 3,200-acre preserve from two trailheads on Skyline Boulevard or one on Higgins Purisima Road in Half Moon Bay. Purisima's trails traverse the slopes between Skyline Ridge and the coast, a 1,600-foot elevation change. Choose any path and you'll have to go up and then down, or down and then up.

This 10-mile loop begins at the preserve's northern entrance on Skyline Boulevard, a mere half-hour drive from San Francisco. This is an "upside down" hike, in which you'll go downhill first, then uphill on your return. Even though it's a relatively mellow ascent, bring plenty of water and snacks to sustain you in the final miles. (If you want to hike the uphill leg first, you could begin the loop at the Higgins Purisima Road trailhead in Half Moon Bay.)

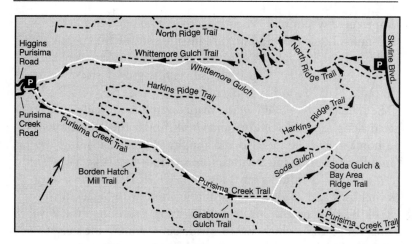

From the Skyline trailhead, follow the single-track, hikers-only trail to the right of the wide fire road. Switchback your way down the trail, enjoying the shade of Douglas firs, tanoaks, and madrones. From February to June, the woodland understory is littered with dense clusters of light blue forget-me-nots. Look down at your feet; it appears as if you are walking amid blue and white clouds.

The narrow trail ends a half-mile out. Turn right on North Ridge Trail, a fir tree-lined fire road, and follow it for a half mile. A left turn on Whittemore Gulch Trail puts you back on single-track. You'll pass through a seasonal gate used for blocking the trail to equestrians and mountain bikers during the wet season, then begin a series of long switchbacks downhill. The path opens out to chaparral-covered slopes with views of Half Moon Bay and the San Mateo coast. A short spur trail leads to an overlook with a railing to lean on; the coast vista is widest from here.

Continue descending and meet up with Whittemore Gulch, a seasonal tributary to Purisima Creek. Whittemore Gulch Trail follows the gulch downhill; the path bottoms out in a beautiful redwood and Douglas fir forest. Big-leaf maples grow in the understory of the conifers; their leaves turn bright yellow in the fall. You may want to linger in this lovely creekside woodland.

At 3.8 miles from the trailhead, you reach the trail's end and two junctions. Bypass Harkins Ridge Trail on the left and continue across the bridge over Purisima Creek to join Purisima Creek Trail. (The Higgins Purisima Road trailhead is located 100 feet west.)

Wide, redwood-lined Purisima Creek Trail climbs practically

imperceptibly alongside Purisima Creek, gaining only 400 feet in 2.3 miles. Large redwood stumps are interspersed among the young redwoods, giving you a hint of what this forest looked like before it was logged in the late 1800s. Purisima's first-growth trees were used to build Half Moon Bay and San Francisco after the Gold Rush. The trail itself is an old logging road; seven lumber mills once operated along the banks of Purisima Creek. Today the stream canyon is home to a variety of ferns and a multitude of banana slugs. Its middle reaches are lined with impressive redwood deadfall.

Two miles from its start, Purisima Creek Trail makes a long switchback and heads northward to junction with Soda Gulch Trail. Bear left on this hikers-only pathway, a section of the Bay Area Ridge Trail, which makes a wide curve around the steep slopes of Soda Gulch. You'll traverse both sides of the canyon, crossing several smaller ravines on footbridges. Some of the tallest redwoods found in the preserve grow in the fertile soil around Soda Gulch.

As the trail gains elevation, the redwood canopy gives way to mixed hardwoods and chaparral-covered slopes. Soda Gulch Trail's last mile offers occasional inspiring views of the Santa Cruz Mountains and distant Pacific Ocean. At a junction with Harkins Ridge Trail, turn right and hike the final 1.4 miles back to the trailhead. In the last half-mile, you can turn right on North Ridge Trail or cross North Ridge and take the single-track trail you began the day on.

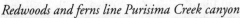
Redwoods and ferns line Purisima Creek canyon

Trip notes: There is no fee. Dogs are not allowed. Bikes are allowed on some trails. Free trail maps are available at the trailhead. For more information, contact the Midpeninsula Regional Open Space District, 330 Distel Circle, Los Altos, CA 94022; (650) 691-1200. Website: www.openspace.org

77. TAFONI & FIR TRAIL LOOP
El Corte de Madera Open Space Preserve

DISTANCE: 6.0 miles round-trip; 3 hours **LEVEL:** Easy

ELEVATION CHANGE: 600 feet **RATING:** ★ ★ ★

DIRECTIONS: From San Francisco, drive south on Interstate 280 for 19 miles to the Highway 92 west exit. Go west on Highway 92 for 2.7 miles, then turn left (south) on Highway 35 (Skyline Boulevard). Drive 8.5 miles to the Skeggs Vista Point parking area on your left. (It's 1.6 miles south of the intersection with Kings Mountain Road and 3.8 miles north of Skylonda.) You can't turn left into the parking area; you must drive farther south and find a safe place to make a U-turn. After parking, walk 50 yards north on Skyline and cross the road to access Tafoni Trail. Or, continue 0.4 miles south on Skyline from Skeggs Vista Point to the small parking area on the west side of the road. From there, begin hiking on Sierra Morena Trail.

The main attraction of the 2,800-acre El Corte de Madera Open Space Preserve is the monolithic sandstone formations at the end of the Tafoni Trail. Similar in appearance to the rock outcrops at nearby Castle Rock State Park (see the story on page 259), the sandstone at El Corte de Madera is composed of a softer, more fragile substance. You won't find any rock climbers here.

The formations stand completely alone in the forest; they're unlike anything else you see along the trail. The rest of the preserve is primarily trees and more trees, including some magnificent old Douglas firs and younger redwoods. You hike through acres of forest, then suddenly they appear—huge sandstone beasts looming 50 feet high. Just as suddenly, there are no more of them, just dense trees again. It's as if Mother Nature told the delivery company to drop the sandstone off at the wrong location.

The preserve has several access points along Skyline Boulevard; unfortunately, most of them don't have ample parking. The two best parking areas are at Caltrans' Skeggs Vista Point, where there is a paved lot on the east side of the road, or a half-mile farther south, where there is parking for about 10 cars on the west side of the road. The latter trailhead has immediate access to the preserve's Sierra Morena Trail. From Skeggs Point, you must walk north along Skyline Boulevard for about 50 yards, then cross the road to access Tafoni Trail at a gated dirt road.

This six-mile figure-eight loop combines stints on Tafoni Trail, El Corte de Madera Creek Trail, Resolution Trail, and Fir Trail. The following description starts on Tafoni Trail; if you are beginning from the southern trailhead, take Sierra Morena Trail north (right) to Fir Trail, then turn right and join the start of Tafoni Trail. This will add an extra 1.2 miles to your round-trip.

Hike on a gentle uphill grade through big Douglas firs for the first 1.2 miles on Tafoni Trail. At a four-way junction, turn sharply right to head to the sandstone formations. In just a few hundred yards, you'll reach a sign announcing the "tafoni" ahead. Turn right on a single-track path (this is the only trail in the preserve that is reserved for hikers only) and descend to the 50-foot-high outcrops. Following steep use paths, you can circle around the big rocks and explore their nooks and crannies. Be careful not to touch the sandstone; the pressure of human hands speeds erosion.

Looking up at the sandstone monoliths

Although it sounds like an Italian dessert, tafoni is a type of sandstone that is formed by years of weathering. A unique combination of coastal fog, tectonic upthrust, and sandstone cliffs provide the right ingredients for tafoni. The "glue" that holds the sandstone's indi-

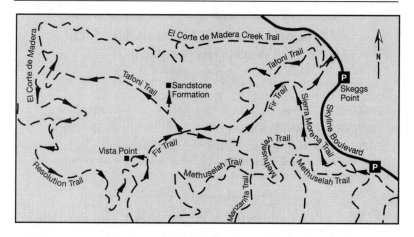

vidual sand grains together eventually erodes away, leaving honeycomb patterned, lace-like crevices and holes in the smooth rock.

After visiting the outcrops, retrace your steps back uphill to Tafoni Trail and continue northwest. The old logging road continues for another mile in oak and fir forest to El Corte de Madera Creek Trail. Turn left and head mostly downhill for nine-tenths of a mile, paralleling a seasonal creek in the final stretch. Turn left on Resolution Trail and follow it for just over a mile, climbing gradually among some good-sized redwoods. Among the second-growth trees, you'll see burned-out stumps left from logging days.

After you've gained a few hundred feet in elevation, you'll emerge from the forest into chaparral. At a sizeable clearing, Resolution Trail meets up with Fir Trail; turn left and then left again on the spur path signed for Vista Point. This ridgetop site offers a nice view of the coast and a level, open area for picnicking, in abrupt contrast to the dense woods you've been hiking in. The ocean vista is somewhat obstructed by foliage; in another decade it may be completely obliterated.

When you rejoin the main Fir Trail, it's only 1.1 miles farther to the Tafoni trailhead or 0.9 miles to the turnoff for Sierra Morena Trail and the southern parking area.

Trip notes: There is no fee. Dogs are not allowed. Bikes are allowed on fire roads only. Free trail maps are available at the trailhead. For more information, contact the Midpeninsula Regional Open Space District, 330 Distel Circle, Los Altos, CA 94022; (650) 691-1200. Website: www.openspace.org

78. BEAR GULCH & ALAMBIQUE LOOP
Wunderlich County Park

DISTANCE: 5.4 miles round-trip; 2.5 hours   **LEVEL:** Easy

ELEVATION CHANGE: 600 feet   **RATING:** ★ ★

DIRECTIONS: From Interstate 280 at Woodside, take the Highway 84 west exit. Drive west for 2.5 miles, through Woodside, to the park entrance on the right. (The sign is small and easy to miss.)

Wunderlich is wonderful in the springtime. This San Mateo County park is a mix of redwoods, Douglas firs, creeks, meadows, wildflowers, and windings trails, ideally suited for either short walks or long day-hikes. Located just a few minutes from the tony community of Woodside and Interstate 280, Wunderlich Park is an easy getaway for anyone living or working on the Peninsula.

The park's German name comes from its last private owner, a contractor named Martin Wunderlich, who deeded the land to San Mateo County in 1974. Prior to Wunderlich's ownership, the land belonged to the James A. Folger family of coffee fame.

Wunderlich is especially popular with runners, who appreciate the smooth, easy grades of its trails. Equestrians also share the paths; bicyclists and dogs are not allowed. The following loop tour circles the eastern half of the park.

Start your trip on the wide dirt road to the left of the stables, signed as Bear Gulch Trail. A bunch of easy switchbacks on Bear Gulch Trail lead you uphill through a mixed forest of black oaks, bay laurel, madrones, Douglas fir, and shrub-like California hazelnut. A half-mile from the trailhead, you enter a second-growth redwood forest and soon reach Redwood Flat, near the park border and Bear Gulch Road.

Follow Bear Gulch Trail for another eight-tenths of a mile to The Meadows, elevation 1,430 feet, the high point on this loop. The Meadows is a pleasant, sunny clearing, where you could easily while away an afternoon with a blanket and a book. Contrary to its name, this isn't an area of grasslands. Ceanothus, coyote brush, and Scotch broom have taken over.

From The Meadows, continue on Bear Gulch Trail, now start-

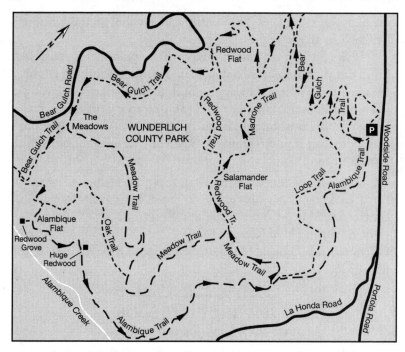

ing to descend. Where Bear Gulch Trail joins Alambique Trail at Alambique Flat, watch for a spur trail on the right. The spur leads 50 feet to a lovely redwood grove along Alambique Creek. This is the most tranquil and inviting spot yet. Stay a while and savor the sound of the creek and the peace of the big trees.

Returning to the junction of Alambique and Bear Gulch trails, follow wide Alambique Trail downhill. In less than a half mile, you'll pass by a huge virgin redwood right alongside the dirt road, on your left. It's at least 12 feet in diameter.

While you consider why the loggers chose to spare this particular tree, continue downhill, now coming closer to the steep canyon of Alambique Creek. At a junction with Meadow Trail, an old ranch road, turn left.

Follow this wide road through a eucalyptus grove to Redwood Trail. Not surprisingly, the forest changes to redwoods. Where the trail reaches Salamander Flat, a dense grove of big trees, you'll find an old reservoir remaining from this land's ranching days. Why is it called Salamander Flat? Because the reservoir now serves as a major breeding ground for California newts every winter.

Bear right on level Madrone Trail to return to Bear Gulch Trail, the path you started on. Then backtrack downhill on those many switchbacks all the way to your car.

If you just remembered an important appointment, you could finish out your loop on Alambique Trail instead of turning left on Meadow Trail. This will bring you back to the trailhead in less time (it's a mile shorter). The trail offers some nice views of the South Bay, including the obvious landmark of Hoover Tower at Stanford University, but it suffers from too much car noise from nearby La Honda Road.

Trip notes: There is no fee. Dogs and bikes are not allowed. A free trail map is available at the trailhead. For more information, contact San Mateo County Parks and Recreation, 455 County Center, Fourth Floor, Redwood City, CA 94063; (650) 363-4020. Or contact neighboring Huddart Park at (650) 851-1210 or (650) 851-0326.

---

79. WINDY HILL LOOP
Windy Hill Open Space Preserve

DISTANCE: 8.0 miles round-trip; 4 hours   **LEVEL:** Moderate
ELEVATION CHANGE: 1,100 feet   **RATING:** ★ ★ ★
DIRECTIONS: From Interstate 280 at Woodside, take Highway 84 west for 6.5 miles to its junction with Highway 35 (Skyline Boulevard). Turn left (south) on Skyline and drive 2.2 miles to the main Windy Hill Open Space entrance on the left. (There are picnic tables at the trailhead.)

Or, from Interstate 280 in Palo Alto, take the Page Mill Road exit west. Drive 8.9 winding miles to Skyline Boulevard (Highway 35). Turn right (north) on Skyline and drive 4.9 miles to the main Windy Hill Open Space entrance on the right. (There are picnic tables at the trailhead.)

Windy Hill Open Space Preserve is best known to two kinds of people: those who love easy-to-reach, panoramic views and those who fly kites. The former includes dog-walkers and sunset watchers who set out on the three-quarter-mile Anniversary Trail for an easy walk with fine views of the Peninsula and South Bay. The latter includes hang gliders, paragliders, remote-control airplane fliers, and your basic kid with a five-dollar kite, all of whom are drawn to the near-constant updrafts on Windy Hill.

The Anniversary Trail and the high, grassy summit of Windy Hill are well worth a visit on any clear day. But after you walk the short path and admire the 360-degree view from the top of Windy Hill (which includes the Pacific Ocean and even San Francisco on high visibility days), you'll be primed for further exploration in the preserve. The eight-mile Windy Hill Loop is just the ticket.

The loop trail provides some of the same wide vistas of the Peninsula as the short Anniversary Trail, but also includes long stints through fir and oak forests on a lovely single-track path. Windy Hill Loop is best hiked in a clockwise direction, following the trails in this order: Hamms Gulch Trail, Eagle Trail, Razorback Ridge Trail, Lost Trail. Note that dogs are allowed on Hamms Gulch Trail, Eagle Trail, and the short Anniversary Trail, but not on the other legs of the loop.

Starting at the picnic area, follow the connector trail to the right (the Anniversary Trail leads left). The path roughly parallels Skyline Boulevard as it travels through chaparral for just under a half mile. A well-placed bench affords wide views of the valley.

At the first trail junction, turn left on Hamms Gulch Trail and bid farewell to road noise and other signs of civilization. Hamms Gulch Trail, an old road, travels through a forest of tanoaks, firs, and madrones as it heads gently downhill, losing 1,100 feet in 2.6 miles. The immense Douglas fir trees shading the trail are a sight to

Lichens, moss, and ferns cover the slopes of Hamms Gulch in Windy Hill

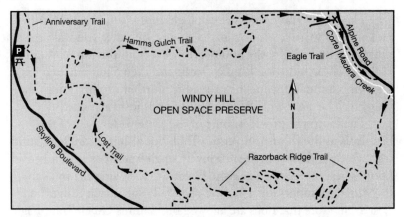

behold—some are as large as eight feet in diameter. A few branches are large enough to be individual trees. In spring, the woodland understory is lined with trillium, hounds-tongue, and milkmaids.

The trail bottoms out near Corte Madera Creek and the gated entrance to Rancho Corte Madera, a private inholding within the preserve. Cross its driveway and bridge and pick up Eagle Trail, which runs in between Corte Madera Creek and Alpine Road. This six-tenths of a mile stretch is the least appealing leg of the loop, due to the proximity of the road and several private homes. Corte Madera Creek is a pleasant distraction in the wet season.

A short stint on Alpine Road, then a bridge crossing on a dirt road, puts you on Razorback Ridge Trail. Head into a well-graded climb through numerous switchbacks under a high forest canopy of oaks and madrones. This 2.3-mile stretch gains nearly 1,000 feet, but the gradient is so mellow that you hardly notice you're climbing. Where the trail nears Skyline Boulevard, turn right on Lost Trail, still gently ascending through the forest. In between the trees you gain peek-a-boo views of the valley below.

Where Lost Trail junctions with Hamms Gulch Trail at the start of your loop, continue straight on the connector trail back to Windy Hill's parking lot.

Trip notes: There is no fee. Dogs are allowed on some trails, but not on the entire Windy Hill Loop. Bikes are not allowed. Free trail maps are available at the trailhead. For more information, contact the Midpeninsula Regional Open Space District, 330 Distel Circle, Los Altos, CA 94022; (650) 691-1200. Website: www.openspace.org

80. RUSSIAN RIDGE LOOP

Russian Ridge Open Space Preserve

DISTANCE: 4.4 miles round-trip; 2 hours   **LEVEL:** Easy

ELEVATION CHANGE: 550 feet   **RATING:** ★ ★ ★

DIRECTIONS: From Interstate 280 in Palo Alto, take the Page Mill Road exit west. Drive 8.9 winding miles to Skyline Boulevard (Highway 35). Cross Skyline Boulevard to Alpine Road. Drive 200 feet on Alpine Road and turn right into the Russian Ridge entrance.

Russian Ridge Open Space Preserve is more than 1,500 acres of windswept ridgetop paradise. We're talking location, location, location, as in directly off Skyline Boulevard (Highway 35), near the well-to-do town of Woodside. The weather may be foggy along the coast, but the sun is usually shining brightly on Skyline. From the preserve's 2,300-foot elevation, you can look out and above the layer of fog blanketing the ocean. What pleasure to appreciate its cotton candy appearance without being stuck in the thick of it.

In spring, Russian Ridge will charm you with colorful wild-flowers and verdant grasslands. In summer and fall, the hillsides turn to gold and the grasses sway in unison to the ridgetop winds. On the rare days of winter when snow dusts this ridge, you can pull out your cross-country skis and glide along the slopes! On a clear day in any season, you'll be wowed by the vistas from 2,572-foot Borel Hill, the highest named point in San Mateo County.

Although many people visit this preserve for the views, Russian Ridge offers much more. Its acreage combines several plant environments, including lush grasslands, creeks, springs, and oak-shaded canyons. It is home to substantial wildlife, including a variety of raptors, coyotes, and mountain lions. Most impressive are the spring

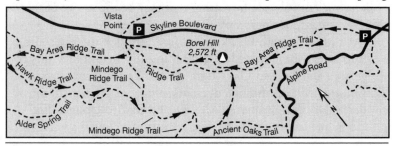

Mule's ears in Russian Ridge Open Space Preserve

wildflowers. Every April and May, the grasslands explode in a fire-works display of colorful mule's ears, poppies, lupine, goldfields, johnny jump-ups, and blue-eyed grass. Russian Ridge is considered to be one of the best places in the Bay Area to see wildflowers.

This 4.4-mile loop circles the park. Take the Bay Area Ridge Trail uphill from the parking lot, heading for the top of grassy Borel Hill in less than a mile. (Stay right at two junctions.) The 2,572-foot summit of Borel Hill is just high enough to provide a 360-degree view of the South Bay, Skyline Ridge, and all the way west to the Pacific Ocean. Mount Diablo looms in the eastern horizon and Mount Tamalpais guards the north. This has to be one of the most inspiring lookouts on the Peninsula.

From the summit, descend gently for a half-mile to a major junction of trails near Skyline Boulevard. Bear left on Mindego Ridge Trail, then shortly turn right on Bay Area Ridge Trail. Ridge Trail narrows, curving around grassy knolls and offering more views of the coast and the bay. To the southwest you can see Mindego Hill, an ancient volcanic formation that may be the source of this ridge's scattered rock outcrops.

At a junction with Hawk Ridge Trail, turn left to head south-east and start your loop back. Descend to the junction of Mindego Ridge Trail and Ancient Oaks Trail, then follow Ancient Oaks Trail. This short trail leads through a remarkable forest of gnarled, moss-covered oak trees interspersed with equally gnarled Douglas firs, plus some madrones and ferns. You may want to linger a while in this strange, enchanted woodland, at least long enough to climb a few trees. Then turn left at the next junction and cruise back out into the sunlight to rejoin Bay Area Ridge Trail. Watch for a wooden bench along this open stretch that is nearly overwhelmed by bright orange California poppies in spring. A plaque on its side reads: "There is great peace in this natural beauty. We must all help to preserve it."

Trip notes: There is no fee. Dogs are not allowed. Bikes are allowed. Free trail maps are available at the trailhead. For more information, contact the Midpeninsula Regional Open Space District, 330 Distel Circle, Los Altos, CA 94022; (650) 691-1200. Website: www.openspace.org

81. BLACK MOUNTAIN & STEVENS CREEK LOOP
Monte Bello Open Space Preserve

DISTANCE: 6.0 miles round-trip; 3 hours   **LEVEL:** Moderate

ELEVATION CHANGE: 1,300 feet   **RATING:** ★ ★ ★

DIRECTIONS: From Interstate 280 in Palo Alto, take the Page Mill Road exit west. Drive 7.2 winding miles on Page Mill Road to the signed preserve entrance on the left.

Or, from the junction of highways 35 and 9 at Saratoga Gap, drive six miles north on Highway 35 (Skyline Boulevard). Turn right on Page Mill Road and drive 1.7 miles to the preserve entrance on the right.

People who live on the Peninsula are well acquainted with 2,800-foot Black Mountain, the peak that forms a rounded green backdrop for the communities around Palo Alto. The town of Mountain View was named for its vista of the verdant peak. It's always there, anchoring the background of the lives of thousands.

Black Mountain doesn't have a singular peaked summit; rather it's the highest point on long and narrow Monte Bello Ridge. It's also the most prominent feature of Monte Bello Open Space Preserve, a park that displays a lovely mix of grasslands, conifers, and chaparral. This six-mile loop trip tours Monte Bello and pays a visit to the summit of Black Mountain.

Begin you hike at the preserve's main entrance on Stevens Creek Nature Trail. The path leads a level few hundred feet to a

Rock outcrops on Black Mountain's summit

stone bench and overlook. There you gaze at the source of Stevens Creek, which follows the San Andreas fault zone. Mount Umunhum appears far in the distance.

Take the left fork in the nature trail, heading to Canyon Trail in three-tenths of a mile. Turn right on wide Canyon Trail, walk two-tenths of a mile, then leave that road for the mountain bikers and bear left on Bella Vista Trail. A wide single-track trail, Bella Vista Trail climbs steadily but moderately and offers lovely views over the Stevens Creek canyon. Contouring along grassy slopes, the trail provides excellent opportunities for spotting wildlife. We watched a coyote gallop across the grasslands while two curious deer watched us. During the autumn mating season, large herds of deer are often seen in this preserve.

After almost a mile of climbing, you've nearly reached the ridgetop. Bear right on Old Ranch Trail and in a half mile you come to Black Mountain Backpack Camp, the only campground in the Midpeninsula Regional Open Space District. Four family campsites and one group campsite are available for backpackers who have obtained a permit from the district office. You must pack in your own water and camp stove; no fires are permitted. Oddly, the camp has one modern amenity: a pay telephone.

Walk around the camp and join Monte Bello Road in a few hundred feet. It's only a quarter-mile to the microwave-covered summit of Black Mountain, elevation 2,800 feet even. Black Mountain Trail intersects with Monte Bello Road at the summit. This popular trail is for hikers and equestrians only. Starting from the Duveneck Windmill Pasture Area of Rancho San Antonio Open Space Preserve, it's an eight-mile round-trip to the summit with a 2,300-foot elevation gain.

From Black Mountain's summit, you have a wide view of the Peninsula and Santa Clara valley. But the lovelier view is to the west. To see it best, follow Monte Bello Road for another 150 feet, then exit the trail on the right near an odd marker: a 15-mile-per-hour speed limit sign. Here, at a fascinating outcrop of scattered rocks, is the best picnic site and finest view of the day. Stevens Creek canyon lies below you. Untrammeled grassland hills spread to the north and south along Skyline Ridge. In springtime, blue-eyed grass, checkerbloom, farewell-to-spring, and California poppies bloom in the hilltop grasses. It's time to throw down your pack and have lunch.

After admiring the view, backtrack to just before the camp and bear left on Indian Creek Trail. You'll face a steep downhill on the ranch road with lovely views of Indian Creek canyon. (Be sure to take the short spur trail on the left with more views of the densely forested canyon.) Hiking through chaparral, toyon, and lichen-covered oaks, descend 1.2 miles to Canyon Trail. Bear right, walk a quarter mile, then turn left on Stevens Creek Nature Trail.

Soon you'll cross a footbridge over Stevens Creek and travel alongside the stream. Ferns, Douglas firs, and oaks line the banks of Stevens Creek. This lush riparian area is in extreme contrast to the open grasslands of Black Mountain. After crossing two more footbridges, bear right to stay on Stevens Creek Nature Trail, now on single-track.

The final 1.2 miles of the trip are an easy, streamside ascent with plenty of shade and switchbacks. You'll climb out of the stream canyon, head back into the grasslands, and wind up right back at the stone bench and overlook where you began the hike. Turn left to walk back to your car.

Trip notes: There is no fee. Dogs are not allowed. Bikes are allowed. Free trail maps are available at the trailhead. For more information, contact the Midpeninsula Regional Open Space District, 330 Distel Circle, Los Altos, CA 94022; (650) 691-1200. Website: www.openspace.org

82. PETER'S CREEK & LONG RIDGE LOOP
Long Ridge Open Space Preserve

DISTANCE: 4.6 miles round-trip; 2 hours   **LEVEL:** Easy

ELEVATION CHANGE: 400 feet   **RATING:** ★ ★ ★

DIRECTIONS: From Interstate 280 in Palo Alto, take the Page Mill Road exit west. Drive 8.9 winding miles to Skyline Boulevard (Highway 35). Turn left on Skyline Boulevard and drive 4.8 miles to the Long Ridge/ Grizzly Flat parking area on the left. The trail is located across the road.

Or, from Saratoga, take Highway 9 west to its junction with Skyline Boulevard. Turn right on Skyline and drive 3.2 miles to the Long Ridge/ Grizzly Flat parking area on the right. The trail is located across the road.

Long Ridge Open Space is a peaceful 2,000-acre preserve along Skyline Boulevard near Saratoga Gap. Its hiking, biking, and equestrian trails are perfect in all seasons—warm and windy in summer, crisp and golden in autumn, fern-laden and mossy in winter, and gilded with wildflowers in spring.

From the Grizzly Flat trailhead, only one pathway enters Long Ridge. It's the start of Peter's Creek Trail, which soon junctions with the Bay Area Ridge Trail. The latter makes a tight switchback and heads north; you'll continue straight on Peter's Creek Trail. Once you get moving, the sight and sound of Skyline Boulevard quickly disappear as the trail drops below the road and into a pristine canyon of grasslands and forest. Fields of wildflowers and rolling grasses in the foreground are framed by a forest of Douglas firs and oaks ahead. Some people walk only as far as this first open meadow, spread out a picnic, then head home.

At a junction with Long Ridge Trail, turn left to stay on Peter's Creek Trail and begin a gentle ascent through oaks, firs, and bay laurel. Babbling Peter's Creek, a major tributary of Pescadero Creek, meanders along at your side. Ferns and moss-covered boulders line the stream. Woodland wildflowers include tiny two-eyed violets (heart-shaped leaves with white and purple flowers) and purple shooting stars.

The trail wanders in and out of meadows and forest, passing an old apple orchard and ranch site. The trees still bear delicious apples in autumn; in winter, their bare branches are lined with a shaggy, grey-green lichen. At 1.6 miles, you'll reach a small pond with huge reeds and a sea of horsetails growing around its edges. Watch for pond turtles sunning themselves. On the far side of the pond is private property belonging to the Jikoji Buddhist retreat center.

The spring flower show continues as you hike. Look for brodiaea, columbine, wild roses, blue-eyed grass, white irises, poppies, lupine, and huge ceanothus bushes with sprays of blue flowers. The variety of species is remarkable.

A few switchbacks lead you to the top of the ridge, where you meet up with Long Ridge Road. At this 2,500-foot elevation, expansive views are yours for the taking. Turn right on Long Ridge Road and traipse along, oohing and aahing at the panorama of neighboring Butano Ridge and the forests of the Pescadero Creek watershed. Be sure to pause at the bench commemorating Pulitzer prize-winning author Wallace Stegner, who lived in this area and aided in the conservation of Long Ridge.

After this sunny, view-filled stint, take Long Ridge Trail back into the forest to finish out the loop. The path makes a wide circle around to the north and then east, then reconnects with the start of Peter's Creek Trail.

Long Ridge's trails are multi-use; you may share your trip with mountain bikers or equestrians. If that concerns you, wait until the rainy season to visit, when the Open Space District closes the trails to everyone but hikers. The preserve is at its finest then anyway; the best time to visit is on a clear winter day soon after a rainstorm.

Long Ridge's sunny, exposed ridgeline

Trip notes: There is no fee. Dogs are not allowed. Bikes are allowed. Free trail maps are available at the trailhead. For more information, contact Midpeninsula Regional Open Space District, 330 Distel Circle, Los Altos, CA 94022; (650) 691-1200. Website: www.openspace.org

83. JONES GULCH & BROOK TRAIL LOOP
Pescadero Creek County Park

DISTANCE: 10.0 miles round-trip; 6 hours   **LEVEL:** Moderate

ELEVATION CHANGE: 1,000 feet   **RATING:** ★ ★ ★

DIRECTIONS: From Interstate 280 at Woodside, take Highway 84 west for 13 winding miles to La Honda. Turn left (southeast) on Pescadero Road and drive one mile, then bear right to stay on Pescadero Road. Continue 4.2 miles farther to Wurr Road on the left. (It's a quarter-mile before the entrance to Memorial County Park.) Turn left and drive a quarter-mile to the Hoffman Creek Trailhead.

Or, from Highway 1 at Pescadero, turn east on Pescadero Road and drive 9.8 miles. Turn right at the second entrance to Wurr Road, a quarter-mile past the entrance to Memorial Park. Drive a quarter-mile to the Hoffman Creek Trailhead.

They call it the Pescadero Creek Park Complex—three side-by-side county parks in the stream- and redwood-studded canyons south of La Honda. Accessible only by long, winding country roads from either the coast or the Peninsula, the three county parks—Memorial, Pescadero Creek, and Sam McDonald—are a piece of hiking heaven. Because the parks are contiguous, few people even realize when they've left one and entered another.

Of the three parks, Pescadero Creek is the largest, covering 6,500 acres. Bordered to the north and west by Memorial and Sam McDonald county parks and to the east by Portola State Park, Pescadero Creek Park isn't set on a major road. Its two trailheads are located off quiet side streets. The park doesn't have family or group campgrounds, only a couple of backpacking camps, so it gets missed by a lot of people. Its peaceful trails are perfect for a day-hike in the redwoods. For sun-lovers, the park also has meadows and ridges with open views.

This 10-mile loop begins at the park's western trailhead, Hoffman Creek, located off Wurr Road near Memorial Park. Purchase a park map at Memorial Park or Sam McDonald Park; the loop has numerous junctions. (Fortunately, the trails are well signed.) Be forewarned that if you're hiking in the rainy season, you'll need to make two unbridged stream crossings to complete the loop. Prepare to take off your shoes and socks. If Pescadero Creek is running high, these fords could be potentially dangerous, so use good judgment. Still, the wet season is the best time for this trip, when equestrians are barred from most of its single-track stretches and the neighboring parks' campgrounds are deserted.

From the Hoffman Creek Trailhead, head east on Old Haul Road through a recently logged redwood forest. The trail is bordered by private property in the first half mile. Bear left where the wide road forks, following the sign for Pomponio Trail. Here, just 20 minutes from the trailhead, you'll face your first crossing of Pescadero Creek. If the bridge is in place, you're in luck. If not, be ready for cold ankles.

After replacing your shoes and socks, continue on the wide road on the far side of the stream. Watch for a sign directing you to the right on Pomponio Trail. (The left fork is not shown on the park map; it's private property.) The single-track path will lead you to Worley Flat, a large meadow dotted with a few oaks.

Continue on well-signed Pomponio Trail through an oak forest and downhill to Jones Gulch Creek. Turn left on Jones Gulch Trail. Although you could bypass this stretch to shorten the trip by two miles, don't miss a little exploration in Jones Gulch, heading up one side of the ravine and then down the other. The gorgeous redwood forest is worth the effort. Narrow Jones Gulch Trail meanders among the big trees and passes by the stream's musical cascades. A short stint brings you to an open clearing, then a bridge crossing over deep Jones Gulch. On the far side, the trail widens again; turn sharply right to backtrack down the east slope. A highlight of Jones Gulch is Granger's Bridge, near the confluence of Jones Gulch and Towne Creek. Be sure to pause at this beautiful spot and admire the small waterfall just 20 feet upstream of the bridge. The narrow, deep canyon is carved from sandstone and lined with five-finger ferns.

Where Jones Gulch Trail ends, join Brook Trail Loop. At a three-way junction, where Pomponio Trail and Brook Trail each have left and right options, turn left on Brook Trail. This is the formal start of Brook Trail Loop, and from here on out there are fewer junctions to negotiate.

Departing Towne Creek canyon, the path's many easy switchbacks lead you uphill through large and small redwoods. The amount of old-growth in this canyon is surprising; perhaps the loggers left the trees because it would have been too difficult to haul the lumber out.

The ascent bring you out of the redwoods and into a mixed forest of oaks and Douglas firs. You'll near Towne Fire Road and the horse camp in Sam McDonald County Park. Brook Trail Loop

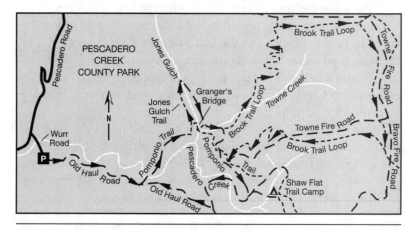

Fallen redwood in Jones Gulch

parallels the fire road for a long, scenic stretch with many open views of the park's forested canyons and Butano Ridge. Where the trail crosses Towne Fire Road, you could shave a little distance off the trip by following the fire road three-quarters of a mile to Brook Trail's next crossing. Thereafter Brook Trail makes a long series of downhill switchbacks. These deposit you back in the redwoods in one of the finest groves of the day.

Too soon you leave Brook Trail Loop and follow Towne Fire Road back to Pescadero Creek. This requires a second crossing; if you're lucky, the seasonal bridge will be in place. Another quarter-mile brings you back to Old Haul Road. Turn right and walk out the last two miles to the trailhead. You'll pass many enormous redwood stumps along the way.

If you get confused at any junctions on the return trip, just follow the signs pointing to Memorial Ranger Station (not the signs pointing to McDonald Ranger Station!). These will lead you back to the Old Haul Road and eventually to your car.

Trip notes: There is no fee at the Hoffman Creek Trailhead. Dogs are not allowed. Bikes are allowed on fire roads only. A park map is available for $1 at Memorial or Sam McDonald county park ranger stations. For more information, contact San Mateo County Parks and Recreation, 455 County Center, Fourth Floor, Redwood City, CA 94063; (650) 363-4020 or Memorial Park Visitor Center at (650) 879-0212.

84. HERITAGE GROVE & HIKER'S HUT LOOP

Sam McDonald County Park

DISTANCE: 5.0 miles round-trip; 2.5 hours   **LEVEL:** Easy

ELEVATION CHANGE: 600 feet   **RATING:** ★ ★ ★

DIRECTIONS: From Interstate 280 at Woodside, take Highway 84 west for 13 winding miles to La Honda. Turn left (southeast) on Pescadero Road and drive 1.8 miles to Sam McDonald County Park on the right. (Bear right after the first mile to stay on Pescadero Road.) The trail begins across the parking lot from the ranger station.

If you've ever taken the tortuous drive on Alpine Road between Portola State Park Road and La Honda, you've seen some of the marvelous first-growth redwoods of the Heritage Grove. The big trees are so enchanting that it makes the snaking, serpentine road a pleasure. After all, you don't want to drive fast through these giants.

To see them at an even slower pace, take this five-mile loop hike at Sam McDonald County Park. From the main parking lot, take the Big Tree Trail across from the ranger station. The path leads through tall redwoods and across Pescadero Road (use caution in crossing). After merging with and then departing from Towne Fire Road, Big Tree Trail begins a gentle uphill with many switchbacks and wooden stairsteps, passing the well-named Big Tree. It then curves around to the west to join Heritage Grove Trail. (Don't miss this turnoff or you'll loop right back to Pescadero Road).

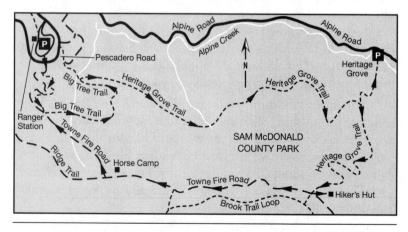

Sierra Club Hiker's Hut in Sam McDonald County Park

Take Heritage Grove Trail east for 1.2 miles to the Heritage Grove turnoff. The path leads through a forest of mostly Douglas firs with a few redwoods among them. On clear days, sunlight filters through the trees and cascades down the hillside. On rainy days, you'll have the pleasure of staying nearly dry underneath the dense forest canopy.

Follow the trail to the left all the way downhill to near Alpine Road and wander among the big trees growing along Alpine Creek. These 37 acres of virgin redwoods were scheduled to be logged in the early 1970s, but were saved by a group of citizen activists who raised funds to purchase the grove. After admiring the giant trees, backtrack uphill and take the opposite fork of Heritage Grove Trail.

The trail tops out at a big open meadow and Towne Fire Road. Look for the single-track spur trail on your left signed for Hiker's Hut, only 150 yards away. Amid huge Douglas firs and ridgetop chaparral and grasslands, you'll find the Sierra Club Hiker's Hut. Run by the Loma Prieta Chapter of the Sierra Club, this inviting A-frame building is open to the public and available for rent. It holds up to 14 people at the low cost of $10 per person per night. (Sierra Club members receive a discount.) The Hiker's Hut has a full kitchen, electricity, a wood stove, a big deck with a picnic table out front, and best of all, a view of the Pescadero Creek canyon and the coast from its backyard on Towne Ridge.

(To reserve the Hiker's Hut, phone 650/390-8411 or 650/390-8494. If you don't have at least six people in your party, you may have to share the hut with others on Friday and Saturday nights in summer and fall. The rest of the year, the place is all yours no matter how small your group is.)

Retrace your steps on the spur trail to Towne Fire Road, then head west (right). In less than a mile, you'll pass an equestrian camp. Turn right just beyond it and follow Towne Fire Road downhill. It leads all the way back to Pescadero Road, but a more scenic option is to take Towne Fire Road to its junction with Big Tree Trail, then take either fork of the Big Tree Trail back to the ranger station.

Trip notes: A $4 day-use fee is charged per vehicle. Dogs and bikes are not allowed. A park map is available for $1 at the ranger station. For more information, contact San Mateo County Parks and Recreation, 455 County Center, Fourth Floor, Redwood City, CA 94063; (650) 363-4020 or Memorial Park Visitor Center at (650) 879-0212.

85. MOUNT ELLEN & POMPONIO TRAIL LOOP
Memorial County Park

DISTANCE: 4.0 miles round-trip; 2 hours   **LEVEL:** Easy
ELEVATION CHANGE: 450 feet   **RATING:** ★ ★ ★
DIRECTIONS: From Interstate 280 at Woodside, take Highway 84 west for 13 winding miles to La Honda. Turn left (southeast) on Pescadero Road and drive one mile, then bear right to stay on Pescadero Road. Continue 4.5 miles farther to the entrance to Memorial County Park on the left. The trail begins across the road from the entrance station.

At an elevation of less than 700 feet, Mount Ellen isn't the kind of summit you brag about climbing. But if you're camping at Memorial County Park or just looking for a leg-stretching hike in a quiet forest, the Mount Ellen and Pomponio Trail Loop makes a perfect two-hour walk.

From the entrance station at Memorial County Park, cross Pescadero Road to access the trailhead on the north side. A sign states that the Nature Trail is 1.0 mile, Mount Ellen Summit Trail is 1.6 miles, and Pomponio Trail is 3.5 miles. This loop trip combines all three. (If the visitor center is open at Memorial County Park, pick up an interpretive brochure for the nature trail. It's posted with alphabetical letters that correspond to the brochure.)

Begin hiking through the redwoods. The forest floor is lined with ferns and sorrel year-round and the bright blooms of hound's tongue and trillium in early spring. Bear right at the first trail intersection, leaving the nature trail and switchbacking uphill to the summit of Mount Ellen. The trail is extremely well graded, making an easy ascent. You'll quickly leave the noise from Pescadero Road behind you. Peeking between the branches of big redwoods and Douglas firs, you'll glimpse Pescadero Creek canyon. Mount Ellen's 680-foot summit is overgrown with bays and madrones and lacks much of a vista, but if you continue slightly downhill along the ridge for another few hundred feet, views open up to the north.

The path junctions with Pomponio Trail. Bear right and travel along this well-built ridgetop trail, emerging from the forest and entering a long stretch in open sunshine. The ridgetop is comprised of sandstone and lined with chaparral. Considering the shady redwoods in the valley below, you may be surprised to find you need to put on your sunscreen up here.

Enjoy this long, level stretch with fine canyon views. A bench along the trail is located just before the path begins to loop back on the other side of the canyon. Watch for a fenced area on your right; a spur path leads to a high overlook a few hundred feet off the trail.

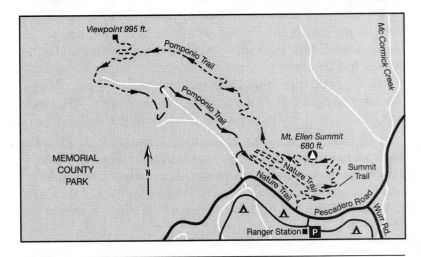

Canyon views from Pomponio Trail

From it, you can look north and west for the widest view of the day, although oak trees obscure some of the scenery. On the best days, you can see all the way to the ocean.

Note a cluster of non-native pampas grass as you make a hairpin turn around the back of the canyon. Cross a footbridge over a trickling stream and enter a grove of gnarled, twisted tanoaks. These trees are lovely in winter when they are coated in wet moss.

Pomponio Trail suddenly widens, becoming a dirt road. Walls of ferns line the southern slope. After a nice, easy downhill cruise on the wide path, you meet up with a gurgling stream at the canyon bottom. Big second-growth redwoods thrive in the rich, damp, streamside soil. One particularly massive stump is at least 10 feet wide at its base.

Continue straight ahead, walking through the big trees along the canyon bottom. You'll wind up back on the Nature Trail, which will take you back to Pescadero Road and the ranger station.

Trip notes: A $4 day-use fee is charged per vehicle. Dogs and bikes are not allowed. A park map is available for $1 at the ranger station. For more information, contact San Mateo County Parks and Recreation, 455 County Center, Fourth Floor, Redwood City, CA 94063; (650) 363-4020 or Memorial Park Visitor Center at (650) 879-0212.

86. PETERS CREEK GROVE
Portola Redwoods State Park

DISTANCE: 13.0 miles round-trip; 7 hours   **LEVEL:** Strenuous

ELEVATION CHANGE: 1,400 feet   **RATING:** ★ ★ ★ ★

DIRECTIONS: From the junction of highways 35 and 9 at Saratoga Gap, drive six miles north on Highway 35 (Skyline Boulevard). Turn left (west) on Alpine Road, drive 3.2 miles and turn left on Portola State Park Road. Drive 3.3 miles to park headquarters.

Or, from Interstate 280 in Palo Alto, take the Page Mill Road exit. Turn west and drive 8.9 miles to Highway 35 (Skyline Boulevard). Cross Highway 35 and continue on Alpine Road as above.

Old-growth redwood trees are indisputably majestic. Even when a highway or a paved trail is built right alongside them, or when they are hemmed in by fences and signs, the big trees retain their profound dignity and grace. Gazing at the ancient redwoods, humans feel awed and humbled.

But seeing a grove of old-growth redwoods that isn't accessible by car or an easy walk makes the experience even more compelling. That's why a trip to the Peters Creek Grove in Portola Redwoods State Park may be the most awe-inspiring hike in the Bay Area. Simply put, the sanctity of this grove will move you. It is pristine, unspoiled, and spectacular.

The trip is long and on the strenuous side, mostly because of the steep descent required to reach the grove. You'll need most of a day to complete the 13-mile round-trip, plus plenty of water and food. Because Portola Redwoods State Park is such a long, circuitous drive from just about everywhere, you should get an early morning start from your house if you aren't camping at the park. (Portola's car campground is booked in advance almost every weekend in summer. If you want to camp, be sure to make reservations.)

Those who would rather turn the 13-miler into a backpacking trip can stay at Slate Creek Trail Camp located halfway along the route. Again, reservations are necessary, but you shouldn't have a problem obtaining a site. You will need to pack in your own water.

That said, the trip is entirely doable as a day-hike for most people. Because most of the route is shaded, it never gets too hot.

Redwood "goosepen" in Peters Creek Grove

The trail is well graded and the total elevation change is only 1,400 feet. Seeing the Peters Creek Grove is worth every step.

Start your trip on either Summit Trail or Slate Creek Trail. (The ascent on Slate Creek Trail is slightly more gradual. A full description of these trails is found in the following story.) The two trails meet up after a 600 foot gain and about 1.5 miles. From their junction, head north on the continuation of Slate Creek Trail, following a mellower grade through redwoods, Douglas firs, and huckleberries for 1.5 miles to Slate Creek Trail Camp. If it isn't occupied, the camp makes a good rest stop. There are six campsites, picnic tables, and a pit toilet.

From the trail junction near the camp, take the north fork on Bear Creek Trail, an old jeep road. (This is the old Page Mill Road.) You'll climb for another mile up a ridge through a mixed forest of Douglas firs, oaks, and bay laurel. The jeep trail ends and you follow a narrower, steeper footpath into high chaparral country. The manzanita and pines are a surprising contrast to the dense forest you've been traveling in. Ascend a bit more along this dry ridge before beginning a one-mile, 750-foot descent into the canyon of Bear Creek and Peters Creek. The forest returns to a mix of bay laurel and Douglas firs as you make your way steeply downhill. (This may seem like it's going to be a nightmare climb out on the way back, but in fact, it's not as bad as it looks.)

Where the trail crosses Bear Creek, 5.8 miles from the start, you're about to enter the big trees. Parallel Bear Creek down to its confluence with Peters Creek, then meet up with Peters Creek Loop Trail. Take either fork to circle the grove, following both banks of Peters Creek.

Acquired by the Save the Redwoods League, the Peters Creek Grove is one of the most precious gems of the Santa Cruz Mountains. Some trees are more than 12 feet in diameter and 200 feet tall. Most are at least 1,000 years old. No one is quite sure why these redwoods weren't logged along with other groves in the area. Probably the canyon was too steep to make it feasible to haul out the lumber. A highlight of the grove is the huge Grandfather Tree, the largest redwood at Peters Creek. But what makes this place magical is not any one single tree but the sacred ambience created by the sum total. Isolated from the civilized world, the Peters Creek Grove is one of the most pristine places in the Bay Area.

Trip notes: A $6 day-use fee is charged. Dogs and bikes are not allowed. A park map is available for $1 at the visitor center. For more information, contact Portola Redwoods State Park, 9000 Portola State Park Road, La Honda, CA 94020; (650) 948-9098.

87. SLATE CREEK, SUMMIT, & IVERSON LOOP
Portola Redwoods State Park

DISTANCE: 5.0 miles round-trip; 2.5 hours   **LEVEL:** Easy

ELEVATION CHANGE: 600 feet   **RATING:** ★ ★ ★

DIRECTIONS: From the junction of highways 35 and 9 at Saratoga Gap, drive six miles north on Highway 35 (Skyline Boulevard). Turn left (west) on Alpine Road, drive 3.2 miles and turn left on Portola State Park Road. Drive 3.3 miles to park headquarters.

Or, from Interstate 280 in Palo Alto, take the Page Mill Road exit. Turn west and drive 8.9 miles to Highway 35 (Skyline Boulevard). Cross Highway 35 and continue on Alpine Road as above.

Portola Redwoods State Park is located at the end of a country road, a few winding miles from Alpine Road and Skyline Boulevard. A smaller, less visited cousin of nearby Big Basin Redwoods State Park, Portola is a favorite of Peninsula campers who retreat to the

Tiptoe Falls

shade of the redwoods on summer weekends. Day-hikers also fare well by making the circuitous drive to the park, particularly in winter and spring when the campers have vanished but the park's streams are running full. This five-mile loop trip offers a sample of Portola's best features: redwoods, ferns, clear-running creeks, and even a small waterfall.

Drive in to the park, pay your day-use fee at the visitor center, then continue along the park road, following the signs toward the campfire center. Park in the pullouts on the right, near the entrance to the campground. The Old Tree Trail/Slate Creek Trail begins on the opposite side of the road. (Depending on how crowded the park is, you may have to leave your car at park headquarters and walk to this point.)

Begin hiking on Old Tree Trail. Before turning left to join Slate Creek Trail, walk the quarter-mile stint to see the Old Tree. The path deadends at a 12-foot-wide, fire-scarred redwood. The old giant is an impressive sight and good for photo opportunities.

Retrace your steps and take Slate Creek Trail uphill, following a gentle, steady grade through second-growth redwoods, Douglas firs, tanoak, and hemlock. Some of the larger redwoods have "goose-pens" or hollows in their bases large enough for you to walk inside. Be sure to make a stop at the signed Bolton Grove. It features a bench situated in perfect position to admire the afternoon light cascading through the redwood canopy.

At 1.5 miles, you'll junction with Summit Trail; bear right. (The continuation of Slate Creek Trail to the left leads to the spectacular Peters Creek Grove of virgin redwoods. See the previous story.) Summit Trail continues uphill for 25 yards to an anticlimactic summit, offering only a partial view between the trees of distant forested ridges. Then the path descends, contouring down a drier slope covered with madrones.

Where Summit Trail reaches a paved service road, turn right and hike uphill for a few hundred feet. Take the left turnoff signed for Tiptoe Falls and drop steeply downhill on wooden stairsteps. Cross wide Pescadero Creek, then bear left and walk a level stretch through a lush meadow of woodwardia ferns and horsetails. Signs point the way to Tiptoe Falls. You'll cross Fall Creek and reach the diminutive waterfall and its secluded grotto in short order. The cataract drops on Fall Creek, which flows even in the dry autumn months, but the waterfall is prettiest after a period of rain. Lacy five-finger ferns frame Tiptoe Falls and its wide pool perfectly.

From the waterfall, backtrack to Pescadero Creek. Don't cross the creek; instead follow Iverson Trail along its southern banks. Enjoy this final leg along the coursing stream, then follow the trail signed for the visitor center. This will deposit you in the general proximity of your car.

Trip notes: A $6 day-use fee is charged per vehicle. Dogs and bikes are not allowed. A park map is available for $1 at the visitor center. For more information, contact Portola Redwoods State Park, 9000 Portola State Park Road, La Honda, CA 94020; (650) 948-9098.

88. SARATOGA GAP & RIDGE TRAIL LOOP
Castle Rock State Park

DISTANCE: 5.2 miles round-trip; 2.5 hours   **LEVEL:** Moderate

ELEVATION CHANGE: 800 feet   **RATING:** ★ ★ ★ ★

DIRECTIONS: From Saratoga, take Highway 9 west to its junction with Skyline Boulevard (Highway 35). Turn left (south) on Skyline and drive 2.5 miles to the Castle Rock State Park parking area on the right. The trailhead is on the west side of the parking lot, opposite the entrance.

Or, from Interstate 280 in Palo Alto, take Page Mill Road west for 8.9 miles to Skyline Boulevard (Highway 35). Turn left (south) on Skyline and drive 13 miles, past Highway 9, to the Castle Rock State Park parking area on the right.

Hello, hikers, and welcome to Swiss Cheese State Park. Oops, that's Castle Rock State Park, of course, but all those holey sandstone rocks look more like *fromage* than *châteaus*. Call it what you like, Castle Rock is one of the most surprising and spectacular parks in the entire Bay Area. In five miles of hiking, you visit a 50-foot waterfall in winter and spring, gaze at miles of Santa Cruz Mountains wildlands, and explore several large sandstone formations, including the local rock climbers' favorite, Goat Rock.

In recent years, Castle Rock has also become one of the most popular parks in the Bay Area. Because the park is used by rock climbers as well as hikers, weekends can be very crowded. For the best experience, plan your trip for a weekday, or get an early morning start on the weekends.

Take Saratoga Gap Trail from the far side of Castle Rock's parking lot, heading right. (The trail is signed "to campground.") The pleasure begins immediately as you travel downhill, walking along rocky, fern-lined Kings Creek through a mixed forest of Douglas firs, black oaks, and madrones. The seasonal stream begins as a trickle at the parking lot, then picks up flow and intensity as it heads downhill alongside the trail.

It's a mere eight-tenths of a mile to Castle Rock Falls, which flow with vigor in the wet season. After 15 minutes on the trail, you find yourself standing on a large wooden viewing deck, perched on top of the waterfall. Because you're at its brink, the fall is a bit difficult to see. You'll be torn between searching for the best view of its 50-foot drop and admiring the miles of uninhabited Santa Cruz Mountains' wildlands. It's hard to say whether this deck was built for viewing the waterfall or the canyon vista. Both are incredible.

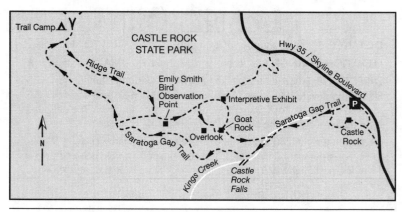

From the viewing deck, continue on Saratoga Gap Trail for another 1.8 miles. The terrain changes quickly from a shady mixed woodland to a sunny, exposed slope with views all the way out to Monterey Bay and the Pacific Ocean. Spring and summer bring forth colorful blooms on bush monkeyflower and other sun-loving chaparral plants. As you progress along the trail, you'll notice an ever-increasing number of sandstone outcrops that have been hollowed and sculpted by wind

Castle Rock State Park's holey sandstone

erosion. In some places, the sandstone becomes the trail surface. You'll have to scramble over a few small boulders to continue on your way.

At 2.5 miles from its start, Saratoga Gap Trail junctions with Ridge Trail and the spur to Castle Rock Trail Camp. Pay a visit to the pleasant, forested campsites if you wish (water and picnic tables are available), or just turn sharply right on Ridge Trail, beginning the return of your loop. After a half-mile uphill hike through a beautiful madrone forest, you emerge on an open ridge. (Ridge Trail roughly parallels Saratoga Gap Trail, but at a higher elevation.)

Another half-mile of gentle ascent takes you past a connector trail to Saratoga Gap Trail. Just beyond is a short spur to the Emily Smith Bird Observation Point. This forested knoll is a good spot to look for raptors, although views are severely limited by the leafy black oaks.

Nearly four miles into the loop you reach the spur trail for

Goat Rock. Turn right and follow it for a quarter mile. (The left fork leads to a fascinating interpretive exhibit on the park's geology; you can also loop around to Goat Rock from there.)

You're likely to see rock climbers strutting their stuff on the steep south side of Goat Rock, but the north side is easily accessible on two feet. Signs along the path encourage hikers to visit a neighboring overlook area instead of climbing on the 100-foot-high rock, due to its steep and potentially dangerous dropoffs. Take your pick. The overlook features a great view of the Santa Cruz Mountains parading down to the Pacific Ocean, and often more solitude than Goat Rock. If you're sure-footed and cautious, the smooth back side of Goat Rock is a great place to examine the sandstone close up and enjoy more fine views.

Beyond Goat Rock, Ridge Trail continues eastward until it reconnects with Saratoga Gap Trail just above Castle Rock Falls. Turn left and make a short, four-tenths-of-a-mile climb back up the creek canyon to the trailhead.

Don't leave the park without walking the half-mile loop trail to Castle Rock, the park's namesake rock formation. A spur trail on your right, just before you return to the parking lot on Saratoga Gap Trail, will take you there. Photo opportunities abound.

Trip notes: A $5 day-use fee is charged per vehicle. Dogs and bikes are not allowed. A park map is available at the trailhead for 50 cents. For more information, contact Castle Rock State Park, 15000 Skyline Boulevard, Los Gatos, CA 95020; (408) 867-2952 or (831) 429-2851.

89. BERRY CREEK, SILVER, & GOLDEN FALLS
Big Basin Redwoods State Park

DISTANCE: 10.4 to 12.0 miles round-trip; 5-6 hours   **LEVEL:** Strenuous
ELEVATION CHANGE: 1,900 feet   **RATING:** ★ ★ ★ ★
DIRECTIONS: From the junction of highways 35 and 9 at Saratoga Gap, drive six miles west on Highway 9 to Highway 236. Turn west on Highway 236 and drive 8.4 winding miles to Big Basin Redwoods State Park Headquarters. Park in the lot across from park headquarters, then begin hiking from the west side of the lot on a signed connector trail to the Skyline to the Sea Trail.

Big Basin Redwoods was established in 1902 as California's first state park. It was well-loved a century ago and it's equally loved today. Featuring an incredible diversity of terrain, some of the Bay Area's loveliest waterfalls, a freshwater marsh at the ocean's edge, 1,500-year-old redwood trees, and 80 miles of well-built trails, the park leaves little to be desired.

Not surprisingly, Big Basin is heavily visited. But on weekdays in winter and early spring (or early in the morning on weekends) precious solitude can still be found among the redwoods and even at the base of Big Basin's waterfalls. Time your trip carefully and don't be afraid to visit on a gray or rainy day. Nothing is prettier than a redwood forest in a light rain.

This 12-mile loop is the park's premier hike, beginning at park headquarters and passing three waterfalls: Berry Creek, Silver, and Golden. Although you can also access these falls by following the Skyline to the Sea Trail from Highway 1 near Davenport, that route is shared with mountain bikers and equestrians. The path described is luscious single-track for nearly its entire length, and only hikers are permitted. If you get tired along the way, the trail length can be reduced by a couple of miles by skipping the loop return.

Begin at the large parking lot by park headquarters. Take the connector trail from the west side of the lot, Redwood Nature Trail, past the campfire circle. After crossing Opal Creek, you'll turn left on Skyline to the Sea Trail.

The trail starts out good and stays that way as it meanders among virgin redwoods, some larger than 12 feet in diameter. After climbing 250 feet to gain a ridge in the first mile, the trail angles to the right across Middle Ridge Fire Road, then drops down the other side. After a pleasant descent through more huge redwoods, Skyline to the Sea Trail parallels Kelly Creek and then West Waddell Creek. As you hike, keep an eye out for huge yellow banana slugs slowly crossing the trail and plentiful California newts that always seem to be right under your boots.

At 4.2 miles, just before Skyline to the Sea Trail meets up with Berry Creek Falls Trail, you get your first glimpse of Berry Creek Falls through the redwood branches. It's enough to make you quicken your pace. Turn right on Berry Creek Falls Trail and in moments you'll be standing in front of the breathtaking 65-foot cataract. Berry Creek Falls inspires admiration as it tumbles gracefully over a fern-lined black cliff surrounded by redwoods.

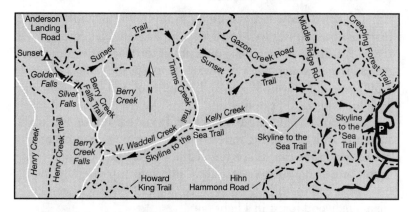

Many hikers go no farther. A picnic lunch on the wooden viewing platform and a turnaround here makes a fine nine-mile round-trip. But since you've come this far, it would be a pity not to hike the rest of the loop. The remaining two waterfalls are no slouches and the remaining scenery is far from anticlimactic.

Follow the trail up the left side of Berry Creek Falls, obtaining an interesting perspective looking down on its brink. You'll leave Berry Creek and join West Berry Creek, a narrower and more channeled stream. Another 20 minutes of gentle climbing brings you to the base of Silver Falls. The 70-foot freefall spills over sandstone and limestone in hues of tan, gold, and orange. It's a colorful contrast to Berry Creek Falls' dark cliff. In summer, you can walk right up to Silver Falls' flow and stick your head under the water. Several redwoods have fallen around the waterfall's base, making good seats.

You'll see more orange sandstone glowing underneath white water as you climb the wooden steps alongside Silver Falls. The trail takes you to the falls' brink, where you walk on rocky sandstone steps. Steel cables are in place along the trail. In high water, it's wise to use them.

In moments, you're looking at the lower tumble of Golden Falls Cascade, a long drop of slippery orange sandstone. In one area the water funnels and plunges in a cascade, but most of Golden Falls is more horizontal, like a water slide for sea otters. The color of the rock is so striking, and the shape of the fall is so unusual, that you'll find it hard to believe that you're less than a mile from classic-looking, postcard-like Berry Creek Falls.

Some hikers make Golden Falls Cascade their turnaround point for a 10.4-mile roundtrip. Backpackers can continue for an easy quarter-mile to Sunset Trail Camp, a lovely spot to spend the night near West Berry Creek. Hikers opting for the 12-mile loop continue to the trail camp turnoff, then bear right on Sunset Trail. The path soon enters a vastly different world filled with knobcone pines, chinquapin, live oak, and madrone. A brief stretch on an exposed sandstone ridge may prompt you to put on your sunglasses for the first time all day.

Soon enough you head back into the forest canopy. Tanoaks and young

Berry Creek Falls

redwoods border the steeply descending trail. After crossing West Waddell Creek, Sunset Trail climb again, touring grassland slopes and mixed forests. Spring wildflowers are often good in this area.

When the trail meets up with Middle Ridge Fire Road, cross it and descend again. Turn right on Dool Trail, then right again on Skyline to the Sea Trail. A left turn puts you back on Redwood Nature Trail to finish out the loop back at the parking lot. You'll be able to count this as one of the finest days you've ever spent.

Trip notes: A $6 day-use fee is charged per vehicle. Dogs and bikes are not allowed. A park map is available at the entrance station for $1. For more information, contact Big Basin Redwoods State Park, 21600 Big Basin Way, Boulder Creek, CA 95006; (831) 338-8860 or (831) 429-2851.

90. SEQUOIA AUDUBON TRAIL

Pescadero Marsh Natural Preserve

DISTANCE: 2.4 miles round-trip; 1 hour   **LEVEL:** Easy

ELEVATION CHANGE: Negligible   **RATING:** ★ ★ ★

DIRECTIONS: From Highway 1 in Half Moon Bay, drive south for 17 miles to just north of Pescadero Road, near Pescadero State Beach. Park in the state beach parking lot south of the highway bridge over Pescadero Creek, on the west side of the highway. Walk to the north side of the bridge (use the pedestrian walkway on the west side), take the stairs to the sand, then follow the trail underneath the bridge and up the canyon.

Pescadero Marsh Natural Preserve is a 500-acre coastal marsh that backs the spectacular San Mateo Coast along Highway 1. Considered to be one of the largest and most important freshwater and brackish marshes in California, Pescadero Marsh serves the important function of water filtration, water storage, and ground-water recharge for Pescadero and Butano creeks. In addition, it provides critical habitat for a diverse assemblage of wildlife, including thousands of migratory birds traveling on the Pacific Flyway.

There's one other thing about Pescadero Marsh: it's beautiful. Despite being bordered by Highway 1 to the west, the preserve is a peaceful oasis that is marked by the deep, rich blues and greens of plentiful water and foliage. *Plein-air* painters often drive up alongside the preserve, pull out their brushes and canvases, and try to capture the marsh's voluptuous hues.

One of the best ways to see Pescadero Marsh is on a guided walk with a naturalist; free tours are offered every weekend year-round. If you choose to explore on your own, the preserve has three trails, which unfortunately are not contiguous. The southern trail along Butano Creek is accessed from a trailhead on Pescadero Road, just 75 yards from its junction with Highway 1. The preserve's North Pond Trail is accessed by parking at the northernmost Pescadero State Beach parking lot. (Walk across the highway, then follow the trail as it curves around the east side of Pescadero Marsh's freshwater pond.) Sequoia Audubon Trail is the longest of the three trails, and it is accessed by parking in the state beach lot just south of the highway bridge over Pescadero Creek.

Because of its length and diversity, Sequoia Audubon Trail is the preference of most hikers. The trail travels alongside Pescadero Creek for 1.2 miles, providing an excellent chance for wildlife watching. It begins on the beach on soft sand. Walk underneath the highway bridge and head inland, soon gaining hard earth beneath your shoes. You'll notice that the ground heats up as you get away from the coastal winds and move into thick vegetation. Spring and summer wildflowers bloom along the trail, including coastal paint-

Great egret fishing at Pescadero Marsh

brush, monkeyflower, yellow bush lupine, and nonnative purple and yellow ice plant. A couple of gnarled, low-lying eucalyptus trees grow along the path.

A veritable jungle of wetlands and coastal foliage, the marsh attracts more than 200 species of birds (more than 60 species nest here), as well as numerous mammals and amphibians. Almost everyone who comes to Pescadero Marsh gets rewarded with wildlife sightings. On one trip, we saw two deer wading up to their knees through the marsh waters, half a dozen bullfrogs under a footbridge by the creek, one large turtle, scads of minnows and water bugs, and birds galore—ducks, great egrets, redwing blackbirds, swallows, egrets, godwits, and four great blue herons doing a little fishing. The herons nest in the eucalyptus trees above the marsh.

In late winter, you might get the chance to see steelhead trout swimming up Pescadero Creek to spawn. Or watch for the endangered San Francisco garter snake slithering along the trail.

The far end of Sequoia Audubon Trail climbs above the marsh to a viewing area, where a bench affords a vista of the entire wetlands and the ocean beyond. An interpretive sign identifies different birds of prey you may see soaring above you. Hawks, kites, and owls are most common.

If birdwatching is your thing, the best birding times at Pescadero Marsh are late fall and early spring. But there's one prerequisite for a spring hike in the marsh—make sure you wear long pants and long sleeves. Pescadero Marsh happens to be the tick capital of the world, and it may be one of California's greatest natural greenhouses for poison oak. If the trail hasn't been cleared recently, you may think they grow the stuff commercially here.

A side trip that's a must is a little coastal walk along Pescadero's rocky beaches, starting from the lot where you parked your car. The coastline features long sandy stretches, interesting rock formations, tidepools, and plentiful harbor seals lounging around on the rocks.

Trip notes: There is no fee. Dogs and bikes are not allowed. A map of San Mateo Coast State Parks and Beaches, which includes Pescadero Marsh, is available for $1 from the address below. For more information, contact California State Parks, Bay Area District, 250 Executive Park Boulevard, Suite 4900, San Francisco, CA 94135; (415) 330-6300. Or phone Pescadero State Beach at (650) 879-2170.

91. BUTANO GRAND LOOP
Butano State Park

DISTANCE: 11.0 miles round-trip; 6 hours **LEVEL:** Strenuous
ELEVATION CHANGE: 1,300 feet **RATING:** ★ ★ ★
DIRECTIONS: From Highway 1 in Half Moon Bay, drive south for 17 miles to the Pescadero Road turnoff. Turn left (east) and drive 2.5 miles to Cloverdale Road. Turn right on Cloverdale Road and drive 4.2 miles to the park entrance. Turn left and drive three-tenths of a mile to the entrance kiosk. Park in the small lot just beyond it.

There's a forested canyon along the Half Moon Bay coast that looks much the same as it did a century ago. Filled with redwoods, Douglas firs, calypso orchids, and ferns, that canyon is found in 3,200-acre Butano State Park, just outside the coastal town of

Butano State Park

Pescadero. It's far enough away from the Bay Area's major population centers that its trails are never crowded. An 11-mile loop trip
through the park is about as close as you can get to a wilderness
experience on a day-hike in the Bay Area.

You can hike this loop in either direction—the gradient doesn't
change much no matter which way you go. (The route described
saves the best grove of redwoods for the end.) But before you start,
you must learn how to pronounce the park's name. It's *Byu*-tin-o,
with the accent on the first syllable. Almost nobody gets this right
on their first visit.

Park by the entrance kiosk and begin on the Año Nuevo Trail.
The narrow path switchbacks up and up through dense vegetation,
primarily thimbleberry, huckleberry, and poison oak vines. The
ascent will get your heart pumping immediately. Finally you climb
high enough to claim a vista through the lichen-covered branches of
Douglas fir trees. The panorama includes the coast and the forested
canyon inland; hawks soar over the beautiful grassy hills. Take the
right spur to a bench 20 feet off the trail. A second bench, a little
farther up the trail, has more obstructed views. At one time it had
a clear view of Año Nuevo Island, giving this trail its name.

Año Nuevo Trail drops downhill and joins Olmo Fire Road.
Follow it for a quarter mile to the right turnoff for single-track
Gazos Trail, which roughly parallels the fire road but makes much

more pleasant walking. Excellent views of the coast are provided as you cruise up and down along the ridgetop. The high ridge is composed of light-colored shale and sandstone—proof that the entire area was once undersea. Manzanita, chinquapin, and knobcone pines line the exposed, gravelly slopes.

At Gazos Trail's end is a fine vista of the coast, worth stopping to admire before you rejoin Olmo Fire Road and continue to climb. A highlight along the wide dirt road is the 25-foot-tall root ball of a huge fallen Douglas fir. On the day I visited, it was covered with bright yellow banana slugs, busy doing the important business of decomposition.

Just before the road junctions with narrow Indian Trail on the left, it becomes noticeably steeper. Where the vegetation opens up, you can clearly see the ridge's sandy shale soil. If you can withstand another 100 feet of climbing, follow the road a short distance past Indian Trail to a high overlook just off the trail. This sunny spot is probably the best picnic site of the day.

Then follow Indian Trail into a dense oak and madrone forest, curving around the steep slopes of Little Butano Creek canyon to begin the loop's return leg. Where Indian Trail forks right a half mile from its start, the path leads to Trail Camp. A few no-frills backpacking sites are hidden in the forest; a pit toilet is the only amenity. At the turnoff, bear left on chaparral-lined Canyon Trail. You'll have a few more glimpses of the coast through the ceanothus and occasional Douglas firs.

Canyon Trail connects with Jackson Flats Trail, the final leg of this loop. The last 2.8 miles on Jackson Flats are an easy cruise through the park's loveliest stretch of forest. The woodland features fern gardens, many big and small redwoods, and moss-covered

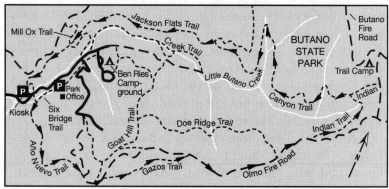

Douglas firs in some interesting configurations—they have trunks and limbs growing every which way. Watch for banana slugs and California newts; the redwood duff is their home and you don't want to step on them. From February to April, keep your eyes trained to the forest floor in search of the rare calypso orchid, a small and delicate purple flower.

Trip notes: A $5 day-use fee is charged per vehicle. Dogs and bikes are not allowed. A park map is available for $1 at the kiosk. For more information, contact Butano State Park, 1500 Cloverdale Road, Pescadero, CA 94060; (650) 879-2040 or (415) 330-6300.

92. AÑO NUEVO POINT TRAIL
Año Nuevo State Reserve

DISTANCE: 3.0 miles round-trip; 2 hours   **LEVEL:** Easy
ELEVATION CHANGE: Negligible   **RATING:** ★ ★ ★
DIRECTIONS: From Half Moon Bay at the junction of Highway 92 and Highway 1, drive south on Highway 1 for 28 miles to the right turnoff for Año Nuevo State Reserve. (From Santa Cruz, drive 21 miles north on Highway 1.)
SPECIAL NOTE: From December 15 to March 31, entry to the elephant seal area is by guided walk only. Walks are offered daily and reservations are recommended. The fee is $4 per person (in addition to a $5 per vehicle parking fee). Tickets go on sale as early as 56 days in advance; call 1-800-444-4445 to make a reservation. Unreserved tickets are sold daily at the park on a first-come, first-served basis.

When was the last time you saw thousands of animals in one spot? Those kinds of numbers don't happen often for wildlife watchers, but they occur regularly at Año Nuevo State Reserve. Every year from December to March, Año Nuevo Island is the breeding ground for more than 3,000 elephant seals. It's a wildlife show you'll never forget.

It's not just the number of animals that's impressive. It's their immense size. Elephant seals are the kings of the pinniped family. The males can grow longer than 18 feet and weigh more than two tons. The females reach as long as 12 feet and weigh more than one ton. Baby elephant seals increase their weight from 60 pounds to

200 pounds in only four weeks after birth. Aside from their huge size, the elephant seal's most elephantine characteristic is its snout. Particularly on the male elephant seal, the snout resembles a short version of an elephant's trunk. It is used primarily for vocalization—to amplify the animal's strange roars.

You can show up any time of year and see pinnipeds at Año Nuevo State Reserve. The mainland beaches, as well as the shores of Año Nuevo Island, are popular with California sea lions and harbor seals year-round. From mid-May to mid-August, stellar sea lions breed on an isolated reef surrounding the island.

But in the winter months, it's the northern elephant seals that steal the show. The huge males arrive in late November to claim the best spots on the beaches; the pregnant females come to shore two to three weeks later to give birth and breed. In a few months the adults and their young all disappear back into the ocean and are usually not seen again until the following winter.

Given all this, the Año Nuevo Point Trail at Año Nuevo State Reserve is a basic requirement on the resume of any Bay Area hiker. The trail is an easy three miles round-trip, most of which is nearly level. In addition to the elephant seal show, the path leads to a gorgeous stretch of sand called Cove Beach, where you could easily while away an entire day.

The rules at Año Nuevo are as follows: From April through November you may visit the preserve and hike on your own. From December through March, entry is by guided walks only and prior reservations are recommended. It's unwise to drive all the way to the park if you don't have reservations. January is usually the busiest month, when the baby elephant seals are born.

(Those who can't plan more than a day in advance should wait until the end of March, then call the park to find out when the "entry by guided walks only" period ends. If you show up soon thereafter, plenty of elephant seals will still be hanging around.)

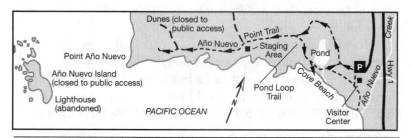

Besides the elephant seals, the trail has many other charms. From the parking lot, you set out through the coastal scrub and soon reach a fork with Pond Loop Trail. At the fork is a large, odd piece of old wood. It's a piece of the wreck of the steam schooner *Point Arena,* which was battered on the rocks along the coast in 1913.

Bear right to loop around the high side of the pond, gaining lovely

Año Nuevo beach and lighthouse

views of its blue waters and the ocean beyond. Three-quarters of a mile from the trailhead is a kiosk and staging area for the Wildlife Protection Area. The kiosk features interesting displays on the pinnipeds that call Año Nuevo home.

From here you continue toward Año Nuevo Point, where you gain a fine view of the multitudes of elephant seals on Año Nuevo Island and the mainland beaches. An abandoned lighthouse, built in 1890 to warn mariners away from the rock-strewn coastline, has been taken over by seals and sea lions. When the light was still in use, the lighthouse keeper and his family had to constantly battle the pinnipeds, who called the island their own and even forced their way into the keeper's house. In 1948, the lighthouse was replaced by an automatic buoy and the building was left to the animals.

As you near Año Nuevo Point, the cacophony of barking and snorting is tremendous. From your vantage point about 25 feet from the seals, you are close enough to see them brawling with each other and watch their strange, jerking movements as they go from sand to sea and back.

While you stare at the giant creatures, consider that their presence here is a remarkable testament to the healing power of nature. By the year 1900, less than 100 elephant seals were left in the world; the rest had been killed for their fur and the oil contained in their blubber. Miraculously, one small surviving group of seals located on an island west of Baja, California slowly began to multiply. By the 1920s, elephant seals were occasionally seen off the coast of Southern California and in 1955 they returned to Año Nuevo Island, one of their traditional breeding grounds.

On your return hike, be sure to walk the other leg of the loop around the pond, then take the short cutoff trail to Cove Beach. It's a great spot for a picnic or a long walk on the sand. And don't miss a visit to the terrific visitor center at Año Nuevo.

Trip notes: A $5 day-use fee is charged per vehicle. In addition, from December 15 through March 31 guided walks to see the elephant seals cost $4 per person. Dogs and bikes are not allowed. A park map is available at the entrance station for $1. For more information, contact Año Nuevo State Reserve, New Years Creek Road, Pescadero, CA 94060; (650) 879-2025 or (650) 879-0227. Website: www. anonuevo.org

---

93. ANTLER POINT LOOP
Joseph D. Grant County Park

DISTANCE: 8.8 miles round-trip; 5 hours   **LEVEL:** Strenuous
ELEVATION CHANGE: 1,800 feet   **RATING:** ★ ★ ★
DIRECTIONS: From Interstate 680 in San Jose, take the Alum Rock Avenue exit and drive east for 2.2 miles. Turn right on Mount Hamilton Road and drive 7.9 miles to the sign for Joseph D. Grant County Park on the right. Don't turn here; continue for another 100 yards to the Grant Lake parking lot on the left side of the road.

Joseph D. Grant County Park is a world apart from the rest of Santa Clara County. Just down the hill lies the hustle and bustle of the Silicon Valley, but up at Grant Park, all is tranquil. A few cows graze on the hillsides, ancient oaks and wildflowers dot the grasslands, bluebirds flit among the trees, and golden eagles soar the skies. If you spend a day hiking the park's trails, the biggest excitement you may encounter is the sudden appearance of wild pigs, who will scatter and run when they hear you coming.

A few warnings, just so you know what you're in for. Grant County Park, called "Grant Ranch" by the locals, lies due north of better known Henry Coe State Park, and it shares the same summer weather—hot as Hades. There is very little shade in the park, so plan your trip for autumn, winter, or spring. April and May are the best months to visit, when the grasslands are green and the slopes are gilded with blue-eyed grass, poppies, brodiaea, and lupine.

The trails at Grant County Park are predominantly multi-use dirt roads and are very popular with mountain bikers. (If you turn up your nose at anything wider than single-track, you won't be happy here.) The path described is designed to avoid a good deal of bike traffic, but it won't eliminate it. For the least chance of sharing the trails with bikes, plan your visit for a weekday, when the park is usually empty.

This semi-loop trip takes you to the highest point in the park, Antler Point at 2,995 feet. The first two miles feature some steep uphill pitches, but the rest of the walk is moderate. Begin your hike at the Grant Lake Trailhead and follow the wide road edging large, shallow Grant Lake. (Bass and bluegill fishing from shoreline is popular here.) About halfway along the lakeshore, turn right on Halls Valley Trail. A quarter-mile farther, turn right on Los Huecos Trail. Because most mountain bikers follow the continuation of Halls Valley Trail uphill, you'll have less company on steep Los Huecos Trail.

The next 1.8 miles are a steady uphill with a few pitches that will leave you gasping for breath. Hopefully you've picked a cool

Woodpeckers' acorn granary in an oak tree at Grant County Park

day. Expanding vistas of Grant Lake and the park's western ridge are fair compensation for the climb. As you gain elevation, you'll have surprising views of the South Bay's distant shimmering waters.

Birdwatching is excellent on Los Huecos Trail. Hawks, golden eagles, and other raptors perch on the tall oaks and hunt the grasslands. Songbirds such as western bluebirds and tanagers may be seen in springtime. Black and white magpies are present year-round and acorn woodpeckers are frequently heard and seen. The woodpeckers form a social group centered around an acorn granary, a chosen tree in which the birds drill holes, filling each one with an acorn to be eaten later. A single granary may contain thousands of acorns.

Where the trail tops out at Cañada de Pala Trail, turn left and enjoy an easier, more rolling grade. More views of the South Bay are seen to the northwest and Mount Hamilton shows up to the east. Although spring wildflowers are good throughout the park's grasslands, the most abundant displays are found on this high, bald ridge. (I hope you timed your trip for April or May.)

Your destination, Antler Point, is visible straight ahead, the highest hill around. After three quarters of a mile, bear right on Pala Seca Trail. Another 1.6 miles through grasslands and occasional grazing bovines brings you to the spur trail to Antler Point. Turn right and walk the final quarter mile uphill to the bald, grassy overlook. This is the day's best view of the South Bay, San Jose, Grant Park's rolling grasslands, and Lick Observatory on top of 4,209-foot Mount Hamilton.

For your return trip, retrace your steps on the spur to Antler Point, then turn right and loop back on Cañada de Pala Trail, enjoying more ridgetop views. Don't miss the right turnoff for Halls Valley Trail for your downhill return to Grant Lake. Mountain bikers are allowed to go uphill only on this trail, so you don't have to worry about being mowed down from behind as you descend.

A surprise for many first-time visitors may be the sudden appearance of wild pigs along the trail, especially in the oak- and laurel-shaded canyon of Halls Valley. More than 500 wild pigs live in the park; rangers keep tabs on their numbers so they don't get out of control. The large animals are descendants of European wild pigs that were brought in by ranchers for sport hunting in the early twentieth century. They have thrived and multiplied throughout large areas of California. Most of the pigs in Grant Park are black, although some have bred with domestic pigs and their descendants are multi-colored. Pigs seen along the trail will most likely run from you; the bolder ones have taken to rooting around the park's campgrounds.

One more tip to optimize your trip: If you can, time your exit from the park so that you leave right at sunset when the gates are locked. Then you'll have the pleasure of driving back down Mount Hamilton Road with a lovely view of glowing city lights.

Trip notes: A $4 day-use fee is charged per vehicle. Dogs are not allowed. Bikes are allowed. A free map is available at the trailhead. For more information, contact Joseph D. Grant County Park at (408) 274-6121, or Santa Clara County Parks and Recreation Department, 298 Garden Hill Drive, Los Gatos, CA 95032; (408) 358-3741. Website: www.parkhere.org

94. COYOTE PEAK LOOP
Santa Teresa County Park

DISTANCE: 4.0 miles round-trip; 2 hours   **LEVEL:** Easy

ELEVATION CHANGE: 500 feet   **RATING:** ★ ★

DIRECTIONS: From U.S. 101 in Morgan Hill, take the Bernal Road exit and drive west 1.5 miles to the park entrance. Continue uphill for a quarter mile (past the golf course) and turn left at the sign for Muriel Wright Residential Center. Drive three-quarters of a mile to the end of the road by the corral at the far end of the Pueblo Day-Use Area.

Santa Teresa County Park isn't the largest or most wilderness-like park in Santa Clara County. It's better known for its golf course and picnic areas than for its hiking trails. Similarly, the park's high point, Coyote Peak, isn't the tallest summit in the county. But considering its location just off Bernal Road south of San Jose, the park and its 1,155-foot peak are clear winners for an afternoon hike with a stellar South Bay view. A bonus is that Santa Teresa's grasslands are fertile soil for a bounty of spring wildflowers. Can a park this close to an urban area feel like a nature preserve? Surprisingly, yes.

You drive through a large portion of this county park to access the trailhead at the far end of the Pueblo Day-Use Area. (Make sure

Coyote Peak summit, Santa Teresa County Park

you turn left off Bernal Road at the sign for Muriel Wright Residential Center.) At present, a section of the described loop is not shown on the park map, but the path is clearly signed.

From the trailhead parking lot, head west along the wide road by the corral, signed as Mine Trail. Walk a mere 75 yards, then turn left on single-track Rocky Ridge Trail, the trail that's absent from the park map.

Begin a zig-zagging climb through the grasslands of Big Oak Valley. The narrow path is open to mountain bikers; you may have to step aside to let them pass. Because you are going uphill, you'll have plenty of time to see bikes coming downhill toward you. Those going uphill will be traveling at a much slower pace. Take a few side trips off the trail to admire the occasional ancient, sprawling oaks and lichen-covered serpentine outcrops. Springtime brings lovely displays of fiddleneck, poppies, goldfields, and yarrow.

(Wildflower lovers, take note: Although most of the park offers good wildflower viewing, the park's best flower trail is Stile Ranch Trail. Access it from the trailhead at the junction of Fortini Road and San Vicente Avenue in San Jose.)

The path meanders gently up and down in a rollercoastering fashion; it was clearly built with mountain biking in mind but it makes a fine hiking trail as well. As you ascend the ridge, keep following the trail toward the white building located on a high point. Just below it, Rocky Ridge Trail connects with wide Coyote Peak Trail; turn left. Now it's an easy half-mile to the top of Coyote Peak, elevation 1,155 feet. A bench and railing are placed on the flat summit. Views are to the north and east of the Santa Clara Valley. Look for the white dome of Lick Observatory on top of Mount Hamilton, and gaze in wonder at what the South Bay has become.

After you've seen (and perhaps admired) the wild sprawl of civilization below, backtrack down the summit spur to Coyote Peak Trail, then turn right and follow it steeply downhill. The route drops into a canyon lined with bay laurel and oaks. At a junction with Hidden Springs Trail, turn left to head back to the Pueblo Day-Use Area in a little more than a half mile. You'll have to walk past the various picnic areas to reach the lot where you left your car.

Trip notes: There is no fee. Leashed dogs and bikes are allowed. A free park map is available at the trailhead. For more information, contact Santa Teresa County Park at (408) 268-3883 or Santa Clara County Parks and Recreation Department, 298 Garden Hill Drive, Los Gatos, CA 95032; (408) 358-3741. Website: www.parkhere.org

95. FLAT FROG, MIDDLE RIDGE, & FISH TRAIL LOOP
Henry W. Coe State Park

DISTANCE: 8.0 miles round-trip; 4 hours   **LEVEL:** Moderate
ELEVATION CHANGE: 1,000 feet   **RATING:** ★ ★ ★
DIRECTIONS: From U.S. 101 in Morgan Hill, take the East Dunne Avenue exit and drive east for 13 miles to Henry W. Coe State Park headquarters.

The closest thing to a wilderness park in the South Bay Area is Henry W. Coe State Park. This well known but little traveled state park is the second largest in California (the largest is Anza-Borrego Desert State Park near San Diego). Comprised of tall ridges bisected by deep, steep ravines, the park is notoriously hilly and rugged. Its varied terrain includes grasslands, oaks, chaparral, pines, and mixed hardwoods.

Henry Coe is so large—80,000 acres—and its terrain is so rugged that to see much of it, you need to take a backpacking trip of at least a few days. But day-hikers can tour the western part of

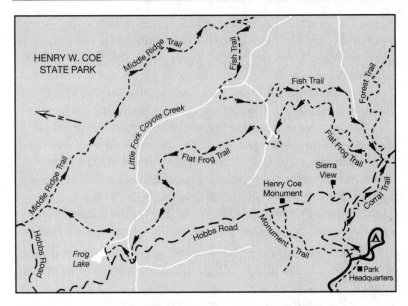

the park on this eight-mile loop around Middle Ridge.

Two requirements for the trip: First, pick a cool day to hike, ideally in late winter or spring when Coe Park's streams are running. The park is notoriously hot in summer. Second, bring plenty of water, even if the weather is cool.

The loop begins by state park headquarters. For the most part, it avoids the wide, exposed ranch roads and sticks to narrow footpaths. Take the single-track trail leading north from the parking lot and in a short distance, bear right on Corral Trail, which parallels Manzanita Point Road. In typical Coe Park fashion, Corral Trail passes through three distinct ecosystems in short order—mixed oak woodland, grasslands, and chaparral. Spring wildflowers are plentiful, especially iris, poppies, buttercups, and popcorn flowers. Watch for the more unusual purple monkeyflowers.

In less than a mile, turn left on Spring Trail to cross Manzanita Point Road, then immediately bear left on Flat Frog Trail to begin a gentle ascent to Frog Lake. This 2.9-mile trail isn't the shortest route to the tiny lake; it's nearly double the length of Hobbs Road to the west. But it offers a pleasant, single-track ramble with excellent views of Middle Ridge, and it leads through a surprising mixed woodland. Ponderosa pines are mingled with the black oaks and madrones. In spring, look for giant trillium in the forest understory. Its large, mottled leaves are easy to identify. Bright red columbine, purple shooting stars, and Chinese houses are also common.

Flat Frog Trail connects with Hobbs Road just before Frog Lake; you can take either trail to the tiny former cattle pond. A backpacking camp is located nearby. One-acre Frog Lake is spring-fed; even in dry years it usually has a little water in it. It supports a few bass and bluegill, but they aren't easy to catch. Frequently the surface of the water is completely covered with green algae. Still, the pond is an excellent place for birdwatching. Acorn woodpeckers use the dead snags around the lake as granaries for their acorns. On one April trip, we spotted a pair of colorful western tanagers flitting around the trees bordering the lake. We watched their bright-hued feathers for almost an hour.

Cross Frog Lake's inlet stream and continue steeply uphill to Middle Ridge. The oak-dotted grasslands above Frog Lake support goldfields, lupine, poppies, and even a few dogtooth violets. They give you something to look at while you stop to catch your breath on the steep climb.

Frog Lake, Henry Coe State Park

Once you reach Middle Ridge, look forward to a roller-coastering walk with many lovely views of Coyote Creek canyon. Although the trail initially leads through alternating grassy clearings and groves of pines and black oaks, it later enters a grove of giant, tree-sized manzanitas growing 15 feet tall.

Follow the ridge for just over a mile to the right turnoff for Fish Trail. Enjoy a pleasant descent through two canyons filled with black oaks, bay laurels, and willows. Cross the Little Fork of Coyote Creek.

Where the trail parallels Fish Creek, you'll have the good company of this small cascading stream. The final leg of the trail brings you back into grasslands dotted with huge valley oaks. Many bear large clumps of mistletoe growing high in their branches.

Where Fish Trail ends, cross Manzanita Point Road, take Spring Trail to Corral Trail and follow it west for the final stretch back to park headquarters and your car.

Trip notes: A $5 day-use fee is charged per vehicle. Dogs are not allowed. Bikes are allowed only on fire roads. Park maps are available for $1 at the visitor center. For more information, contact Henry W. Coe State Park, P.O. Box 846, Morgan Hill, CA 95038; (408) 779-2728. Website: www.coepark.parks.ca.gov

96. WATERFALL LOOP TRAIL
Uvas Canyon County Park

DISTANCE: 3.5 miles round-trip; 2 hours   **LEVEL:** Easy

ELEVATION CHANGE: 700 feet   **RATING:** ★ ★ ★

DIRECTIONS: From U.S. 101 heading south in Morgan Hill, take the Bernal Road exit. At the stoplight, turn right, then right again, to access Monterey Highway. Turn left (south) on Monterey Highway. Turn right on Bailey Avenue and drive 2.8 miles to McKean Road. Turn left on McKean Road and drive six miles (McKean Road becomes Uvas Road). Turn right on Croy Road and drive 4.5 miles to the park (continue past Sveadal, a private camp/resort). Park near park headquarters or in one of the picnic area parking lots. The trail is the gated dirt road at Black Oak Picnic Area.

Uvas Canyon County Park is a little slice of waterfall heaven on the east side of the Santa Cruz Mountains. Although the drive to reach it is a long journey from the freeway through grasslands and oaks, it delivers you to a surprising redwood forest at the park entrance. Suddenly, you've entered another world.

Uvas Canyon is a small park, offering camping and picnicking facilities and a short stretch of hiking trails in its 1,200 acres, but it's living proof that good things come in small packages. If you're short on time, you can walk the one-mile Waterfall Loop Trail and see Black Rock Falls and several smaller cascades on Swanson Creek. If you're in the mood to stretch your legs, you can make a 3.5-mile loop out to Alec Canyon, then take the uphill trail a half-mile to Triple Falls on Alec Creek.

The park has enough waterfalls to make any waterfall-lover happy. Just make sure you show up in the rainy season, because that's when Uvas Canyon is at its best. Water seems to pour from every crack in the hillsides. By mid-summer, the falls run dry. The canyon is filled with oaks, laurels, big-leaf maples, and Douglas firs, all thriving in the moist environment around Swanson Creek.

Start your trip at the Black Oak Group Picnic Area by the gated dirt road. Head straight (not uphill on the road) to connect to the short loop trail through the canyon. Cross Swanson Creek on a footbridge, then bear right at the fork and head directly for Black Rock Falls, a quarter-mile away. You'll find the waterfall on your right, pouring 30 feet down a side canyon over—you guessed it— black rock. Take a few pictures, then continue on the trail, heading for Basin Falls. This waterfall is 20 feet high and surrounded by moss-covered rocks. It makes a lovely S-curve at it carves its way downcanyon. Next you'll reach Upper Falls, a little shorter in height than the other falls, but just as enchanting.

At Upper Falls, it's decision time: Either head back and take the other side of the Waterfall Loop Trail for a short and level one-mile hike, or continue up Swanson Creek and follow the winding Contour Trail to Alec Canyon and Triple Falls. For the longer trip, follow Contour Trail through a dense oak and Douglas fir forest, crossing a few small ravines. Where the trail junctions with Alec Canyon Trail, turn right and hike a half-mile to Manzanita Point.

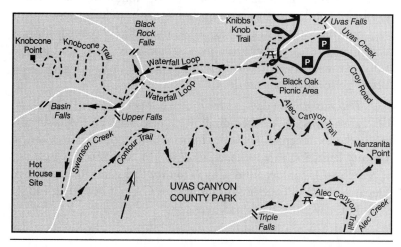

Upper Falls at Uvas Canyon County Park

Here, at an opening in the abundant manzanita bushes, you gain wide views of the South Bay and Diablo Range on clear days.

A short distance farther in the chaparral and soon you enter Alec Canyon's second-growth redwood forest. In the late 1800s, the virgin redwoods in this canyon were cut for lumber to build the nearby mining town of New Almaden. The trail you're following is an old logging road.

Turn right on the short spur trail to Triple Falls. True to its name, Triple Falls is a series of three cascades, totaling 40 feet in height. If you wish, you can find a seat right alongside the cascading fall. Or backtrack to Alec Canyon Trail, turn right, and head for a picnic table right alongside the creek. To finish the loop, follow the road back to Black Oak Picnic Area, a steep three-quarter mile descent.

So which waterfall at Uvas Park is the best? Uvas rangers say that if you're only going to see one cataract in the park, see Upper Falls. My favorites are Basin Falls and Triple Falls. Your favorite? Better go see them all and decide.

Trip notes: A $4 day-use fee is charged per vehicle. Leashed dogs are allowed. Bikes are not allowed. Free maps are available at the park visitor center. For more information, contact Uvas Canyon County Park, 8515 Croy Road, Morgan Hill, CA 95037; (408) 779-9232. Or contact Santa Clara County Parks and Recreation Department, 298 Garden Hill Drive, Los Gatos, CA 95032; (408) 358-3741. Website: www.parkhere.org

97. LOCH TRAIL & HIGHLANDS LOOP
Loch Lomond Recreation Area

DISTANCE: 5.2 miles round-trip; 3 hours   **LEVEL:** Moderate

ELEVATION CHANGE: 700 feet   **RATING:** ★ ★ ★

DIRECTIONS: From Interstate 280 in San Jose, take Highway 17 south for 24 miles to Scotts Valley. Take the Mount Hermon Road exit, turn right, and drive 3.5 miles. Turn left on Graham Hill Road, then turn left immediately on Zayante Road. Drive three miles to Lompico Road. Turn left and drive 1.7 miles to West Drive. Turn left and drive a half-mile to Sequoia Road, then enter the park. (The route is clearly signed for Loch Lomond Recreation Area.) Follow the park road to its end near the boat ramp and store. Loch Trail begins by the boat ramp.

SPECIAL NOTE: Check your calendar before you go: Loch Lomond Recreation Area is open only from March 1 through September 15.

Every summer when I was a kid, my parents took my sisters and me hiking and fishing at a big lake surrounded by a beautiful forest. We'd explore around the lake, learn about the trees and plants that grew there, watch for wildlife, and go fishing in our little motor boat. We'd always take a break at midday, pull up our boat on an island on the lake, sit on a rock, and eat some sandwiches. Then we'd hike in the woods or just sit on the shoreline and admire the scenery.

As an adult, I never thought I'd find any place in urban California to match that lake of my memories. But then I went to Loch Lomond Reservoir, just 10 miles north of Santa Cruz, and found just such a place.

The Loch Trail at Loch Lomond Recreation Area follows the shoreline of a large, deep blue reservoir through a Douglas fir and redwood forest. After a pleasant mile along the water's edge, the trail connects with Highlands Trail, which ascends the hillside above the lake. With a gentle climb of only a few hundred feet, you rise above the treetops for lovely high views of Loch Lomond. The entire loop is only five miles; it's perfect for a morning or afternoon walk.

The key to the trip is to show up in the right season. The reservoir and its surrounding land are locked up for six months of the year in order to protect the water supply for the city of Santa Cruz.

Loch Lomond

But each year on March 1, the gates are opened and the public recreation season begins. The park is open all spring and summer, usually until September 15.

As you hike the Loch Trail, you could stop to drop a line in the water or picnic at one of the many shaded tables near the shoreline. Or you might just meander along, admiring the pretty lake. The only thing you can't do is swim; Loch Lomond is a public water supply so no human contact is allowed. The footpath winds gently around one tree-lined cove after another: Cunningham, MacGregor, Stewart, Fir, and Huckleberry. At Deer Flat, 1.2 miles out, Loch Trail meets up with Highlands Trail, a wide fire road. Continue on Highlands Trail farther north along the lakeshore and then uphill through the redwoods, climbing 500 feet. The road tops out and loops back to the south, now in a more open forest of knobcone pines, chaparral, and nonnative but pretty Scotch broom. Fine views of the lake and Newell Creek canyon are provided. Where the trail nears the park road, be sure to walk the short Big Trees Nature Trail before following the pavement back downhill to your car.

Trip notes: A $4 day-use fee is charged per vehicle. Leashed dogs are allowed. Bikes are not allowed. A free trail map is available at the park entrance. For more information, contact Loch Lomond Recreation Area, 100 Loch Lomond Way, Felton, CA 95018; (831) 335-7424.

98. FALL CREEK LOOP
Henry Cowell Redwoods State Park - Fall Creek Unit

DISTANCE: 8.0 miles round-trip; 4 hours   **LEVEL:** Moderate

ELEVATION CHANGE: 1,500 feet   **RATING:** ★ ★ ★ ★

DIRECTIONS: From Interstate 280 in San Jose, take Highway 17 south for 24 miles to Scotts Valley. Take the Mount Hermon Road exit, turn right, and drive 3.5 miles. Turn right on Graham Hill Road and drive one-tenth of a mile to Highway 9. Continue straight across Highway 9 onto Felton Empire Road. Drive six-tenths of a mile on Felton Empire Road to the Fall Creek trailhead on the right. (The main Henry Cowell State Park entrance requires a left turn on Highway 9.)

Or, from Highway 1 in Santa Cruz, take Highway 9 north for 7.5 miles to Felton Empire Road. Turn left and continue as above.

Question: Where in the Bay Area can you find a fast running, full flowing stream even in the driest months of summer and fall? Answer: Almost nowhere, except at the Fall Creek Unit of Henry Cowell Redwoods State Park.

The Fall Creek Unit is not the best known section of Henry Cowell Park. More famous is the northern park unit with its family campgrounds and Roaring Camp steam trains. (See the following story.) But the less developed Fall Creek Unit is perfectly suited for hikers, with crystal-clear Fall Creek tumbling, cascading, and pooling alongside the park's main trail even in the traditional summer and fall drought months.

The Fall Creek Unit isn't huge, so you can make an eight-mile loop around the park and see much of it in one day. In addition to its natural beauty, the park features three 1870s lime kilns and other evidence of its history as an important lime producer. The lime was used to make mortar to build the brick buildings of San Francisco and other California cities.

Starting from the Felton Empire Road trailhead just west of Felton, take Bennett Creek Trail gently downhill from the parking lot for a quarter-mile. Immediately you are serenaded by the music of Fall Creek, which quickly drowns out the sound of the nearby road. A left turn on Fall Creek Trail sends you traipsing alongside the stream, nestled in a cool, shady forest of mixed hardwoods—

tanoaks, Douglas firs, big-leaf maples, and bay laurel. (The colorful big-leaf maples are worth a special visit in the fall.)

As the trail keeps to the clear, rocky stream, you'll witness a marvelous fern forest, including some huge woodwardia ferns. The park is home to more than 12 fern species. Sorrel and sugar scoop carpet the spaces between them.

Three quarters of a mile from the trailhead, turn left at the path signed for "lime kilns." Now following South Fork Trail along South Fall Creek, you'll approach the kiln area in less than a half mile. Evidence of past homesteading is seen along the trail, including spreading purple vinca, English ivy, and low rock walls. About 40 kiln workers and their families lived in this canyon in the late 1800s. The kilns were built by the IXL Lime Company to process limestone from nearby Blue Cliff Quarry. For thirty years, these kilns were one of the major lime producers in California.

You can climb up on the remaining walls of the three kilns and look inside their yawning pits. Imagine the time when the 1,700-degree heat from their fires would have kept you far away. Today, maidenhair ferns grow inside the kiln's walls.

Behind the kilns is the old railroad grade that carried limestone from the quarry. The rock was transported up and down the hill via a gravity cable system.

From the kiln area, head to your right and cross South Fall Creek on Cape Horn Trail. Follow Cape Horn Trail a half mile to Lost Empire Trail, where you turn sharply left and head uphill. Climbing above Fall Creek canyon, you'll face a healthy ascent for almost a mile. The trail levels out for a half-mile stretch to Lost Camp, where Barrel Mill Creek runs through. In the autumn, it's wise to bring your hard hat for this stretch—acorns from the tanoaks come pelting down like raindrops through the forest.

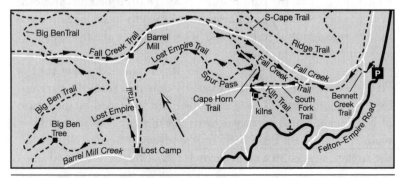

Lime kilns at Fall Creek Unit, Henry Cowell Redwoods State Park

Next comes a second climb on Lost Empire Trail for three-quarters of a mile to the Big Ben Tree, a virgin redwood and the high point on this loop at 1,800 feet. The tree is clearly marked at the junction of Lost Empire, Big Ben, and Sunlit trails. After a break to admire Big Ben, head downhill on Big Ben Trail for 1.4 miles through a forest of big, twisted madrones and Douglas firs. Soon you'll descend back into the redwoods along Fall Creek.

Turn right on Fall Creek Trail to finish out the loop. You have only three miles left to return to the trailhead; the majority of this will be spent right alongside splashing Fall Creek. The upstream area, where the canyon is squeezed, exhibits a tremendous amount of deadfall. The redwoods growing on its steep slopes don't always last through the heavy rains of winter. Fall Creek Trail narrows and becomes more rough in this section; you'll have to duck under fallen trees and watch your step on the slippery streamside trail. Look for wild ginger and giant trillium growing nearby. In mid-summer, you may get lucky and spot bright orange leopard lilies blooming along the creek's edges.

On the way back to the trailhead, be sure to stop at the Barrel Mill site. This water-powered mill manufactured parts for the barrels that were used to ship the lime. Massive timbers and some abandoned machinery remain at the streamside site.

Trip notes: There is no fee at the Fall Creek Unit parking lot. Dogs and bikes are not allowed. A park map is available at the Henry Cowell Visitor Center at the main state park area on Highway 9. For more information, contact Henry Cowell Redwoods State Park, 101 North Big Trees Park Road, Felton, CA 95018; (831) 335-4598 or (831) 429-2851.

99. OBSERVATION DECK & BIG ROCK HOLE LOOP
Henry Cowell Redwoods State Park

DISTANCE: 6.4 miles round-trip; 3.5 hours   **LEVEL:** Moderate

ELEVATION CHANGE: 1,000 feet   **RATING:** ★ ★ ★

DIRECTIONS: From Interstate 280 in San Jose, take Highway 17 south for 24 miles to Scotts Valley. Take the Mount Hermon Road exit, turn right, and drive 3.5 miles. Turn right on Graham Hill Road and drive one-tenth of a mile to Highway 9. Turn left on Highway 9 and drive six-tenths of a mile to Henry Cowell Redwoods State Park on the left. Continue past the entrance kiosk to the visitor center and main parking lot. Follow the signs to the Redwood Grove and Redwood Loop Trail.

Or, from Highway 1 in Santa Cruz, take Highway 9 north for six miles to the right turnoff for the park.

Henry Cowell Redwoods State Park is celebrated for its ancient groves of coast redwoods. It's famous for its Roaring Camp Railroad steam trains, whose whistles blow as they steam around tracks that carve through the center of the park. And the park is well known for the San Lorenzo River, which offers rushing waters for runs of salmon and steelhead in winter, and good swimming and wading for humans in summer.

But surprisingly, most visitors never hike any farther in the park than the three-quarter-mile Redwood Loop Trail that starts by the visitor center. Too bad, because miles of footpaths roll gently alongside the river, cruise through dense groves of redwoods, laurels, and Douglas firs, and traverse chaparral-covered slopes. This loop trip tours these areas and visits many of the park's highlights.

Note that the loop described requires two unbridged crossings of the San Lorenzo River. If you're hiking when the river is running too high, you'll have to shorten the loop to bypass the fords. Use good judgment about crossing. Also, carry a park map to help you negotiate your way through this loop's many junctions.

Begin your hike by following the short Redwood Loop Trail. This popular path through huge first-growth redwoods is worth seeing; the rest of the park's redwoods are mostly second-growth. Take either leg of the loop into the marvelous virgin grove, then exit the trail at the far end of the loop. Follow the signed path to paved Pipeline Road, which is popular with dog-walkers and bicyclists. Cross the pavement and pick up the hikers-only San Lorenzo River Trail, which parallels Pipeline Road and closely follows the east bank of the river. Although the river is only a few inches deep in summer, it can be 20 to 30 feet deep during winter rains. Its banks are lined with willows, cottonwoods, and sycamores.

In short order you'll pass under a railroad trestle crossing the San Lorenzo River. Chances are good that at some point during your hike you'll hear the wail of a train screeching around a curve in the canyon. The privately operated Roaring Camp Railroad runs through the park (the ticket office and station are located near the parking lot by the nature center). When you hear one of its trains, you may think it sounds more like the "Wailing" Camp Railroad.

A quarter-mile beyond the trestle, River Trail and neighboring Pipeline Road meet up with Eagle Creek and its namesake trail. Bear left on Eagle Creek Trail, heading through the redwoods and Douglas firs to begin a moderate ascent into higher, madrone- and manzanita-covered slopes. The trail gets steeper as you go, offering lovely views of small cascades and pools after winter rains.

Soon after crossing Eagle Creek on a footbridge, turn right on Pine Trail. The earth beneath your feet suddenly becomes sandy, and walking becomes more difficult on the sunny, exposed ridge. Follow the signs leading through sun-loving chaparral to the park's observation deck.

This 15-foot-high concrete structure is surrounded by a picnic table, hitching post, and water fountain, plus two surprising kinds of trees—knobcone pines and ponderosa pines. The latter, with its distinctive jigsaw puzzle bark, usually is found at much higher elevations in places like the Sierra Nevada. Here at 800 feet in elevation in the Santa Cruz Mountains, the ponderosa pine grows only in this strange "sand hill chaparral" community. This region's sandy soil is what remains of an ancient ocean floor. Four million years ago a shallow sea completely covered the area.

Walk up the observation platform's stairs and you'll get a some-what obstructed view of Monterey Bay. Even if the view is only fair, the sunny platform is a fine place to sit down and have lunch, or maybe take a cat nap.

If the San Lorenzo River looked wide and deep at the start of your trip, now is the time to cut this loop short and follow Ridge Fire Road downhill and back to River Trail. If the river looked safe to cross, continue on Pine Trail to its junction with Powder Mill Fire Road. Follow Powder Mill downhill for a half mile to where it crosses Pipeline Road, then take single-track Buckeye Trail downhill for another half-mile through several switchbacks and across the San Lorenzo River. This is the first of two fords. On the river's far side, Buckeye Trail winds along the riverbank, then crosses it again. Pass an obvious swimming hole on your left, Big Rock Hole, which is lined with granite boulders.

After a dip and a rest, you'll be ready to climb again. Follow Big Rock Hole Trail steeply uphill for a half-mile to its junction with Rincon Fire Road, where you'll find the lovely Cathedral Redwoods Grove. These trees aren't as large or old as those on the Redwood Loop Trail, but they offer more solitude and a chance to catch your breath after the challenging climb.

Rincon Fire Road continues northward back to a junction with River Trail. The latter will bring you back to the Eagle Creek junc-

Observation deck at Henry Cowell Redwoods State Park

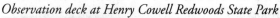

tion, the railroad trestle, Pipeline Road, Redwood Loop Trail, and finally, the visitor center and your car.

Trip notes: A $6 day-use fee is charged per vehicle. Leashed dogs are allowed only on paved Pipeline Road. Bikes are allowed on some trails. A park map is available from the visitor center for $1.50. For more information, contact Henry Cowell Redwoods State Park, 101 North Big Trees Park Road, Felton, CA 95018; (831) 335-4598 or (831) 429-2851.

100. OLD LANDING COVE TRAIL
Wilder Ranch State Park

DISTANCE: 2.5 miles round-trip; 1.5 hours   **LEVEL:** Easy

ELEVATION CHANGE: Negligible   **RATING:** ★ ★ ★

DIRECTIONS: From Santa Cruz, drive north on Highway 1 for four miles. Turn left into the entrance to Wilder Ranch State Park, then follow the park road to its end and park in the main parking area. Take the trail marked "Nature Trail" from the southwest side of the parking lot.

One foggy November afternoon, we tossed off our responsibilities and headed for the coast south of Davenport and Wilder Ranch State Park. Bundled in our fleece jackets to ward off the gloomy weather, we set off on Old Landing Cove Trail.

In our first 10 minutes of walking we spotted a bobcat as he leapt off the trail and into the surrounding bushes. Moments later we admired the soaring flight of a hawk on land and pelicans over the sea. In a few more footsteps we peered down on dozens of harbor seals hauled out on rocks just off the coast. Leaving the blufftop trail for the sands of Fern Grotto Beach, we marveled at two remarkably divergent creatures that had washed up onshore: a six-inch-long, bright orange sea sponge and the decaying remains of a 20-foot grey whale.

You never know quite what you'll find at Wilder Ranch State Park. A walk on the park's Old Landing Cove Trail is short and easy, but the rewards are numerous. Spotting wildlife is nearly a given considering the plentiful pinnipeds and sea birds. But even if you aren't fortunate enough to have a bobcat cross your path, you're certain to enjoy the trail's other highlights, including a seal rookery, spectacular jagged bluffs and sandy beaches, and a hidden fern cave.

Many people think of Wilder Ranch as a mountain biker's park, but the reality is that most bicyclists stick to the trails on the inland side of the park, across Highway 1, where ranch roads criss-cross the grassy hillside. The few bikers you'll find on the short, level Old Landing Cove Trail are absolute beginners or those who are there for the scenery. They won't be traveling very fast.

The Old Landing Cove Trail starts from the parking lot at a sign that simply reads "Nature Trail." Bordered by 10-foot-tall stalks of anise, the trail is a wide ranch road that makes a short and direct path to the edge of the ocean. Soon you'll be walking along-side the park's brussels sprouts fields. Some say that Wilder Ranch's biggest claim to fame is not its historic ranch buildings, nor its excellent trail system, nor its spectacular beaches and coastal vistas. It's the fact that 12 percent of our national brussels sprouts produc-tion happens right here within the park's boundaries. One question: Who's eating all of them, anyway?

Follow the trail toward the coast, then turn right and head out along the sandstone and mudstone bluffs. The first beach you'll reach, Wilder Beach, is a critical habitat area for the endangered snowy plover and is fenced off and protected as a natural preserve. An overlook platform with a bench provides a good viewing spot.

In another eighth of a mile you'll reach the trail's namesake, the old landing cove. The cove is a remarkably narrow inlet where small schooners pulled in to anchor and load lumber in the late 1800s. Just off Old Landing Cove is a huge flat rock where harbor

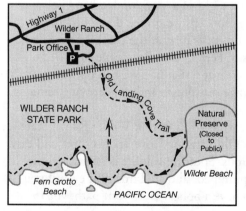

seals haul out at low tide. They require sunshine to warm their flippers, the only part of their body that isn't well insulated. Your best view of the harbor seals comes after you pass the cove and look back, or on your return trip.

The trail continues along the blufftops. The

highlight of this hike is the descent to the beach to see Wilder Ranch's fern cave, the oceanside home of a collection of bracken and sword ferns. They hang from the small cave's ceiling just low enough to tickle the top of your head.

The fern cave is hidden in the back of a U-shaped cove; it is accessible from the blufftops via a spur path. Watch for post number 8 along the main trail. The spur is located a few yards beyond it.

The fern cave's location in the back of the oval cove keeps it somewhat protected from the salty ocean air.

Rugged bluffs at Wilder Ranch State Park

An underground spring gives the ferns life and keeps them moist and cool. The floor of the cave is covered in driftwood of all shapes and sizes that has been collected from the sea by the constant motion of the tide. Water drips continually from the cave's ceiling.

After exploring and admiring the sea cave, return to the top of the bluffs and Old Landing Cove Trail. Walk a quarter mile farther north, heading to the next beach cove. This one has a wider and more visible trail leading down to it and it displays a perfect crescent-shaped strip of sand—the ideal place to have a picnic lunch or sit and watch the waves come in.

Trip notes: A $6 day-use fee is charged per vehicle. Dogs are not allowed. Bikes are allowed. A free park map is available at the entrance kiosk. For more information, contact Wilder Ranch State Park, 1401 Old Coast Road, Santa Cruz, CA 95060; (831) 423-9703 or (831) 429-2851.

101. LOMA PRIETA GRADE & BRIDGE CREEK LOOP
The Forest of Nisene Marks State Park

DISTANCE: 7.0 or 9.0 miles round-trip; 4-5 hours   **LEVEL:** Moderate

ELEVATION CHANGE: 600 feet   **RATING:** ★ ★ ★

DIRECTIONS: From Santa Cruz, drive south on Highway 1 for six miles to the Aptos exit. Bear left at the exit, then turn right on Soquel Drive and drive a half-mile. Turn left on Aptos Creek Road. Stop at the park entrance kiosk, then continue up the road to Georges Picnic Area or Porter Picnic Area. (Parking at Porter Picnic Area will cut two miles off your round-trip, but the park road is closed beyond Georges Picnic Area in winter.)

The Forest of Nisene Marks is a relatively undeveloped state park. It's the kind of park that doesn't have car campgrounds, a visitor center, or even paved parking lots. Sounds good, yes? It just gets better. In terms of scenery, the park is like a young cousin to popular Big Basin Redwoods State Park, filled with second-growth redwoods, more ferns than you can shake a stick at, and banana slugs and newts by the dozen. And just like Big Basin, Nisene Marks even boasts a couple of pretty waterfalls.

Two major forces have shaped the land here: the railroad and unstable geology. Although virgin redwoods remained untouched in this steep and winding canyon for hundreds of years, the Loma Prieta Lumber Company procured the valley in 1881 and teamed up with Southern Pacific Railroad to destroy it—oops, I mean log it. They built a railroad along Aptos Creek and worked the land with trains, oxen, skid roads, inclines, horses, and as many men as they could recruit, removing 140 million board feet of lumber over the course of 40 years. In 1922, when the loggers finally put their saws down, there were no trees left.

Luckily, Mother Nature has been busy in the last eighty years. Today the canyon is filled with Douglas firs and second-growth redwoods; the higher ridges are lined with oaks and madrones.

Mother Nature was especially busy on October 17, 1989, when the park was the epicenter of the famous Loma Prieta earthquake, which forcefully shook the entire Bay Area. You can visit the epicenter via a hike on Aptos Creek Trail, but there is little to see except a sign marking the spot.

A more interesting hike is the seven- or nine-mile semi-loop up Loma Prieta Grade to Maple Falls, returning via Bridge Creek Trail. The mileage varies according to where you leave your car. In winter, the park road is usually closed off at Georges Picnic Area, requiring a longer walk. If you can park up the road at Porter Picnic Area, you'll save a couple miles.

From either trailhead begin hiking on Aptos Creek Road, a wide multi-use trail that travels under a thriving canopy of second-growth redwoods. A quarter-mile past Porter Picnic Area, Loma Prieta Grade takes off on the left. Follow this old railroad grade and leave Aptos Creek Road and the mountain bikers behind. The rest of the loop is open to hikers only.

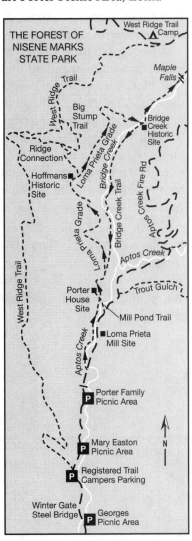

As soon as you're on single-track, what was good becomes gorgeous. You hike among tall trees and ferns alongside Aptos Creek. Considering the lush green canopy of redwoods and Douglas firs in the canyon, it's hard to imagine the clear-cutting that took place here. At a fork signed for Bridge Creek Historic Site to the right, bear left to stay on Loma Prieta Grade. The right fork will be the return of your loop to Maple Falls.

The worn old railroad grade enters into its prettiest stretch as it climbs gently up the slopes above Bridge Creek. The trail is often quite narrow and eroded, so watch your footing. You'll pass Hoffmans Historic Site, the location of a logging camp that was nicknamed "Camp Comfort." It housed 300 workers and was used until 1921. The camp's ruins are slowly rotting away.

Four miles from Porter Picnic Area, Loma Prieta Grade ends at Bridge Creek Historic Site, the location of another former logging camp. From here, you'll make a half-mile stream scramble up Bridge Creek to Maple Falls (there is no formal trail, but the route is obvious). Bridge Creek's canyon walls squeeze tighter as you travel upstream, providing close-up looks at the millions of ferns and mini-waterfalls dropping among the rocks and crevices. When Bridge Creek is running strong, you'll have to walk in the creekbed and cross the stream a dozen or more times, so wear your waterproof boots. In summer, the canyon scramble is much easier, but the waterfall is less impressive.

Keep going until you reach the back of the canyon, where its walls pinch together and 30-foot Maple Falls pours over a sandstone wall, blocking any farther progress. A few big-leaf maple trees frame the falls. After paying homage to the pretty cataract, retrace your steps down the canyon to Bridge Creek Historic Site and take the left fork on Bridge Creek Trail. As you hike through the redwood-lined canyon, look carefully for fossils embedded in the soft sandstone lining the stream. You'll cross Bridge Creek one more time, then rejoin Loma Prieta Grade where you started your loop. Retrace your steps back to the parking area.

Trip notes: A $3 day-use fee is charged per vehicle. Dogs are not allowed. Bikes are allowed only on fire roads. A free park map is available at the entrance kiosk. For more information, contact The Forest of Nisene Marks State Park, 201 Sunset Beach Road, Watsonville, CA 95076; (831) 763-7063 or (831) 429-2851.

APPENDICES

- **Best Peak Vistas in the Bay Area**
  Bald Mountain, Sugarloaf Ridge State Park, pp. 23-25
  Mount St. Helena, Robert Louis Stevenson State Park, pp. 33-37
  Mount Wittenberg, Point Reyes National Seashore, pp. 64-66
  Barnabe Peak, Samuel P. Taylor State Park, pp. 80-83
  Mount Tamalpais, Mount Tamalpais State Park, pp. 100-103
  Hill 88, Golden Gate National Recreation Area, pp. 129-132
  Mount Livermore, Angel Island State Park, pp. 141-144
  Wildcat Peak, Tilden Regional Park, pp. 154-156
  Mount Diablo, Mount Diablo State Park, pp. 174-178
  Mission Peak, Mission Peak Regional Preserve, pp. 193-196
  San Bruno Mountain, San Bruno Mountain State & County Park,
  pp. 214-217
  Montara Mountain, McNee Ranch State Park, pp. 220-223

- **Bay Area Waterfalls**
  Alamere Falls, Point Reyes National Seashore, pp. 74-77
  Stairstep Falls, Samuel P. Taylor State Park, pp. 80-83
  Cascade Falls, Marin County Open Space District, pp. 86-88
  Carson Falls, Marin Municipal Water District, pp. 92-94
  Cataract Falls, Marin Municipal Water District, pp. 95-96
  Abrigo Falls, Briones Regional Park, pp. 157-160
  Mount Diablo's Donner Canyon Falls, Mount Diablo State Park,
  pp. 180-183
  Murietta Falls, Ohlone Regional Wilderness, pp. 202-206
  Brooks Falls, San Pedro Valley County Park, pp. 223-225
  Tiptoe Falls, Portola Redwoods State Park, pp. 257-259
  Castle Rock Falls, Castle Rock State Park, pp. 259-262
  Berry Creek, Silver, & Golden Falls, Big Basin Redwoods State Park,
  pp. 262-265
  Black Rock, Triple, Upper, and Basin Falls, Uvas Canyon County Park,
  pp. 282-284
  Maple Falls, The Forest of Nisene Marks State Park, pp. 296-298

- **Special Places for Wildlife Watching & Birdwatching**
  Rush Ranch, Solano County Open Space, pp. 40-42 (river otters)
  Tomales Point, Point Reyes National Seashore, pp. 44-46 (tule elk)
  Chimney Rock Trail, Point Reyes National Seashore, pp. 61-64 (whales
  and elephant seals)
  Abbotts Lagoon, Point Reyes National Seashore, pp. 50-52 (birds)
  Audubon Canyon Ranch, Bolinas Lagoon Preserve, pp. 77-80 (nesting
  egrets and herons)
  Muir Woods National Monument, pp. 116-121 (spawning steelhead
  trout and coho salmon)

- **Special Places for Wildlife Watching & Birdwatching, cont.**
  Rodeo Lagoon, Golden Gate National Rec. Area, pp. 126-129 (birds)
  Wall Point, Mount Diablo State Park, pp. 178-180 (birds)
  Round Valley Regional Preserve, pp. 183-185 (San Joaquin kit fox)
  Cogswell Marsh, Hayward Regional Shoreline, pp. 188-190 (birds)
  Bay View Trail, Coyote Hills Regional Park, pp. 190-193 (birds)
  Sunol Regional Wilderness, pp. 196-202 (birds)
  Alcatraz Island, Golden Gate National Rec. Area, pp. 211-213 (birds)
  Fitzgerald Marine Reserve, pp. 225-228 (tidepools)
  Pescadero Marsh Natural Preserve, pp. 266-268 (birds)
  Año Nuevo Point Trail, Año Nuevo State Reserve, pp. 271-273 (elephant seals)
  Joseph D. Grant County Park, pp. 274-277 (wild pigs, birds)
  Old Landing Cove Trail, Wilder Ranch State Park, pp. 293-295 (birds, sea lions, whales)

- **Exceptional Wildflower Displays**
  Chimney Rock Trail, Point Reyes National Seashore, pp. 61-64
  Coastal Trail, Mount Tamalpais State Park, pp. 110-112
  Phyllis Ellman Trail, Ring Mountain Preserve, pp. 135-138
  Morgan Territory Regional Preserve, pp. 185-187
  Sunol Regional Wilderness, pp. 196-202
  Summit Loop, San Bruno Mountain State & County Park, pp. 214-217
  Russian Ridge Open Space Preserve, pp. 239-241

- **Best Redwood Forests**
  Steep Ravine, Mount Tamalpais State Park, pp. 103-106
  Bootjack, Ben Johnson, and Hillside Trail Loop, Muir Woods National Monument, pp. 119-121
  Stream Trail, Redwood Regional Park, pp. 163-166
  Purisima Creek Redwoods Open Space Preserve, pp. 228-231
  Jones Gulch & Brook Trail, Pescadero Creek County Park, pp. 246-249
  Heritage Grove, Sam McDonald County Park, pp. 250-252
  Peters Creek Grove, Portola Redwoods State Park, pp. 255-257
  Berry Creek Falls Trail, Big Basin Redwoods State Park, pp. 262-265
  Redwood Loop Trail, Henry Cowell Redwoods State Park, pp. 290-293

- **Best Short Backpacking Trips in the Bay Area**
  Point Reyes National Seashore, Sky & Coast camps, pp. 64-68
  Black Diamond Mines Regional Preserve, Stewartville Camp, pp. 171-174
  Monte Bello Open Space Preserve, Black Mountain Camp, pp. 241-243
  Portola Redwoods State Park, Slate Creek Trail Camp, pp. 255-257
  Castle Rock State Park, Castle Rock Trail Camp, pp. 259-262
  Big Basin Redwoods State Park, Sunset Trail Camp, pp. 262-265
  Butano State Park, Trail Camp, pp. 268-271
  Henry Coe State Park, Frog Lake Camp, pp. 279-282

• Long Distance Trails in the Bay Area

Coastal Trail: Running through Point Reyes National Seashore, Mount Tamalpais State Park, and Golden Gate National Recreation Area, the Coastal Trail is a spectacular oceanside route. The only downer is that it isn't contiguous. But no matter, enough of the trail is connected so that you could easily put together a three - or four-day backpacking trip. Also called the Pacific Coast Trail or just the Coast Trail, the Coastal Trail begins in the Marin Headlands near Sausalito and runs continuously to Muir Beach. It then breaks off and begins again near Muir Beach Overlook and Slide Ranch, then runs through Mount Tamalpais State Park.

The most popular section for backpacking is the 15-mile Point Reyes' stretch that runs from the Palomarin Trailhead near Bolinas to the Point Reyes Youth Hostel near Limantour Beach. Most people hike it from north to south, ending up at Palomarin.

Skyline to the Sea Trail: This book details a short section of the Skyline to the Sea Trail leading to Berry Creek Falls in Big Basin Redwoods State Park (see page 262), but the trail in its entirety is a 38-mile one-way trek from Saratoga Gap at the junction of Highways 9 and 35 to Waddell Beach at Highway 1 near Davenport. Aside from the spectacular Santa Cruz Mountains scenery, a major plus on this trail is that most of it is downhill. It makes an ideal three- or four-day backpacking trip. Trail camps are conveniently spaced along the route in Castle Rock State Park and Big Basin Redwoods State Park.

The Bay Area Ridge Trail: The grandaddy of Bay Area long distance trails and a 400-mile trail-in-progress, the Bay Area Ridge Trail will eventually circle the entire Bay Area, connecting 75 parks. It is designed as a multi-use path (for hikers, horseback riders, and mountain bikers). The Bay Area Ridge Trail Council is the volunteer organization putting it all together.

East Bay Skyline National Trail: A 31-mile ridge trail in the East Bay begins near Castro Valley and ends in Richmond. The only downer? There are no trail camps, so don't think about doing the whole thing as a backpacking trip. You can make several nice day-hikes out of it, though. (The only camping available is at Anthony Chabot Family Campground, near the southern terminus of the trail.) For a free brochure on the East Bay Skyline National Trail, contact the East Bay Regional Parks District, (510) 635-0135 or (510) 562-7275. Website: www.ebparks.org

Ohlone Wilderness Trail: A 29-mile trail that runs from Del Valle Regional Park in Livermore to Mission Peak Regional Park in Fremont. Trail camps are located in the Sunol Regional Wilderness and Ohlone Regional Wilderness. Highlights of the trail include Rose Peak (3,817 feet) and Murietta Falls. The East Bay Regional Parks District has more information; (510) 635-0135 or (510) 562-7275.

INDEX

ABOUT THE AUTHOR

Ann Marie Brown has lived and hiked in the San Francisco Bay Area for 15 years. She is the author of eight books on the California outdoors, all published by Foghorn Press. Her titles include:

101 Great Hikes of the San Francisco Bay Area
Day-Hiking California's National Parks
California Waterfalls
California Hiking (with Tom Stienstra)
Easy Hiking in Northern California
Easy Biking in Northern California
Easy Hiking in Southern California
Easy Camping in Southern California

Will you have enough stories to tell your grandchildren?

Yahoo! Travel

Do You
YAHOO!
?